MW01051222

Cython

Kurt W. Smith

Beijing · Cambridge · Farnham · Köln · Sebastopol · Tokyo

Cython

by Kurt W. Smith

Copyright © 2015 Kurt W. Smith, PhD. All rights reserved.

Printed in the United States of America.

Published by O'Reilly Media, Inc., 1005 Gravenstein Highway North, Sebastopol, CA 95472.

O'Reilly books may be purchased for educational, business, or sales promotional use. Online editions are also available for most titles (*http://safaribooksonline.com*). For more information, contact our corporate/institutional sales department: 800-998-9938 or *corporate@oreilly.com*.

Editors: Mike Loukides and Meghan Blanchette
Production Editor: Matthew Hacker
Copyeditor: Rachel Monaghan
Proofreader: Rachel Head

Indexer: Ellen Troutman Zaig
Cover Designer: Ellie Volckhausen
Interior Designer: David Futato
Illustrator: Rebecca Demarest

January 2015:   First Edition

Revision History for the First Edition:

2015-01-09:   First release

See *http://oreilly.com/catalog/errata.csp?isbn=9781491901557* for release details.

The O'Reilly logo is a registered trademark of O'Reilly Media, Inc. *Cython*, the cover image of a South African python, and related trade dress are trademarks of O'Reilly Media, Inc.

While the publisher and the author have used good faith efforts to ensure that the information and instructions contained in this work are accurate, the publisher and the author disclaim all responsibility for errors or omissions, including without limitation responsibility for damages resulting from the use of or reliance on this work. Use of the information and instructions contained in this work is at your own risk. If any code samples or other technology this work contains or describes is subject to open source licenses or the intellectual property rights of others, it is your responsibility to ensure that your use thereof complies with such licenses and/or rights.

ISBN: 978-1-491-90155-7

[LSI]

For Ellen, Zélie, Leo, and Hugh—my muses.

*An inconvenience is only an adventure wrongly considered; an adventure
is an inconvenience rightly considered.*

— GKC

A dead thing can go with the stream, but only a living thing can go against it.

— GKC

Table of Contents

Preface. xi

1. Cython Essentials. 1
   Comparing Python, C, and Cython   2
      Function Call Overhead   5
      Looping   6
      Math Operations   6
      Stack Versus Heap Allocation   6
   Tempering Our Enthusiasm   7
   Wrapping C Code with Cython   8
   Summary   10

2. Compiling and Running Cython Code. 11
   The Cython Compilation Pipeline   12
      Installing and Testing Our Setup   13
   The Standard Way: Using distutils with cythonize   14
      Our distutils Script   15
      Compiling with distutils on Mac OS X and Linux   15
      Compiling with distutils on Windows   16
      Using Our Extension Module   17
   Interactive Cython with IPython's %%cython Magic   19
   Compiling On-the-Fly with pyximport   21
      Controlling pyximport and Managing Dependencies   22
      pyximport Example with External Dependencies   23
   Rolling Our Own and Compiling by Hand   24
   Using Cython with Other Build Systems   26
      CMake and Cython   26
      SCons and Cython   26
      Make and Cython   26

Compiler Directives   28
Summary   29

3. Cython in Depth... 31
Interpreted Versus Compiled Execution   31
Dynamic Versus Static Typing   32
Static Type Declaration with cdef   34
  Automatic Type Inference in Cython   36
  C Pointers in Cython   37
  Mixing Statically and Dynamically Typed Variables   39
  Statically Declaring Variables with a Python Type   41
  Static Typing for Speed   43
  Reference Counting and Static String Types   45
Cython's Three Kinds of Functions   46
  Python Functions in Cython with the def Keyword   46
  C Functions in Cython with the cdef Keyword   49
  Combining def and cdef Functions with cpdef   50
  Functions and Exception Handling   51
  Functions and the embedsignature Compiler Directive   53
Type Coercion and Casting   55
Declaring and Using structs, unions, and enums   56
Type Aliasing with ctypedef   59
Cython for Loops and while Loops   61
  Guidelines for Efficient Loops   61
  Loop Example   62
The Cython Preprocessor   63
Bridging the Python 2 and Python 3 Divide   64
  str, unicode, bytes, and All That   66
Summary   67

4. Cython in Practice: N-Body Simulation........................... 69
Overview of the N-Body Python Code   69
Converting to Cython   71
  Python Data Structures and Organization   72
  Converting Data Structures to structs   73
  Running the Cythonized Version   75
Summary   76

5. Cython and Extension Types.................................. 79
Comparing Python Classes and Extension Types   79
Extension Types in Cython   80
Type Attributes and Access Control   83

C-Level Initialization and Finalization   85
cdef and cpdef Methods   86
Inheritance and Subclassing   89
   Casting and Subclasses   90
   Extension Type Objects and None   91
Extension Type Properties in Cython   92
Special Methods Are Even More Special   94
   Arithmetic Methods   94
   Rich Comparisons   96
   Iterator Support   98
Summary   99

6. Organizing Cython Code. 101
Cython Implementation (.pyx) and Declaration (.pxd) Files   102
The cimport Statement   105
   Predefined Definition Files   107
Include Files and the include Statement   109
Organizing and Compiling Cython Modules Inside Python Packages   110
Summary   113

7. Wrapping C Libraries with Cython. 115
Declaring External C Code in Cython   115
   Cython Does Not Automate Wrapping   117
Declaring External C Functions and typedefs   118
Declaring and Wrapping C structs, unions, and enums   119
Wrapping C Functions   121
Wrapping C structs with Extension Types   122
Constants, Other Modifiers, and Controlling What Cython Generates   125
Error Checking and Raising Exceptions   128
Callbacks   128
   Callbacks and Exception Propagation   133
Summary   134

8. Wrapping C++ Libraries with Cython. 135
Simple Example: MT_RNG Class   135
   The Wrapper Extension Type   137
   Compiling with C++   138
   Using Our Wrapper from Python   139
   Overloaded Methods and Functions   140
   Operator Overloading   142
C++ Exceptions   144
Stack and Heap Allocation of C++ Instances   145

Working with C++ Class Hierarchies   146
C++ Templates   147
    Templated Functions and Cython's Fused Types   148
    Templated Classes   149
    Iterators and Nested Classes   150
    Included STL Container Class Declarations   151
Memory Management and Smart Pointers   154
Summary   157

9. Cython Profiling Tools. 159
Cython Runtime Profiling   159
Performance Profiling and Annotations   164
Summary   170

10. Cython, NumPy, and Typed Memoryviews. 171
The Power of the New Buffer Protocol   172
    The memoryview Type   173
Typed Memoryviews   176
    Typed Memoryview Example   176
    C-Level Access to Typed Memoryview Data   177
    Trading Safety for Performance   178
    Declaring Typed Memoryviews   179
    Using Typed Memoryviews   183
    Beyond Buffers   187
Wrapping C and C++ Arrays   189
    Correct (and Automatic) Memory Management with Cython and C Arrays   189
Summary   192

11. Cython in Practice: Spectral Norm. 193
Overview of the Spectral Norm Python Code   193
Performance Profiling   196
Cythonizing Our Code   197
    Adding Static Type Information   198
    Using Typed Memoryviews   198
Comparing to the C Implementation   200
Summary   200

12. Parallel Programming with Cython. 201
Thread-Based Parallelism and the Global Interpreter Lock   201
    The nogil Function Attribute   202
    The with nogil Context Manager   203
Using prange to Parallelize Loops   204

Using prange   208
prange Options   209
Using prange for Reductions   210
Parallel Programming Pointers and Pitfalls   212
Summary   213

13. Cython in Context.   215
Cython Versus Project X   215
Other Ahead-of-Time Compilers for Python   216
Python Wrapper Projects   217
Just-in-Time Compilers for Python   218
Summary   219

Index.   221

Preface

There should be one-- and preferably only one --obvious way to do it.

Although that way may not be obvious at first unless you're Dutch.

— T. Peters
"The Zen of Python"

Cython: A Guide for Python Programmers covers all you need to know about the eponymous creole programming language and Python-to-C compiler. If you have heard of Cython and want to find out more, or if you have been using Cython and want to go deeper, then this book is for you.

Cython is not another experimental (and all too often minimally maintained) language x–to–language y compiler project. Neither is it limited to an interesting research project that never achieves widespread use. Cython is an integral part of foundational projects in the Python world. It is battle-tested in real-world environments, and it continues to innovate to provide better performance, greater ease of use, and better coverage of new Python features.

Who Should Read This Book?

This book is for you if:

- While programming Python, you have thought, "These nested for loops would run hundreds of times faster in C, but the hassle isn't worth it."

- You have considered using PyPy, Numba, or even Julia but want something more mature and with better support tools.

- You have ever wished Python supported optional static typing to speed up the numeric expression that takes up 40 percent of your runtime.

- You use NumPy, SciPy, Pandas, a scikit, or some other data-intensive package and want to go beyond the prepackaged algorithms *without* compromising performance.

- You have a tested and optimized C or C++ library that you want to wrap with Python without learning the arcana of yet another interfacing language.

- You have considered reprogramming that performance-critical part of your Python application as an extension module but were (rightly) put off by all the fussy details.

Prerequisites

Cython is unique in that it exists between languages. It is a hybrid, a chimera, a saber-toothed moose lion. Cython is *mostly* Python and comes from a Python frame of mind, so this book assumes an intermediate level of Python experience. You should be comfortable with all built-in data types, functions, classes, Python's object model, modules, packages, and the more common packages in the standard library. Knowing a bit—or willingness to learn—about how CPython works under the hood is helpful as well.

Intermediate experience with NumPy is assumed for later chapters.

Cython also speaks C, so at least a beginner's level of knowledge of the C or C++ language is necessary. Familiarity with the built-in C numeric types, pointers, C arrays, structs, unions, enums, and macros is useful. Cython takes a lot of the scariness and danger out of programming in C, but to go really far, the more C knowledge you have, the better. The C and C++ wrapping chapters assume an intermediate level of familiarity with these languages and are self-contained.

Who Should Not Read This Book?

If you are just starting out in Python, you will likely benefit from programming a few stretch projects before diving in here.

If you have had no exposure to C or C++, then you will likely need to have reference material handy to help you understand the C- and C++-specific parts. Going through a C or C++ tutorial and having some familiarity with compiled languages will serve you well.

Outline

Most of this book is written in a combination tutorial/reference style. Most chapters are meant to be read more or less in succession and will often build on previously covered material and concepts:

Chapter 1, Cython Essentials
The whirlwind tour, the 50,000-foot view: come here to marvel at how effortless Cython makes speeding up Python and interfacing with C.

Chapter 2, Compiling and Running Cython Code
Where we get you up and running so you can use Cython in your projects.

Chapter 3, Cython in Depth
Where we come to understand *how* Cython can speed up Python by several orders of magnitude. We also go into the basic elements of the Cython language, and what they do.

Chapter 4, Cython in Practice: N-Body Simulation
The first of our practice chapters. We start with a pure-Python program that simulates the solar system and use what we have learned so far to speed it up by two orders of magnitude.

Chapter 5, Cython and Extension Types
Where we learn how to create new Python types with Cython and see just how fast OOP in Python can be.

Chapter 6, Organizing Cython Code
Where we learn about Cython's definition files; implementation files; and how to create, organize, and work with Cython projects, small and large.

Chapter 7, Wrapping C Libraries with Cython
The first wrapping chapter: this covers the basic wrapping concepts and how to wrap a C library with Cython. Users will never know there is a C library underneath that beautiful Python interface!

Chapter 8, Wrapping C++ Libraries with Cython
Where we go down the rabbit hole of interfacing with C++, and see how Cython makes easy things simple and hard things possible.

Chapter 9, Cython Profiling Tools
Where we learn about Cython's runtime and compile-time profiling tools, and how to use them to help optimize our Cython code.

Chapter 10, Cython, NumPy, and Typed Memoryviews
Where we learn all about Cython's support for efficient array-oriented operations, and how to achieve truly massive performance improvements over Python.

Chapter 11, Cython in Practice: Spectral Norm
Our second practice chapter. This time we focus on optimizing a straightforward but nontrivial array-centric program, and achieve performance on par with a pure-C version.

Chapter 12, Parallel Programming with Cython
> Where we discover Cython's `prange` special function, which allows us to easily turn on thread-based parallelism and bypass the global interpreter lock.

Chapter 13, Cython in Context
> Where we compare Cython with other tools in the same space and indulge in a little prognostication.

Conventions Used in This Book

The following typographical conventions are used in this book:

Italic
> Indicates new terms, URLs, email addresses, filenames, and file extensions.

`Constant width`
> Used for program listings, as well as within paragraphs to refer to program elements such as variable or function names, data types, statements, and keywords.

`Constant width italic`
> Shows text that should be replaced with user-supplied values or by values determined by context.

 This element signifies a tip or suggestion.

 This element signifies a general note.

 This element indicates a warning or caution.

Using Code Examples

Supplemental material and the full source code for the in-text examples is available for download at *https://github.com/cythonbook/examples*.

All Cython code in this book is tested with Cython versions 0.20.2 and 0.21. The Cython language and compiler are fairly stable, and the code in this book will likely work with several earlier and later versions. That said, there is currently no strong backward compatibility constraint for future Cython releases, so some examples may require updating in the future.

This book is here to help you get your job done. In general, if example code is offered with this book, you may use it in your programs and documentation. You do not need to contact us for permission unless you're reproducing a significant portion of the code. For example, writing a program that uses several chunks of code from this book does not require permission. Selling or distributing a CD-ROM of examples from O'Reilly books does require permission. Answering a question by citing this book and quoting example code does not require permission. Incorporating a significant amount of example code from this book into your product's documentation does require permission.

We appreciate, but do not require, attribution. An attribution usually includes the title, author, publisher, and ISBN. For example: "*Cython* by Kurt W. Smith, PhD (O'Reilly). Copyright 2015 Kurt W. Smith, PhD, 978-1-491-90155-7."

If you feel your use of code examples falls outside fair use or the permission given above, feel free to contact us at *permissions@oreilly.com*.

Safari® Books Online

 *Safari Books Online* is an on-demand digital library that delivers expert content in both book and video form from the world's leading authors in technology and business.

Technology professionals, software developers, web designers, and business and creative professionals use Safari Books Online as their primary resource for research, problem solving, learning, and certification training.

Safari Books Online offers a range of plans and pricing for enterprise, government, education, and individuals.

Members have access to thousands of books, training videos, and prepublication manuscripts in one fully searchable database from publishers like O'Reilly Media, Prentice Hall Professional, Addison-Wesley Professional, Microsoft Press, Sams, Que, Peachpit Press, Focal Press, Cisco Press, John Wiley & Sons, Syngress, Morgan Kaufmann, IBM Redbooks, Packt, Adobe Press, FT Press, Apress, Manning, New Riders, McGraw-Hill, Jones & Bartlett, Course Technology, and hundreds more. For more information about Safari Books Online, please visit us online.

How to Contact Us

Please address comments and questions concerning this book to the publisher:

O'Reilly Media, Inc.
1005 Gravenstein Highway North
Sebastopol, CA 95472
800-998-9938 (in the United States or Canada)
707-829-0515 (international or local)
707-829-0104 (fax)

We have a web page for this book, where we list errata, examples, and any additional information. You can access this page at *http://bit.ly/cython_1e*.

To comment or ask technical questions about this book, send email to *cython book@gmail.com*.

For more information about our books, courses, conferences, and news, see our website at *http://www.oreilly.com*.

Find us on Facebook: *http://facebook.com/oreilly*

Follow us on Twitter: *http://twitter.com/oreillymedia*

Watch us on YouTube: *http://www.youtube.com/oreillymedia*

Acknowledgments

The Cython core developers—Robert Bradshaw, Stefan Behnel, and Dag Sverre Seljebotn—and Pyrex's main developer, Greg Ewing, deserve the lion's share of praise for conceiving of such a unique and useful tool, and for shouldering the *years* of development effort to make it happen. Without your insight, foresight, and diligence, there would be no reason for this book.

This work emerged rather than being planned, and is the result of several happy circumstances. Thanks to my employer, Enthought, and to the SciPy Conference organizers for providing a platform where Cython can shine. Thanks to Katy Huff (THW FTW!) for putting a bug in O'Reilly's ear; thanks to Mike Loukides for giving this book a hearing and for shepherding it through the proposal process; thanks to Meghan Blanchette for the encouragement and flexibility.

Thanks is due to all the technical editors for your time and investment: Robert Bradshaw, Robert Grant, Jonathan Rocher, Jordan Weaver, and Anthony Scopatz. The manuscript and examples would be half as good without your perspective and input.

Lastly, thanks to my beautiful and talented wife. Little do you realize how much you've had a hand in this work without writing a single word.

## CHAPTER 1

Cython Essentials

> *The test of a first-rate intelligence is the ability to hold two opposed*
> *ideas in mind at the same time and still retain the ability to function.*
>
> — F. Scott Fitzgerald

Cython is two closely related things:

- *Cython* is a programming language that blends Python with the static type system of C and C++.

- cython is a compiler that translates Cython source code into efficient C or C++ source code. This source can then be compiled into a Python extension module or a standalone executable.

Cython's power comes from the way it combines Python and C: it *feels like Python* while providing *easy access to C*. Cython is situated between high-level Python and low-level C; one might call it a *creole programming language*.

But Python and C-like languages are so *different*—why combine them? Precisely because their differences are complementary. Python is high-level, dynamic, easy to learn, and flexible. These positives come with a cost, however—because Python is dynamic and interpreted, it can be *several orders of magnitude* slower than statically typed compiled languages.

C, on the other hand, is one of the oldest statically typed compiled languages in widespread use, so compilers have had nearly half a century to optimize its performance. C is very low level and very powerful. Unlike Python, it does not have many safeguards in place and can be difficult to use.

Both languages are mainstream, but they are typically used in different domains, given their differences. Cython's beauty is this: it combines Python's expressiveness and dynamism with C's bare-metal performance *while still feeling like Python*.

With very few exceptions, Python code (both versions 2.x and 3.x) is already valid Cython code. Cython adds a small number of keywords to the Python language to tap into C's type system, allowing the cython compiler to generate efficient C code. If you already know Python and have a basic understanding of C or C++, you will be able to quickly learn Cython. You do not have to learn yet another interface language.

We can think of Cython as two projects in one. If compiling Python to C is Cython's *yin*, then interfacing C or C++ with Python is its *yang*. We can start with Python code that needs better performance, or we can start with C (or C++) code that needs an optimized Python interface. To speed up Python code, Cython compiles Python source with optional static type declarations to achieve *massive* performance improvements, depending on the algorithm. To interface C or C++ libraries with Python, we can use Cython to interface with external code and create optimized wrappers. Both capabilities—compiling Python and interfacing with external code—are designed to work together well, and each is an essential part of what makes Cython useful. With Cython, we can move in either direction, coming from either starting point.

Cython and CPython

Cython is often confused with *CPython* (mind the P), but the two are very different. CPython is the name of the standard and most widely used Python implementation (*https://www.python.org/*). CPython's core is written in the C language, and the C in CPython is meant to distinguish it from Python the language specification and Python implementations in other languages, such as Jython (Java), IronPython (.NET), and PyPy (Python implemented in Python!). CPython provides a C-level interface into the Python language; the interface is known as the *Python/C API* (*http://docs.python.org/2/c-api/*). Cython uses this C interface extensively, and therefore Cython depends on CPython. Cython is not another implementation of Python—it needs the CPython runtime to run the extension modules it generates.

Let's see an example.

Comparing Python, C, and Cython

Consider a simple Python function fib that computes the *n*th Fibonacci number:[1]

---

1. To follow along with the examples in this chapter, please see *https://github.com/cythonbook/examples*.

```
def fib(n):
    a, b = 0.0, 1.0
    for i in range(n):
        a, b = a + b, a
    return a
```

As mentioned in the introduction, this Python function is already a valid Cython function, and it has identical behavior in both Python and Cython. We will see shortly how we can add Cython-specific syntax to fib to improve its performance.

The C transliteration of fib follows the Python version closely:

```
double cfib(int n) {
    int i;
    double a=0.0, b=1.0, tmp;
    for (i=0; i<n; ++i) {
        tmp = a; a = a + b; b = tmp;
    }
    return a;
}
```

We use doubles in the C version and floats in the Python version to make the comparison direct and remove any issues related to integer overflow for C integral data types.

Imagine blending the types from the C version with the code from the Python version. The result is a statically typed Cython version:

```
def fib(int n):
    cdef int i
    cdef double a=0.0, b=1.0
    for i in range(n):
        a, b = a + b, a
    return a
```

As mentioned previously, Cython understands Python code, so our unmodified Python fib function is also valid Cython code. To convert the dynamically typed Python version to the statically typed Cython version, we use the cdef Cython statement to declare the statically typed C variables i, a, and b. Even for readers who haven't seen Cython code before, it should be straightforward to understand what is going on.

What about performance? Table 1-1 has the results.

Table 1-1. Fibonacci timings for different implementations

Version	fib(0) [ns]	Speedup	fib(90) [ns]	Speedup	Loop body [ns]	Speedup
Pure Python	590	1	12,852	1	12,262	1
Pure C	2	295	164	78	162	76
C extension	220	3	386	33	166	74
Cython	90	7	258	50	168	73

In Table 1-1,[2] the second column measures the runtime for `fib(0)` and the third column measures the speedup of `fib(0)` relative to Python. Because the argument to `fib` controls the number of loop iterations, `fib(0)` does not enter the Fibonacci loop, so its runtime is a reasonable measure of the language-runtime and function-call overhead.

The fourth and fifth columns measure the runtime and speedup for `fib(90)`, which executes the loop 90 times. Both the call overhead and the loop execution runtime contribute to its runtime.

The sixth and seventh columns measure the difference between the `fib(90)` runtime and the `fib(0)` runtime and the relative speedup. This difference is an approximation of the runtime for the loop alone, removing runtime and call overhead.

Table 1-1 has four rows:

Pure Python
> The first row (after the header) measures the performance of the pure-Python version of `fib`, and as expected, it has the poorest performance by a significant margin in all categories. In particular, the call overhead for `fib(0)` is over half a microsecond on this system. Each loop iteration in `fib(90)` requires nearly 150 nanoseconds; Python leaves much room for improvement.

Pure C
> The second row measures the performance of the pure-C version of `fib`. In this version there is no interaction with the Python runtime, so there is minimal call overhead; this also means it cannot be used from Python. This version provides a bound for the best performance we can reasonably expect from a simple serial `fib` function. The `fib(0)` value indicates that C function call overhead is minimal (2 nanoseconds) when compared to Python, and the `fib(90)` runtime (164 nanoseconds) is nearly 80 times faster than Python's on this particular system.

Hand-written C extension
> The third row measures a hand-written C extension module for Python 2. This extension module requires several dozen lines of C code, most of it boilerplate that calls the Python/C API. When calling from Python, the extension module must convert Python objects to C data, compute the Fibonacci number in C, and convert the result back to a Python object. Its call overhead (the `fib(0)` column) is correspondingly larger than that of the pure-C version, which does not have to convert from and to Python objects. Because it is written in C, it is about three times faster than pure Python for `fib(0)`. It also gives a nice factor-of-30 speedup for `fib(90)`.

---

2. Timings were measured on a four-core 2.4 GHz Intel Core i5 with 8 GB of 1,067 MHz DDR3 memory, running Mac OS X version 10.7.5.

Cython

The last row measures the performance for the Cython version. Like the C extension, it is usable from Python, so it must convert Python objects to C data before it can compute the Fibonacci number, and then convert the result back to Python. Because of this overhead, it cannot match the pure-C version for fib(0), but, notably, it has about 2.5 times less overhead than the hand-written C extension. Because of this reduced call overhead, it is able to provide a speedup of about a factor of 50 over pure Python for fib(90).

The takeaways from Table 1-1 are the last two columns: the loop runtime for the pure C, C extension, and Cython versions are all about 165 nanoseconds on this system, and the speedups relative to Python are all approximately 75×.

 For the C-only parts of an algorithm—provided sufficient static type information is available—Cython can usually generate code that is as efficient as a pure-C equivalent.

So, when properly accounting for Python overhead, we see that Cython achieves C-level performance. Moreover, it does better than the hand-written C extension module on the Python-to-C conversions.

 Cython generates highly optimized code that is frequently faster than an equivalent hand-written C extension module. It is often able to generate Python-to-C conversion code that is several factors faster than naive calls into the Python/C API.

As we will learn in Chapter 3, we can go even further and use Cython to create Python-like C functions that have no Python overhead. These functions can be called from other Cython code but cannot be called directly from Python. They allow us to remove expensive call overhead for core computations.

What is the reason for Cython's performance improvements? For this example, the likely causes are function call overhead, looping, math operations, and stack versus heap allocations.

Function Call Overhead

The fib(0) runtime is mostly consumed by the time it takes to call a function in the respective language; the time to run the function's body is relatively small. We see in Table 1-1 that Cython generates code that is nearly an order of magnitude faster than calling a Python function, and more than two times faster than the hand-written extension. Cython accomplishes this by generating highly optimized C code that by-passes some of the slower Python/C API calls. We use these API calls in the preceding C-extension timings.

Looping

Python for loops, as compared to compiled languages, are notoriously slow. One sure-fire way to speed up loopy Python code is to find ways to move the Python for and while loops into compiled code, either by calling built-in functions or by using something like Cython to do the transformation for you. The fib(90) column in the table is running a for loop in each language for 90 iterations, and we see the impact of this operation on the different version runtimes.

Math Operations

Because Python is dynamically typed and cannot make any type-based optimizations, an expression like a + b could do *anything*. We may know that a and b are only ever going to be floating-point numbers, but Python never makes that assumption. So, at runtime, Python has to look up the types of both a and b (which, in this instance, are the same). It must then find the type's underlying __add__ method (or the equivalent), and call __add__ with a and b as arguments. Inside this method, the Python floats a and b have to be unboxed to extract the underlying C doubles, and only *then* can the actual addition occur! The result of this addition has to be packaged in an entirely new Python float and returned as the result.

The C and Cython versions already know that a and b are doubles and can never be anything else, so adding a and b compiles to just one machine code instruction.

Stack Versus Heap Allocation

At the C level, a dynamic Python object is entirely heap allocated. Python takes great pains to intelligently manage memory, using memory pools and internalizing frequently used integers and strings. But the fact remains that creating and destroying objects—*any objects, even scalars*—incurs overhead to work with dynamically allocated memory and Python's memory subsystem. Because Python float objects are immutable, operations using Python floats involve the creation and destruction of heap-allocated objects. The Cython version of fib declares all variables to be stack-allocated C doubles. As a rule, stack allocation is much faster than heap allocation. Moreover, C floating-point numbers are mutable, meaning that the for loop body is much more efficient in terms of allocations and memory usage.

It is not surprising that the C and Cython versions are more than an order of magnitude faster than pure Python, since the Python loop body has to do so much more work per iteration.

Tempering Our Enthusiasm

It can be exhilarating to see massive performance improvements when we add some trivial cdef statements to Python code. It is worth noting at the start, however, that not all Python code will see massive performance improvements when compiled with Cython. The preceding fib example is intentionally CPU bound, meaning all the runtime is spent manipulating a few variables inside CPU registers, and little to no data movement is required. If this function were, instead, memory bound (e.g., adding the elements of two large arrays), I/O bound (e.g., reading a large file from disk), or network bound (e.g., downloading a file from an FTP server), the performance difference between Python, C, and Cython would likely be significantly decreased (for memory-bound operations) or vanish entirely (for I/O-bound or network-bound operations).

When improving Python's performance is the goal, the Pareto principle works in our favor: we can expect that approximately 80 percent of a program's runtime is due to only 20 percent of the code. A corollary to this principle is that the 20 percent is very difficult to locate without profiling. But there is no excuse not to profile Python code, given how simple its built-in profiling tools are to use. Before we use Cython to improve performance, getting profiling data is the first step.

That said, if we determine via profiling that the bottleneck in our program is due to it being I/O or network bound, then we cannot expect Cython to provide a significant improvement in performance. It is worth determining the kind of performance bottleneck you have before turning to Cython—it is a powerful tool, but it must be used in the right way.

Because Cython brings C's type system to Python, all limitations of C data types become relevant concerns. Python integer objects silently convert to unlimited-precision Python long objects when computing large values. C ints or longs are fixed precision, meaning that they cannot properly represent unlimited-precision integers. Cython has features to help catch these overflows, but the larger point remains: C data types are faster than their Python counterparts, but are sometimes not as flexible or general.

Let's consider Cython's other main feature: interfacing with external code. Suppose that, instead of Python code, our starting point is C or C++ code, and that we want to create Python wrappers for it. Because Cython understands C and C++ declarations and can interface with external libraries, and because it generates highly optimized code, it is easy to write efficient wrappers with it.

Wrapping C Code with Cython

Continuing with our Fibonacci theme, let's start with a C implementation and wrap it in Python using Cython. The interface for our function is in *cfib.h*:

```
double cfib(int n);
```

The Cython wrapper code for *cfib.h* is fewer than 10 lines:

```
cdef extern from "cfib.h":
    double cfib(int n)

def fib(n):
    """Returns the nth Fibonacci number."""
    return cfib(n)
```

The cdef extern block may not be immediately transparent, but certain elements are easily identified: we provide the cfib.h header filename in the cdef extern from statement, and we declare the cfib function's signature in the block's indented body. After the cdef extern block, we define a fib Python wrapper function, which calls cfib and returns its result.

After compiling the preceding Cython code into an extension module named wrap_fib (we will cover the details of how to compile Cython code in Chapter 2), we can use it from Python:

```
>>> from wrap_fib import fib
>>> help(fib)
Help on built-in function fib in module wrap_fib:

fib(...)
    Returns the nth Fibonacci number.

>>> fib(90)
2.880067194370816e+18
>>>
```

We see that the fib function is a regular Python function inside the wrap_fib extension module, and calling it with a Python integer does what we expect, calling into the underlying C function for us and returning a (large) result. Overall, it was just a handful of lines of Cython code to wrap a simple function. A hand-written wrapper would require several dozen lines of C code, and detailed knowledge of the Python/C API. The performance benefits we saw in the previous section apply here as well—Cython's wrapper code is better optimized than a hand-written version of the same.

This example was intentionally simple. Provided the values are in range, a Python int converts to a C int without issue, and raises an OverflowError otherwise. Internally the Python float type stores its value in a C double, so there are no conversion issues for the cfib return type. Because we are using simple scalar data, Cython can generate the type conversion code automatically. In future chapters, we will see how Cython helps us wrap arbitrarily complex data structures, classes, functions, and methods. Because Cython is a full-fledged language (and not just a domain-specific language for interfacing like other wrapping tools provide), we can use it to do whatever we like before and after the wrapped function call. Because the Cython language understands Python and has access to Python's standard library, we can leverage all of Python's power and flexibility.

It should be noted that we can use Cython's two *raisons d'être* in one file—speeding up Python alongside calling external C functions. We can even do both inside the same function! We will see this in future chapters.

Cython's Origins

Greg Ewing is the author of Pyrex, Cython's predecessor. When Pyrex was first released, its ability to speed up Python code by large factors made it instantaneously popular. Many projects adopted it and started using it intensively.

Pyrex did not intend to support all constructs in the Python language, but this did not limit its initial success—it satisfied a pressing need, especially for the scientific Python community. As is often the case with successful open source projects, other projects adapted and patched Pyrex to fit their needs. Two forks of Pyrex—one by Stefan Behnel and the other by William Stein—ultimately combined to form the Cython project, under the leadership and guidance of Robert Bradshaw and Stefan Behnel.

Since Cython's inception, William Stein's Sage project has been the major driver behind its development. Sage is a GPL-licensed comprehensive mathematics software system that aims to provide a viable alternative to Magma, Maple, Mathematica, and Matlab. Sage uses Cython extensively to speed up Python-centric algorithms and to interface with dozens of C, C++, and Fortran libraries. It is, bar none, the largest extant Cython project, with hundreds of thousand of lines of Cython code. Without Sage's support, Cython would likely not have had the sustained initial support to become what it is today: a self-standing, widely used, and actively developed open source project.

Since its creation, Cython has had expansive goals, first and foremost being full Python compatibility. It has also acquired features that are specific to its unique position between Python and C, making Cython easier to use, more efficient, and more expressive. Some of these Cython-only features are:

- Features for easier interoperability and conversion between C types and Python types
- Specialized syntax to ease wrapping and interfacing with C++
- Automatic static type inference for certain code paths
- First-class buffer support with buffer-specific syntax (Chapter 10)

- Typed memoryviews (Chapter 10)
- Thread-based parallelism with `prange` (Chapter 12)

The project has in its lifetime received funding and support from the NSF (via Sage), the University of Washington, Enthought (the author's employer), and several Google Summer of Code projects (one of which funded the author's Cython development in 2009). Besides explicit funding, Cython has benefited from a large and active open source community, with many contributions of time and effort to develop new features, to implement them, to report bugs, and to fix them.

Summary

This chapter is meant to whet the appetite. We have seen Cython's essential features, distilled to their most basic elements. The rest of this book explains the Cython language in depth, covers how to compile and run Cython code, describes how to interface with C and C++, and provides many examples to help you use Cython effectively in your own projects.

Compiling and Running Cython Code

I was taught that the way of progress was neither swift nor easy.

— M. Curie

It's not that I'm so smart, it's just that I stay with problems longer.

— A. Einstein

One of the more significant differences between Python and C or C++ is that Python is interpreted while C and C++ are compiled. When developing a Python program, we can immediately run code after making a modification, while C and C++ require an intervening compilation step. Compiling a large C or C++ code base can take hours or days. Using Python can allow much more rapid development, leading to a significant productivity boost.

Like C and C++, Cython requires a compilation step before the source can be run. This compilation step can be explicit or implicit. Both modes have their uses. One nice feature of automatically compiling Cython is that it makes working with Cython feel like working with pure Python. Whether compiling explicitly or implicitly, because Cython can be applied selectively to small sections of a Python code base, Cython's compilation requirement can be minimized.

This chapter will cover the various ways to compile Cython code so that it can be run by Python. There are several options:

- Cython code can be compiled and run interactively from an IPython interpreter.
- It can be compiled automatically at import time.
- It can be separately compiled by build tools like Python's `distutils`.
- It can be integrated into standard build systems such as make, CMake, or SCons.

These options allow us to adapt Cython to particular use cases, from quick interactive exploration on one end to building for the ages on the other.

 It is not necessary to know all the methods to compile Cython code, so this chapter can be read piecemeal.

In all cases, each method passes Cython code through two compilation stages to generate a compiled module that Python can import and use. Before we cover the particulars of each compilation method, it is helpful to understand what is going on in this pipeline.

The Cython Compilation Pipeline

Because the Cython language is a superset of Python, the Python interpreter cannot import and run it directly. So how do we get from Cython source to valid Python? Via the Cython compilation pipeline.

The pipeline's job is to transform Cython code into a Python extension module that can be imported and used by the Python interpreter. This pipeline can be run either automatically, without user involvement (making Cython feel much like Python), or explicitly by the end user when more control is required.

 Cython has a pure-Python mode (*http://docs.cython.org/src/tutorial/pure.html*), which allows the user to bring in Cython-specific declarations in a way that remains valid Python syntax. Code developed in pure-Python mode is more verbose, but can be run directly by the Python interpreter (with no Cython speed improvement) or compiled by Cython. We do not cover pure-Python mode here, leaving its treatment to the online documentation.

The pipeline comprises two stages. The first stage is handled by the cython compiler, which transforms Cython source into optimized and platform-independent C or C++. The second stage compiles the generated C or C++ source into a shared library with a standard C or C++ compiler. The resulting shared library is platform dependent. It is a shared-object file with a *.so* extension on Linux or Mac OS X, and is a dynamic library with a *.pyd* extension on Windows. The flags passed to the C or C++ compiler ensure this shared library is a full-fledged Python module. We call this compiled module an *extension module*, and it can be imported and used as if it were written in pure Python.

Nearly all the complexity of these stages is managed by the tools we will describe in the rest of this chapter. We rarely have to think about what is going on when the compilation pipeline is running, but it is good to keep these stages in mind as we go through the following sections.

 The cython compiler is a source-to-source compiler, and the generated code is highly optimized. It is not uncommon for Cython-generated C code to be faster than typical hand-written C. When the author teaches Cython, students often write C equivalents to Cython's code; the Cython version is nearly always faster, and—for equivalent algorithms—is never slower. Cython's generated C code is also highly portable, supporting all common C compilers and many Python versions simultaneously.

Installing and Testing Our Setup

Now that we know about the two stages in the compilation pipeline, we need to ensure that we have both a C (or C++) compiler and the cython compiler installed and working. Different platforms have different options.

C and C++ compilers

Linux

Refer to the documentation for the distribution's package manager (for example, yum for RedHat-based distros, apt-get for Debian-based, etc.) for how to install GCC and the Python development package (often called python-dev, or some variant) to acquire the Python headers.

Mac OS X

Install the free OS X developer tools via Xcode (*https://developer.apple.com/xcode/ downloads/*); this provides a GCC-like compiler.

Windows

The recommended compiler to use on Windows is Visual Studio, the same version used to compile the Python runtime. If this is not available, then one alternative is the Microsoft-provided minimal Visual C++ compiler (*http://bit.ly/ms_cplus plus_compiler*) for compiling extensions for Python 2.7. Another good alternative is to use the Windows SDK C/C++ compiler (*http://bit.ly/64bit_cython_ext*). These compilers are the only reliable options for compiling 64-bit extensions. Another option on Windows for 32-bit extensions is to use MinGW (*http://bit.ly/installin gonwindows*). It is not as reliable as the Microsoft-provided compilers, but will likely work for simple examples. The MinGW compiler is distributed via several pre-packaged Python software distributions, mentioned in the next section.

Installing Cython

Likely the easiest way to acquire Cython is via a packaged software distribution, such as these popular options:

- The Sage Mathematics software system (*http://www.sagemath.org/*)
- Enthought's Canopy (*https://www.enthought.com/products/canopy/*)
- Anaconda (*https://store.continuum.io/cshop/anaconda/*), from Continuum Analytics
- The GPL-licensed and Windows-centric Python(x,y) (*https://code.google.com/p/pythonxy/*)

Being prepackaged, these options are likely to lag one or two releases behind the most up-to-date version of Cython.

To use the most recent version of Cython, we can install from source. This requires a working C or C++ compiler; see the previous section for details. Likely the easiest way to install from source is via `pip`, which is commonly available via the listed package distributions and is now distributed with Python (version 3.4) itself:

```
$ pip install cython
```

Another option is to download the Cython source code (*https://github.com/cython/cython/releases*). From the Cython source directory, run:

```
$ python setup.py install
```

Once installed—whether via a software distribution or compiled by hand—the `cython` compiler will be available from the command line:

```
$ cython -V
Cython version 0.20.2
```

Once we have a C compiler and the `cython` compiler in place, we are ready to follow along with the `distutils` and `pyximport` sections in this chapter.

Additionally, we will need to have IPython installed to use Cython from within IPython. The packaged distributions include IPython, or we can use `pip` to install it.

The Standard Way: Using distutils with cythonize

Python's standard library includes the `distutils` package (*https://docs.python.org/2/distutils/*) for building, packaging, and distributing Python projects. The `distutils` package has many features; of interest to us is its ability to compile C source into an extension module, the second stage in the pipeline. It manages all platform, architecture, and Python-version details for us, so we can use one `distutils` script and run it anywhere to generate our extension module.

What about the first pipeline stage? That is the job of the `cythonize` command, which is included with Cython: it takes a Cython source file (and any other necessary options) and compiles it to a C or C++ source file, and then `distutils` takes it from there.

By using Python's `distutils` module combined with Cython's `cythonize` command, we have explicit control over the compilation pipeline. This approach requires that we write a small Python script and run it explicitly. It is the most common way for Python projects to compile and distribute their Cython code to end users.

Our distutils Script

For example, consider the *fib.pyx* Cython source code from Chapter 1. Our goal is to use `distutils` to create a compiled extension module—*fib.so* on Mac OS X or Linux, and *fib.pyd* on Windows.

We control the behavior of `distutils` through a Python script, typically named *setup.py*. A minimal *setup.py* script for compiling the *fib.pyx* source file into an extension module is just a few lines long, two of which are imports:[1]

```
from distutils.core import setup
from Cython.Build import cythonize

setup(ext_modules=cythonize('fib.pyx'))
```

The core of the script is in the `setup(cythonize(...))` nested calls. The `cythonize` function in its simplest usage converts Cython source to C source code by calling the `cython` compiler. We can pass it a single file, a sequence of files, or a glob pattern that will match Cython files.

> The `cythonize` command returns a list of `distutils` `Extension` objects that the `setup` function knows how to turn into Python extension modules. It is designed to make `distutils` easier to use for Cython projects.
>
> The `cythonize` command has several other options; see its docstring for details.

Compiling with distutils on Mac OS X and Linux

These two function calls succinctly demonstrate the two stages in the pipeline: `cythonize` calls the `cython` compiler on the *.pyx* source file or files, and `setup` compiles the generated C or C++ code into a Python extension module.

It is a simple matter to invoke this *setup.py* script from the command line:

---

1. To follow along with the examples in this chapter, please see *https://github.com/cythonbook/examples*.

```
$ python setup.py build_ext --inplace
```

The `build_ext` argument is a command instructing `distutils` to build the `Extension` object or objects that the `cythonize` call created. The optional `--inplace` flag instructs `distutils` to place each extension module next to its respective Cython *.pyx* source file.

 To get the full list of options that the `build_ext` subcommand supports, we can run:

```
$ python setup.py build_ext --help
```

Other options allow us to control the preprocessor, include directories, link directories, and link libraries.

The output from this command will look different on Mac OS X, Linux, and Windows—that's `distutils` doing its job for us and handling the platform-specific aspects of the compilation.

For instance, on Mac OS X we will see something like the following, with slight modifications based on our Python version, OS version, architecture, and so on:

```
$ python setup.py build_ext -i
Compiling fib.pyx because it changed.
Cythonizing fib.pyx
running build_ext
building 'fib' extension
creating build
creating build/temp.macosx-10.4-x86_64-2.7
gcc -fno-strict-aliasing -fno-common -dynamic -g -O2
    -DNDEBUG -g -fwrapv -O3 -Wall -Wstrict-prototypes
    -I/Users/ksmith/Devel/PY64/Python.framework/Versions/2.7/include/python2.7
    -c fib.c -o build/temp.macosx-10.4-x86_64-2.7/fib.o
gcc -bundle -undefined dynamic_lookup
    build/temp.macosx-10.4-x86_64-2.7/fib.o
    -o /Users/ksmith/fib.so
```

The line `Cythonizing fib.pyx` is where the call to the `cython` compiler takes place. If we have a syntax error or otherwise invalid Cython code in *fib.pyx*, the `cython` compiler will print out a helpful message and stop things at this step. There are two calls to `gcc`: the first compiles the generated *fib.c* code into an object file, and the second links this object file into a Python extension module, *fib.so*. If the calls are successful, we should see in this directory the generated *fib.c* source file, the compiled extension module *fib.so*, and a directory named *build* with the intermediate build products.

Compiling with distutils on Windows

On Windows we may need to add extra arguments, depending on which compiler we are using and a few other factors:

```
C:\Users\ksmith> python setup.py build_ext -i --compiler=mingw32 -DMS_WIN64
Compiling fib.pyx because it changed.
Cythonizing fib.pyx
running build_ext
building 'fib' extension
creating build
creating build\temp.win-amd64-2.7
creating build\temp.win-amd64-2.7\Release
C:\Users\ksmith\gcc.exe -mno-cygwin -mdll -O -Wall
    -DMS_WIN64=1 -IC:\Users\ksmith\include -c fib.c
    -o build\temp.win-amd64-2.7\Release\fib.o
writing build\temp.win-amd64-2.7\Release\fib.def
C:\Users\ksmith\gcc.exe -mno-cygwin -shared -s
    build\temp.win-amd64-2.7\Release\fib.o
    build\temp.win-amd64-2.7\Release\fib.def
    -LC:\Users\ksmith\libs -LC:\Users\ksmith\amd64
    -lpython27 -lmsvcr90 -o C:\Users\ksmith\fib.pyd
```

Here we use the `mingw` compiler to compile the *fib.pyd* extension module. Because this Python interpreter is a 64-bit executable, we add an extra `-DMS_WIN64` flag to compile in 64-bit mode. Otherwise the steps are the same, with different output that is specific for Windows. The result is the *fib.pyd* extension module, and usage is identical to the Mac OS X version.

If using a different Windows compiler, like Visual Studio or the SDK C/C++ compiler, we should set the `compiler` flag to `msvc` and can remove the `-DMS_WIN64` flag:

```
C:\Users\ksmith> python setup.py build_ext -i --compiler=msvc
...
```

Consult the linked documentation for details.

Using Our Extension Module

Whether on Mac OS X, Linux, or Windows, once we have compiled our extension module, we can bring up our Python or IPython interpreter and import the `fib` module:

```
$ ipython --no-banner

In [1]: import fib
```

If no `ImportError` is raised, then the compilation was likely successful.

We can use IPython's handy introspection features to provide more details about our extension module:

```
In [2]: fib?
Type:        module
String Form:<module 'fib' from 'fib.so'>
File:        /Users/ksmith/fib.so
Docstring:   <no docstring>
```

Putting a single ? after an object instructs IPython to tell us what it knows about the object.

We can also inspect the `fib.fib` function we created:

```
In [3]: fib.fib?
Type:        builtin_function_or_method
String Form:<built-in function fib>
Docstring:   Returns the nth Fibonacci number.
```

Notice that the docstring we defined in Cython shows up in our interactive session. Our `fib` function is a `builtin_function_or_method`; that is one way we can tell that this function is implemented in compiled code rather than in straight Python. It is a full-fledged Python function, though.

To really test things out, let's call `fib.fib`:

```
In [4]: fib.fib(90)
Out[4]: 2.880067194370816e+18
```

When using Cython to wrap C and C++ code, which we will cover in detail in Chapters 7 and 8, we must include other source files in the compilation step.

For example, consider the `distutils` script *setup_wrap.py* that compiles the *cfib.c* wrappers from Chapter 1:

```
from distutils.core import setup, Extension
from Cython.Build import cythonize

# First create an Extension object with the appropriate name and sources.
ext = Extension(name="wrap_fib", sources=["cfib.c", "wrap_fib.pyx"])

# Use cythonize on the extension object.
setup(ext_modules=cythonize(ext))
```

This `distutils` script requires one extra step to wrap an external library: we create an `Extension` object with all C and Cython sources listed and passed in the `sources` argument. We then pass this `Extension` object to `cythonize`, and `cythonize` and the `setup` command ensure that the *cfib.c* file is compiled into the resulting extension module.

If we are provided a precompiled dynamic library *libfib.so* rather than source code, we can instruct `distutils` to link against *libfib.so* at link time:

```
from distutils.core import setup, Extension
from Cython.Build import cythonize

ext = Extension(name="wrap_fib",
                sources=["wrap_fib.pyx"],
                library_dirs=["/path/to/libfib.so"],
                libraries=["fib"])

setup(ext_modules=cythonize(ext))
```

Here we name only *wrap_fib.pyx* in the `sources` argument list, and add a `library_dirs` and a `libraries` argument to our `Extension` object with the appropriate values. For more details on all options that the `distutils Extension` object supports, please see Python's official documentation.

Interactive Cython with IPython's %%cython Magic

Using `distutils` to compile Cython code gives us full control over every step of the process. The downside to using `distutils` is it requires a separate compilation step and works only with *.pyx* source files—no interactive use allowed. This is a definite disadvantage, as one of Python's strengths is its interactive interpreter, which allows us to play around with code and test how something works before committing it to a source file. The IPython project has convenient commands that allow us to interactively use Cython from a live IPython session.

These extra commands are IPython-specific commands called *magic commands*, and they start with either a single (%) or double (%%) percent sign. They provide functionality beyond what the plain Python interpreter supplies. IPython has several magic commands to allow dynamic compilation of Cython code, which we cover here.

Before we can use these magic Cython commands, we first need to tell IPython to load them. We do that with the `%load_ext` metamagic command from the IPython interactive interpreter, or in an IPython notebook cell:

```
In [12]: %load_ext cythonmagic
```

There will be no output if `%load_ext` is successful, and IPython will issue an error message if it cannot find the Cython-related magics.[2]

Now we can use Cython from IPython via the `%%cython` magic command:

```
In [13]: %%cython
   ...: def fib(int n):
   ...:     cdef int i
   ...:     cdef double a=0.0, b=1.0
   ...:     for i in range(n):
```

---

2. If this is the case, an out-of-date IPython is likely the culprit; please update to a more recent version.

```
      ...:          a, b = a+b, a
      ...:      return a
      ...:

In [14]:
```

The %%cython magic command allows us to write a block of Cython code directly in the IPython interpreter. After exiting the block with two returns, IPython will take the Cython code we defined, paste it into a uniquely named Cython source file, and compile it into an extension module. If compilation is successful, IPython will import everything from that module to make the fib function available in the IPython interactive name-space. The compilation pipeline is still in effect, but it is all done for us automatically.

We can now call the fib function we just defined:

```
In [14]: fib(90)
Out[14]: 2.880067194370816e+18
```

 The %%cython magic command recognizes when it has already compiled an identical code block, in which case it bypasses the com-pilation step and loads the precompiled block directly.

There may be a pause after we press return when ending a new Cython code block and before the next input prompt appears: that is IPython compiling and loading the code block behind the scenes.

We can always inspect the generated source file if necessary. It is located in the *$IPYTHONDIR/cython* directory (*~/.ipython/cython* on an OS X or *nix system). The module names are not easily readable because they are formed from the md5 hash of the Cython source code, but all the contents are there.

We can pass optional arguments to the %%cython magic command. The first set of options control the cython compilation stage:

-n, --name
    Specifies the name of the generated *.pyx* file

--cplus
    Instructs cython to generate C++ source

-a, --annotate
    Instructs cython to output an annotated source file (see Chapter 9)

-f, --force
    Forces cython to regenerate C or C++ source

The second set of options allows us to control the second pipeline stage:

-I, --include

Adds extra directories to search for file inclusions and cimports

-c, --compile-args

Allows inclusion of extra C compiler arguments

--link-args

Allows inclusion of extra link arguments

-L

Adds extra library search directories

-l

Adds extra library names to link against

There are other Cython magic commands that are loaded by %load_ext cythonmagic: the %%cython_inline command and the %%cython_pyximport command. These are not as widely used as the %%cython magic command, which is sufficient for quick interactive use and exploration. The %%cython_inline command—as suggested by its name—simply compiles and runs Cython code embedded in the current Python namespace.

Similarly, %%cython_pyximport builds on the pyximport package that comes with Cython, so we'll defer its discussion until the next section.

Compiling On-the-Fly with pyximport

Because Cython is Python-centric, it is natural to want to work with Cython source files as if they were regular, dynamic, importable Python modules. Enter pyximport: it retrofits the import statement to recognize .pyx extension modules, sends them through the compilation pipeline automatically, and *then* imports the extension module for use by Python.

Let's see an example. The pyximport module comes with Cython, and requires just two statements to get it up and running:

```
import pyximport
pyximport.install()  # .install() called before importing
                     # Cython extension modules.
```

We can use pyximport in an interactive IPython session to compile and load our familiar *fib.pyx* example. First, we bring in pyximport itself:

```
In [1]: import pyximport

In [2]: pyximport.install()
Out[2]: (None, <pyximport.pyximport.PyxImporter at 0x101548a90>)
```

With `pyximport` installed, we can `import fib` as if it were *fib.py*, and `pyximport` compiles it automatically:

```
In [3]: import fib
```

Let's check the `__file__` attribute:

```
In [4]: fib.__file__
Out[4]: '/Users/ksmith/.pyxbld/lib.macosx-10.4-x86_64-2.7/fib.so'
```

Everything else checks out, and we can run `fib.fib` as before:

```
In [5]: type(fib)
Out[5]: module

In [6]: fib.fib(90)
Out[6]: 2.880067194370816e+18
```

For simple cases like this example, using `pyximport` removes the need to write a *setup.py* `distutils` script, and we can treat *fib.pyx* as if it were a regular Python module. If a Cython source file is modified, `pyximport` automatically detects the modification and will recompile the source file the next time it is imported in a new Python interpreter session.

Because Cython modules imported via `pyximport` depend on both the `cython` compiler and a properly set up C compiler, it tends not to be used in production environments where these dependencies are not under our control.

Controlling pyximport and Managing Dependencies

The `pyximport` package also handles more complex use cases. For instance, what if a Cython source file depends on other source files, such as C or C++ source or header files, or other Cython source files? In this case, `pyximport` needs to recompile the *.pyx* file if any of its dependencies have been updated, regardless of whether the *.pyx* file itself has changed. To enable this functionality, we add a file with the same base name as the *.pyx* source file and with a *.pyxdeps* extension in the same directory as the Cython source file. It should contain a listing of files that the *.pyx* file depends on, one file per line. These files can be in other directories relative to the directory of the *.pyxdeps* file. The entries can also be glob patterns that match multiple files at once. If a *.pyxdeps* file exists, `pyximport` will read it at import time and compare the modification time of each listed file with the modification time of the *.pyx* file being imported. If any file that matches a pattern in the *.pyxdeps* file is newer than the *.pyx* file, then `pyximport` will recompile on import.

The *.pyxdeps* file is nice to communicate file dependencies to `pyximport`, but how do we tell `pyximport` to compile and link several source files into one extension module? That role is filled by a *.pyxbld* file: its purpose is to customize `pyximport` for this and other use cases. Like *.pyxdeps*, a *.pyxbld* file has the same base name as its Cython source file and replaces the *.pyx* extension with *.pyxbld*. It should be located in the same directory as the *.pyx* file being imported.

What goes inside a *.pyxbld* file? One or two Python functions, each optional:

make_ext(*modname, pyxfilename*)

> If defined, the make_ext function is called with two string arguments before compilation. The first argument is the name of the module, and the second is the name of the *.pyx* file being compiled. It returns a distutils.extension.Extension instance, or (equivalently) it can return the result of a call to Cython.Build.cythonize. This allows the user to customize the Extension being used. By adding files to the sources argument when creating an Extension instance, it instructs pyximport to compile external source files and link them with the compiled *.pyx* file when creating the extension module. See the following example.

make_setup_args

> If defined, pyximport calls this function with no arguments to get an extra argument dictionary to pass to distutils.core.setup. This allows the user to control the setup arguments passed in, which provides full control over distutils.

pyximport Example with External Dependencies

For example, suppose we want to wrap an external Fibonacci implementation in C. Two C files are defined, *_fib.h* and *_fib.c*. Our *fib.pyx* file has a cdef extern from "_fib.h" block and a minimal Python wrapper function to call the C implementation of the Fibonacci function. We can set up pyximport to work with this configuration by creating a *fib.pyxdeps* file that contains one line:

```
_fib.*
```

This glob pattern will match both *_fib.c* and *_fib.h*, so pyximport will recompile *fib.pyx* whenever either of these files changes. We can instruct pyximport to compile and link *_fib.c* together with *fib.pyx* into an extension module by creating a *fib.pyxbld* file that defines make_ext:

```
def make_ext(modname, pyxfilename):
    from distutils.extension import Extension
    return Extension(modname,
            sources=[pyxfilename, '_fib.c'],
            include_dirs = ['.'])
```

The essential line is the sources=[...] argument. It tells distutils to compile *_fib.c* with *fib.pyx* and link everything together. The include_dirs argument tells distutils to look in the current directory for the *_fib.h* header file.

We can import *fib.pyx* as before, and now it will wrap an external C function. If any of *fib.pyx*, *_fib.h*, or *_fib.c* is changed, pyximport will detect it and recompile everything the next time it is used in a new interpreter session.

Rolling Our Own and Compiling by Hand

For the sake of completeness, suppose we want to create an extension module starting with our *fib.pyx* source file, without using distutils, IPython's magic commands, or pyximport. Here we are getting a backstage look at what's going on, which can be helpful if issues arise.

As mentioned, there are two stages in the Cython compilation pipeline: generating C (or C++) code from Cython source, and compiling the C (or C++) code into an extension module.

The first step is easy—we use the cython command:

```
$ cython fib.pyx
```

If there are no compilation errors, then cython will print nothing, and we will see a *fib.c* file that cython has generated. There are several flags that the cython compiler accepts. To see them and a brief description of what they do, call cython with no arguments:

```
$ cython
Cython (http://cython.org) is a compiler for code written in the
Cython language.  Cython is based on Pyrex by Greg Ewing.

Usage: cython [options] sourcefile.{pyx,py} ...

Options:
  -V, --version                Display version number of cython
                               compiler
  -I, --include-dir <directory>  Search for include files in
                               named directory (multiple
                               include directories are
                               allowed).
  -o, --output-file <filename>  Specify name of generated C file
  -f, --force                  Compile all source files
                               (overrides implied -t)
  -v, --verbose                Be verbose, print file names on
                               multiple compilation
  -w, --working <directory>    Sets the working directory for
                               Cython (the directory modules
                               are searched from)
  -D, --no-docstrings          Strip docstrings from the
                               compiled module.
  -a, --annotate               Produce a colorized HTML version
                               of the source.
  --line-directives            Produce #line directives
                               pointing to the .pyx source
```

```
--cplus                          Output a C++ rather than C file.
--embed[=<method_name>]          Generate a main() function that
                                 embeds the Python interpreter.
-2                               Compile based on Python-2 syntax
                                 and code semantics.
-3                               Compile based on Python-3 syntax
                                 and code semantics.
--lenient                        Change some compile time errors
                                 to runtime errors to improve
                                 Python compatibility
--warning-errors, -Werror        Make all warnings into errors
--warning-extra, -Wextra         Enable extra warnings
-X, --directive <name>=<value>[,<name=value,...]
                                 Overrides a compiler directive
```

The preceding example includes only the more common options, most of which we will cover in this and future chapters. The arguments most commonly used are --cplus to generate a C++ source file rather than C; -a to generate an annotated HTML version of the source, useful for performance analysis and covered in depth in Chapter 9; and the -2 or -3 arguments to control which major version of the Python language to use and enforce.

To compile our *fib.c* into a Python extension module, we need to first compile *fib.c* into an object file with the proper includes and compilation flags, and then compile *fib.o* into a dynamic library with the right linking flags. Fortunately, Python provides the python-config command-line utility to help with this process. We can use python-config --cflags to obtain the right compilation flags, and python-config --ldflags gives us the right linking flags:

```
$ CFLAGS=$(python-config --cflags)
$ LDFLAGS=$(python-config --ldflags)
$ cython fib.pyx # --> outputs fib.c
$ gcc -c fib.c ${CFLAGS} # outputs fib.o
$ gcc fib.o -o fib.so -shared ${LDFLAGS} # --> outputs fib.so
```

In the last line, the -shared flag instructs gcc to create a shared library. This is necessary on Mac OS X; different platforms and compilers may require a different argument or arguments. It is strongly recommended to use the same compiler that was used to compile the Python interpreter. The python-config command gives back configuration flags that are tailored to this compiler/Python version combination.

This is fine for a simple project with just one extension module, but what about larger projects that have their own build system? The Cython compilation pipeline can work with these as well.

Using Cython with Other Build Systems

Many build tools know how to take a C or C++ source file and compile it into a Python extension module. These tools often provide simple commands that handle the details for us, much like Python's own `distutils` package does. The benefit of these build tools is that they have improved dependency management and other advanced features that `distutils` lacks, which can be a tremendous productivity enhancement for large projects. Cython can be integrated into these build tools if it is not already, and we will cover a few of them here.

CMake and Cython

CMake is a powerful open source build system created by Kitware, Inc. There are third-party build commands that can properly detect the `cython` compiler and fold Cython code into a standard CMake-compiled project. One version of these commands (*https://github.com/thewtex/cython-cmake-example*) makes it possible to use the following interface:

```
# Detects and activates Cython
include(UseCython)

# Specifies that Cython source files should generate C++
set_source_files_properties(
  ${CYTHON_CMAKE_EXAMPLE_SOURCE_DIR}/src/file.pyx
  PROPERTIES CYTHON_IS_CXX TRUE )

# Adds and compiles Cython source into an extension module
cython_add_module( modname file.pyx cpp_source.cxx)
```

SCons and Cython

SCons is a full build system written in Python. Cython comes with basic SCons support in the *Tools* directory. There we can find *cython.py* and *pyext.py* files to extend SCons with Cython support that can be incorporated into our own SCons-based build system.

Make and Cython

Cython can be incorporated into a `make`-based build system. To help with portability, it is recommended to query the Python interpreter itself to determine the right compilation and linking flags to use. The `python-config` utility that comes with CPython can alternatively be used when available. The `distutils.sysconfig` module can be used to get configuration parameters for these flags. For instance, to access the *include* directory for the Python header file *Python.h* where the Python/C API is declared, we can use the following `make` command:

```
INCDIR := $(shell python -c \
          "from distutils import sysconfig; print(sysconfig.get_python_inc())")
```

To acquire the Python dynamic libraries to link against, we can use:

```
LIBS := $(shell python -c \
        "from distutils import sysconfig; \
         print(sysconfig.get_config_var('LIBS'))")
```

Other configuration settings are available via the `get_config_var` function in the `distutils.sysconfig` module.

 While these build systems do have dependency-tracking features, be aware that they may not recognize all Cython import and include dependencies (Chapter 6), which can result in a dependent module not being compiled when an imported or included dependency changes. It may be necessary to force recompilation in some instances.

Cython Standalone Executables

Because Cython works closely with the Python/C API and runtime environment, Cython source code is nearly always compiled into a dynamic extension module and imported by Python code. But the cython compiler does have an option to embed the Python interpreter inside a main function. This makes it possible to use Cython to create a standalone executable that can be run directly from the command line.

Consider a simple Python—or Cython—script named *irrationals.py*:

```
from math import pi, e

print "e**pi == {:.2f}".format(e**pi)
print "pi**e == {:.2f}".format(pi**e)
```

Here is its output when run:

```
$ python irrationals.py
e**pi == 23.14
pi**e == 22.46
```

To compile this into an executable binary with Cython, we first call cython with the `--embed` flag:

```
$ cython --embed irrationals.py
```

This generates *irrationals.c* with a main entry point that embeds a Python interpreter. We can compile *irrationals.c* on Mac OS X or Linux using `python-config`:

```
$ gcc $(python-config --cflags) $(python-config --ldflags) ./irrationals.c
```

This produces an executable *a.out* that we can run directly:

```
$ ./a.out
e**pi == 23.14
pi**e == 22.46
```

This simple example provides a recipe for embedding the Python interpreter in a Cython-generated source file, which may be useful in certain contexts. Remember that the binary still has a runtime dependency on the Python dynamic library.

Compiler Directives

Cython provides *compiler directives* to control how it compiles Cython source code. Directives can be specified in four separate scopes and can be easily turned on or off for testing and debugging. Not all directives can be set at every scope.

All directives can be set globally for an extension module inside a *directive comment*. These comments must appear at the top of an extension module, and must come before the first line of source code. A directive comment can come after other comments. All directive comments must start with the comment character followed by cython:, the directive name, and its value.

For instance, to globally set the nonecheck directive (covered in detail in Chapter 5) to True for an extension module *source.pyx*, we can say:

```
# cython: nonecheck=True
```

We can have more than one directive specified on one line. To turn off bounds checking for indexing globally (covered in Chapter 10), we can add a boundscheck=False directive:

```
# cython: nonecheck=True, boundscheck=False
```

or we can specify them on separate lines:

```
# cython: nonecheck=True
# cython: boundscheck=False
```

Alternatively, we can set directives from the command line using the -X or -—directive option. *Doing so overrides the value for the directive set in a directive comment.*

For example, to globally set (and overrride) the nonecheck directive in *source.pyx* to False, we can use:

```
$ cython --directive nonecheck=False source.pyx
```

Some directives support function- and context-level scope control, via decorators and context managers, respectively.

For instance, to turn off bounds checking and wraparound checking for an entire function, we can use the decorator forms of the `boundscheck` and `wraparound` directives, both described in Chapter 10:

```
cimport cython

@cython.boundscheck(False)
@cython.wraparound(False)
def fast_indexing():
    # ...
```

If we desire even more local control over these directives, we can use the context-manager form:

```
cimport cython

def fast_indexing(a):
    with cython.boundscheck(False), cython.wraparound(False):
        for i in range(len(a)):
            sum += a[i]
```

These directives are set to `False` only for the body of the context manager, and revert to their default `True` value outside.

Neither the decorator form nor the context-manager form of a directive is affected by directive comments or command-line directives.

In the following chapters we will point out what directives are available and what they do. A comprehensive list of directives is also found in the online Cython documentation (*http://bit.ly/compiler_directives*).

Summary

Now that we have covered the Cython compiler pipeline and various ways to compile Cython source into an importable Python extension module, we have the necessary knowledge to work with the examples throughout the rest of this book.

## CHAPTER 3

Cython in Depth

Readability counts.

Special cases aren't special enough to break the rules.

Although practicality beats purity.

— T. Peters
"The Zen of Python"

The preceding chapters covered what Cython is, why we would want to use it, and how we can compile and run Cython code. With that knowledge in hand, it is time to explore the Cython language in depth.

The first two sections of this chapter cover the deeper reasons *why* Cython works as well as it does to speed up Python code. These sections are useful to help form a mental model of how Cython works, but are not necessary to understand the *what* of Cython's syntax, which comprises the remaining sections.

For those interested in *why* Cython works, it can be attributed to two differences: runtime interpretation versus ahead-of-time compilation, and dynamic versus static typing.

Interpreted Versus Compiled Execution

To better understand how and why Cython improves the performance of Python code, it is useful to compare how the Python runtime runs Python code with how an operating system runs compiled C code.

Before being run, Python code is automatically compiled to Python bytecode. Bytecodes are fundamental instructions to be executed, or *interpreted*, by the Python *virtual machine* (VM). Because the VM abstracts away all platform-specific details, Python bytecode can be generated on one platform and run anywhere else. It is up to the VM to translate each high-level bytecode into one or more lower-level operations that can be executed by the operating system and, ultimately, the CPU. This virtualized design is common and very flexible, bringing with it many benefits—first among them is not having to fuss with picky compilers! The primary downside is that the VM is slower than running natively compiled code.

On the C side of the fence, there is no VM or interpreter, and there are no high-level bytecodes. C code is translated, or *compiled*, directly to machine code by a compiler. This machine code is incorporated into an executable or compiled library. It is tailored to a specific platform and architecture, it can be run directly by a CPU, and it is as low-level as it gets.

There is a way to bridge the divide between the bytecode-executing VM and machine code–executing CPU: the Python interpreter can run compiled C code directly and transparently to the end user. The C code must be compiled into a specific kind of dynamic library known as an *extension module*. These modules are full-fledged Python modules, but the code inside of them has been precompiled into machine code by a standard C compiler. When running code in an extension module, the Python VM no longer interprets high-level bytecodes, but instead runs machine code directly. This removes the interpreter's performance overhead while any operation inside this extension module is running.

How does Cython fit in? As we saw in Chapter 2, we can use the cython and standard C compilers to translate Cython source code into a compiled platform-specific extension module. Whenever Python runs anything inside an extension module, it is running compiled code, so no interpreter overhead can slow things down.

How big of a difference does interpretation versus direct execution make? It can vary widely, depending on the Python code in question, but usually we can expect around a 10 to 30 percent speedup from converting Python code into an equivalent extension module.

Cython gives us this speedup for free, and we are glad to take it. But the real performance improvements come from replacing Python's dynamic dispatch with static typing.

Dynamic Versus Static Typing

Another important difference between high-level languages like Python, Ruby, Tcl, and JavaScript and low-level languages like C, C++, and Java is that the former are *dynamically typed*, while the latter are *statically typed*. Statically typed languages require the type of a variable to be fixed at compile time. Often we can accomplish this by explicitly declaring the type of a variable, or, when possible, the compiler can automatically infer a variable's type. In either case, in the context where it is used, a variable has that type and only that type.

What benefits does static typing bring? Besides compile-time type checking, compilers use static typing to generate fast machine code that is tailored to that specific type.

Dynamically typed languages place no restrictions on a variable's type: the same variable can start out as an integer and end up as a string, or a list, or an instance of a custom Python object, for example. Dynamically typed languages are typically easier to write because the user does not have to explicitly declare variables' types, with the tradeoff that type-related errors are caught at runtime.

When running a Python program, the interpreter spends most of its time figuring out what low-level operation to perform, and extracting the data to give to this low-level operation. Given Python's design and flexibility, the Python interpreter always has to determine the low-level operation in a completely general way, because a variable can have *any* type at *any* time. This is known as *dynamic dispatch*, and for many reasons, fully general dynamic dispatch is slow.[1]

For example, consider what happens when the Python runtime evaluates a + b:

1. The interpreter inspects the Python object referred to by a for its type, which requires at least one pointer lookup at the C level.

2. The interpreter asks the type for an implementation of the addition method, which may require one or more additional pointer lookups and internal function calls.

3. If the method in question is found, the interpreter then has an actual function it can call, implemented either in Python or in C.

4. The interpreter calls the addition function and passes in a and b as arguments.

5. The addition function extracts the necessary internal data from a and b, which may require several more pointer lookups and conversions from Python types to C types. If successful, only then can it perform the actual operation that adds a and b together.

6. The result then must be placed inside a (perhaps new) Python object and returned. Only then is the operation complete.

The situation for C is very different. Because C is compiled and statically typed, the C compiler can determine at compile time what low-level operations to perform and what low-level data to pass as arguments. At runtime, a compiled C program skips nearly *all* steps that the Python interpreter must perform. For something like a + b with a and b both being fundamental numeric types, the compiler generates a handful of machine code instructions to load the data into registers, add them, and store the result.

---

1. For an in-depth and quantitative explication of Python's interpreter and dynamic dispatch performance, see Brandon Rhodes's PyCon 2014 talk "The Day of the EXE Is Upon Us." (*http://bit.ly/day_of_the_exe*)

What is the takeaway? A compiled C program spends nearly all its time calling fast C functions and performing fundamental operations. Because of the restrictions a statically typed language places on its variables, a compiler generates faster, more specialized instructions that are tailored to its data. Given this efficiency, is it any wonder that a language like C can be hundreds, or even thousands, of times faster than Python for certain operations?

The primary reason Cython yields such impressive performance boosts is that it brings static typing to a dynamic language. Static typing transforms runtime dynamic dispatch into type-optimized machine code.

Before Cython (and Cython's predecessor, Pyrex), we could only benefit from static typing by reimplementing our Python code in C. Cython makes it easy to keep our Python code as is and tap into C's static type system. The first and most important Cython-specific keyword we will learn is cdef, which is our gateway to C's performance.

Static Type Declaration with cdef

Dynamically typed variables in Cython come for free: we simply assign to a variable to initialize it and use it as we would in Python:[2]

```
a = [x+1 for x in range(12)]
b = a
a[3] = 42.0
assert b[3] == 42.0
a = 13
assert isinstance(b, list)
```

In Cython, *untyped dynamic variables behave exactly like Python variables*. The assignment b = a allows both a and b to access the same list object created on the first line in the preceding example. Modifying the list via a[3] = 42 modifies the same list referenced by b, so the assertion holds true. The assignment a = 13 leaves b referring to the original list object, while a is now referring to a Python integer object. This reassignment to a *changes a's type*, which is perfectly valid Python code.

To *statically* type variables in Cython, we use the cdef keyword with a type and the variable name. For example:

```
cdef int i
cdef int j
cdef float k
```

Using these statically typed variables looks just like Python (or C) code:

---

2. To follow along with the examples in this chapter, please see *https://github.com/cythonbook/examples*.

```
j = 0
i = j
k = 12.0
j = 2 * k
assert i != j
```

 The important difference between dynamic variables and static variables is that *static variables with C types have C semantics*, which changes the behavior of assignment. It also means these variables follow C coercion and casting rules.

In the previous example, i = j *copies* the integer data at j to the memory location reserved for i. This means that i and j refer to independent entities, and can evolve separately.

As with C, we can declare several variables of the same type at once:

```
cdef int i, j, k
cdef float price, margin
```

Also, we can provide an optional initial value:

```
cdef int i = 0
cdef long int j = 0, k = 0
cdef float price = 0.0, margin = 1.0
```

Inside a function, cdef statements are indented and the static variables declared are local to that function. All of these are valid uses of cdef to declare local variables in a function integrate:

```
def integrate(a, b, f):
    cdef int i
    cdef int N=2000
    cdef float dx, s=0.0
    dx = (b-a)/N
    for i in range(N):
        s += f(a+i*dx)
    return s * dx
```

An equivalent way to declare multiple variables is by means of a cdef block, which groups the declarations in an indented region:

```
def integrate(a, b, f):
    cdef:
        int i
        int N=2000
        float dx, s=0.0
    # ...
```

This groups long lists of cdef declarations nicely, and we will use both forms throughout this book.

What About static and const?

The C `static` keyword is used to declare a variable whose lifetime extends to the entire lifetime of a program. It is not a valid Cython keyword, so we cannot declare C `static` variables in Cython. The C `const` keyword declares an unmodifiable identifier. Cython supports the `const` keyword, but it is not very useful in the context of this chapter. If we try to declare N as `const`, for example, we will get a compilation error ("Error compiling Cython file [...] Assignment to const *N*"). We will see in Chapters 7 and 8 where Cython's `const` support becomes useful.

We can declare any kind of variable that C supports. Table 3-1 gives examples using `cdef` for the more common C types.

Table 3-1. Various cdef declarations

C type	Cython cdef statement
Pointers	`cdef int *p` `cdef void **buf`
Stack-allocated C arrays	`cdef int arr[10]` `cdef double points[20][30]`
typedefed aliased types	`cdef size_t len`
Compound types (structs and unions)	`cdef tm time_struct` `cdef int_short_union_t hi_lo_bytes`
Function pointers	`cdef void (*f)(int, double)`

Cython supports the full range of C declarations, even the cryptic arrays-of-pointers-to-function-pointers-that-return-function-pointers tongue twisters. For example, to declare a function that takes a function pointer as its only argument and *returns* another function pointer, we could say:

```
cdef int (*signal(int (*f)(int))(int)
```

It is not immediately apparent how to make use of the `signal` function in Cython, but we will see later how C function pointers enter the picture with callbacks. Cython does not limit the C-level types that we can use, which is especially useful when we are wrapping external C libraries.

Automatic Type Inference in Cython

Static typing with `cdef` is not the only way to statically type variables in Cython. Cython also performs automatic type inference for untyped variables in function and method bodies. By default, Cython infers variable types only when doing so cannot change the semantics of the code.

Consider the following simple function:

```
def automatic_inference():
    i = 1
    d = 2.0
    c = 3+4j
    r = i * d + c
    return r
```

In this example, Cython types the literals 1 and 3+4j and the variables i, c, and r as general Python objects. Even though these types have obvious corresponding C types, Cython conservatively assumes that the integer i may not be representable as a C long, so types it as a Python object with Python semantics. Automatic inference *is* able to infer that the 2.0 literal, and hence the variable d, are C doubles and proceeds accordingly. To the end user, it is as if d is a regular Python object, but Cython treats it as a C double for performance.

By means of the infer_types compiler directive (see "Compiler Directives" on page 28), we can give Cython more leeway to infer types in cases that may possibly change semantics—for example, when integer addition may result in overflow.

To enable type inference for a function, we can use the decorator form of infer_types:

```
cimport cython

@cython.infer_types(True)
def more_inference():
    i = 1
    d = 2.0
    c = 3+4j
    r = i * d + c
    return r
```

Because infer_types is enabled for more_inference, the variable i is typed as a C long; d is a double, as before, and both c and r are C-level complex variables (more on complex variables in Table 3-2 and "Complex types" on page 41). When enabling infer_types, we are taking responsibility to ensure that integer operations do not overflow and that semantics do not change from the untyped version. The infer_types directive can be enabled at function scope or globally, making it easy to test whether it changes the results of the code base, and whether it makes a difference in performance.

C Pointers in Cython

As we saw in Table 3-1, *declaring* C pointers in Cython uses C syntax and semantics:

```
cdef int *p_int
cdef float** pp_float = NULL
```

As with C, the asterisk can be declared adjacent to the type or to the variable, although the *pointerness* is associated with the *variable*, not the *type*.

This means that to declare multiple pointers on a single line we have to use an asterisk with each variable declared, like so:

```
cdef int *a, *b
```

If we instead use:

```
cdef int *a, b
```

this declares an integer pointer a, and a nonpointer integer b! In recent versions, Cython issues a warning when compiling error-prone declarations such as these.

Dereferencing pointers in Cython is different than in C. Because the Python language already uses the *args and **kwargs syntax to allow arbitrary positional and keyword arguments and to support function argument unpacking, Cython does not support the *a syntax to dereference a C pointer. Instead, we *index into the pointer at location 0* to dereference a pointer in Cython. This syntax also works to dereference a pointer in C, although that's rare.

For example, suppose we have a golden_ratio C double and a p_double C pointer:

```
cdef double golden_ratio
cdef double *p_double
```

We can assign golden_ratio's address to p_double using the address-of operator, &:

```
p_double = &golden_ratio
```

We can now assign to golden_ratio through p_double using our indexing-at-zero-to-dereference syntax:

```
p_double[0] = 1.618
print golden_ratio
# => 1.618
```

And we can access p_double's referent the same way:

```
print p_double[0]
# => 1.618
```

Alternatively, we can use the cython.operator.dereference function-like operator to dereference a pointer. We access this operator by cimporting from the special cython namespace, which is covered in detail in Chapter 6:

```
from cython cimport operator
print operator.dereference(p_double)
# => 1.618
```

This form is not frequently used.

Another difference between Cython and C arises when we are using pointers to structs. (We will cover Cython's struct support in depth later in this chapter.) In C, if p_st is a pointer to a struct typedef:

```
st_t *p_st = make_struct();
```

then to access a struct member a inside p_st, we use arrow syntax:

```
int a_doubled = p_st->a + p_st->a;
```

Cython, however, uses dot access whether we have a nonpointer struct variable or a pointer to a struct:

```
cdef st_t *p_st = make_struct()
cdef int a_doubled = p_st.a + p_st.a
```

Wherever we use the arrow operator in C, we use the dot operator in Cython, and Cython will generate the proper C-level code.

Mixing Statically and Dynamically Typed Variables

Cython allows assignments between statically and dynamically typed variables. This fluid blending of static and dynamic is a powerful feature that we will use in several instances: it allows us to use dynamic Python objects for the majority of our code base, and easily convert them into fast, statically typed analogues for the performance-critical sections.

To illustrate, say we have several (static) C ints we want to group into a (dynamic) Python tuple. The C code to create and initialize this tuple using the Python/C API is straightforward but tedious, requiring dozens of lines of code, with a significant amount of error checking. In Cython, the obvious way to do it just works:

```
cdef int a, b, c
# ...Calculations using a, b, and c...
tuple_of_ints = (a, b, c)
```

This code is trivial, boring even. The point to emphasize here is that a, b, and c are statically typed integers, and Cython allows the creation of a dynamically typed Python tuple literal with them. We can then assign that tuple to the dynamically typed tuple_of_ints variable. The simplicity of this example is part of Cython's power and beauty: we can just create a tuple of C ints in the obvious way without further thought. We *want* conceptually simple things like this to *be* simple, and that is what Cython provides.

This example works because there is an obvious correspondence between C ints and Python ints, so Python can transform things automatically for us. This example would not work as is if a, b, and c were, for example, C pointers. In that case we would have to dereference them before putting them into the tuple, or use another strategy.

Table 3-2 gives the full list of correspondences between built-in Python types and C or C++ types.

Table 3-2. Type correspondence between built-in Python types and C or C++ types

Python type(s)	C type(s)
bool	bint
int long	[unsigned] char [unsigned] short [unsigned] int [unsigned] long [unsigned] long long
float	float double long double
complex	float complex double complex
bytes str unicode	char * std::string (C++)
dict	struct

There are several points worth mentioning regarding Table 3-2, which we'll cover next.

The bint type

The `bint` Boolean integer type is an `int` at the C level and is converted to and from a Python `bool`. It has the standard C interpretation of truthiness: zero is `False`, and non-zero is `True`.

Integral type conversions and overflow

In Python 2, a Python `int` is stored as a C `long`, and a Python `long` has unlimited precision. In Python 3, all `int` objects are unlimited precision.

When converting integral types from Python to C, Cython generates code that checks for overflow. If the C type cannot represent the Python integer, a runtime `OverflowError` is raised.

There are related Boolean `overflowcheck` and `overflowcheck.fold` compiler directives (see "Compiler Directives" on page 28) that will catch overflow errors when we are working with C integers. If `overflowcheck` is set to `True`, Cython will raise an `OverflowError` for overflowing C integer arithmetic operations. The `overflowcheck.fold` directive, when set, may help remove some overhead when `overflowcheck` is enabled.

Floating-point type conversions

A Python `float` is stored as a C `double`. Converting a Python `float` to a C `float` may truncate to `0.0` or positive or negative infinity, according to IEEE 754 conversion rules.

Complex types

The Python `complex` type is stored as a C `struct` of two `doubles`.

Cython has `float complex` and `double complex` C-level types, which correspond to the Python `complex` type. The C types have the same interface as the Python `complex` type, but use efficient C-level operations. This includes the `real` and `imag` attributes to access the real and imaginary components, the `conjugate` method to create the complex conjugate of a number, and efficient operations for addition, subtraction, multiplication, and division.

The C-level complex type is compatible with the C99 `_Complex` type or the C++ `std::complex` templated class.

bytes type

The Python `bytes` type converts to and from a `char *` or `std::string` automatically.

str and unicode types

The `c_string_type` and `c_string_encoding` compiler directives need to be set (see "str, unicode, bytes, and All That" on page 66) to allow `str` or `unicode` types to convert to and from a `char *` or `std::string`.

Statically Declaring Variables with a Python Type

Until now, we have used `cdef` to statically declare variables with a C type. It is also possible to use `cdef` to *statically declare variables with a Python type*. We can do this for the built-in types like `list`, `tuple`, and `dict`; extension types like NumPy arrays; and many others.

Not all Python types can be statically declared: they must be implemented in C and Cython must have access to the declaration. The built-in Python types already satisfy these requirements, and declaring them is straightforward. For example:

```
cdef list particles, modified_particles
cdef dict names_from_particles
cdef str pname
cdef set unique_particles
```

The variables in this example are full Python objects. Under the hood, Cython declares them as C pointers to some built-in Python `struct` type. They can be used like ordinary Python variables, but are constrained to their declared type:

```
# ...initialize names_from_particles...
particles = list(names_from_particles.keys())
```

Dynamic variables can be initialized from statically declared Python types:

```
other_particles = particles
del other_particles[0]
```

Here, deleting the 0th element via `other_particles` will delete the 0th element of `particles` as well, since they are referring to the same list.

One difference between `other_particles` and `particles` is that `particles` can only ever refer to Python `list` objects, while `other_particles` can refer to *any* Python type. Cython will enforce the constraint on `particles` at compile time and at runtime.

 In cases where Python built-in types like `int` or `float` have the same name as a C type, the C type takes precedence. This is almost always what we want.

When we are adding, subtracting, or multiplying scalars, the operations have Python semantics (including automatic Python `long` coercion for large values) when the operands are dynamically typed Python objects. They have C semantics (i.e., the result may overflow for limited-precision integer types) when the operands are statically typed C variables.

Division and modulus (i.e., computing the remainder) deserve special mention. C and Python have markedly different behavior when computing the modulus with signed integer operands: C rounds toward zero, while Python rounds toward infinity. For example, `-1 % 5` evaluates to 4 with Python semantics; with C semantics, however, it evaluates to `-1`. When dividing two integers, Python always checks the denominator and raises a `ZeroDivisionError` when it is zero, while C has no such safeguards in place.

Following the principle of least astonishment, Cython uses Python semantics by default for division and modulus even when the operands are statically typed C scalars. To obtain C semantics, we can use the `cdivision` compiler directive (see "Compiler Directives" on page 28), either at the global module level, or in a directive comment:

```
# cython: cdivision=True
```

or at the function level with a decorator:

```
cimport cython

@cython.cdivision(True)
def divides(int a, int b):
    return a / b
```

or within a function with a context manager:

```
cimport cython

def remainder(int a, int b):
    with cython.cdivision(True):
        return a % b
```

Note that when we are dividing C integers with `cdivision(True)`, if the denominator is zero, the result may lead to undefined behavior (i.e., anything from hard crashes to corrupted data).

Cython also has the `cdivision_warnings` compiler directive (which has a default value of `False`). When `cdivision_warnings` is `True`, Cython emits a runtime warning whenever division (or modulo) is performed with negative operands.

Static Typing for Speed

It may seem odd at first that Cython allows static declaration of variables with built-in Python types. Why not just use Python's dynamic typing as usual? The answer points to a general Cython principle: *the more static type information we provide, the better Cython can optimize the result*. As always, there are exceptions to this rule, but it is more often true than not. For instance, this line of code simply appends a `Particle` object to a dynamic `dynamic_particles` variable:

```
dynamic_particles = make_particles(...)
# ...
dynamic_particles.append(Particle())
# ...
```

The `cython` compiler will generate code that can handle any Python object, and tests at runtime if `dynamic_particles` is a `list`. If it is not, as long as it has an `append` method that takes an argument, this code will run. Under the hood, the generated code first looks up the `append` attribute on the `dynamic_particles` object (using `PyObject_GetAttr`), and then calls that method using the completely general `PyObject_Call` Python/C API function. This essentially emulates what the Python interpreter would do when running equivalent Python bytecode.

Suppose we statically declare a `static_particles` Python `list` and use it instead:

```
cdef list static_particles = make_particles(...)
# ...
static_particles.append(Particle())
# ...
```

Now Cython can generate specialized code that directly calls either the `PyList_SET_ITEM` or the `PyList_Append` function from the C API. This is what `PyObject_Call` in the previous example ends up calling *anyway*, but static typing allows Cython to remove dynamic dispatch on `static_particles`.

Cython currently supports several built-in statically declarable Python types, including:

- `type`, `object`
- `bool`
- `complex`
- `basestring`, `str`, `unicode`, `bytes`, `bytearray`
- `list`, `tuple`, `dict`, `set`, `frozenset`
- `array`
- `slice`
- `date`, `time`, `datetime`, `timedelta`, `tzinfo`

More types may be supported in future releases.

Python types that have direct C counterparts—like `int`, `long`, and `float`—are not included in the preceding list. It turns out that it is not straightforward to statically declare and use `PyIntObjects`, `PyLongObjects`, or `PyFloatObjects` in Cython; fortunately, the need to do so is rare. We just declare regular C `int`s, `long`s, `float`s, and `double`s and let Cython do the automatic conversion to and from Python for us.

A Python `float` corresponds to a C double. For this reason, C doubles are preferred whenever conversions to and from Python are used to ensure no clipping of values or loss of precision.

In Python 2, a Python `int` (more precisely, a `PyIntObject` at the C level) stores its value internally as a C `long`. So a C `long` is the preferred integral data type to ensure maximal compatibility with Python.

Python also has a `PyLongObject` at the C level to represent arbitrarily sized integers. In Python 2, these are exposed as the `long` type, and if an operation with `PyIntObject` overflows, a `PyLongObject` results.

In Python 3, at the C level, all integers are `PyLongObjects`.

Cython properly converts between C integral types and these Python integer types in a language-agnostic way, and raises an `OverflowError` when a conversion is not possible.

When we work with Python objects in Cython, whether statically declared or dynamic, Cython still manages all aspects of the object for us, which includes the tedium of reference counting.

Reference Counting and Static String Types

One of Python's major features is *automatic memory management*. CPython implements this via straightforward reference counting, with an automatic garbage collector that runs periodically to clean up unreachable reference cycles.

Cython handles all reference counting for us, ensuring a Python object (whether statically typed or dynamic) is finalized when its reference count reaches zero.

CPython's automatic memory management has certain implications when mixing static and dynamic variables in Cython. Say, for instance, we have two Python `bytes` objects `b1` and `b2`, and we want to extract the underlying `char` pointer after adding them together:

```
b1 = b"All men are mortal."
b2 = b"Socrates is a man."
cdef char *buf = b1 + b2
```

The `b1 + b2` expression is a temporary Python `bytes` object, and the assignment attempts to extract that temporary object's `char` pointer using Cython's automatic conversion rules. Because the result of the addition is a temporary object, the preceding example cannot work—the temporary result of the addition is deleted immediately after it is created, so the `char` buffer cannot refer to a valid Python object. Fortunately, Cython is able to catch the error and issue a compilation error.

Once understood, the right way to accomplish what we want is straightforward—just use a temporary Python variable, either dynamically typed:

```
tmp = s1 + s2
cdef char *buf = tmp
```

or statically typed:

```
cdef bytes tmp = s1 + s2
cdef char *buf = tmp
```

These cases are not common. It is an issue here only because a C-level object is *referring* to data that is managed by a Python object. Because the Python object owns the underlying string, the C `char *` buffer has no way to tell Python that it has another (non-Python) reference. We have to create a temporary `bytes` object so that Python does not delete the string data, and we must ensure that the temporary object is maintained as long as the C `char *` buffer is required. The other C types listed in Table 3-2 are all value types, not pointer types. For these types, the Python data is copied during assignment (C semantics), allowing the C variable to evolve separately from the Python object used to initialize it.

Just as Cython understands both dynamic Python variables and static C variables, it also understands functions in both languages, and allows us to use either kind.

Cython's Three Kinds of Functions

Much of what we have learned about dynamic and static variables applies to functions as well. Python and C functions have some common attributes: they both (usually) have a name, take zero or more arguments, and can return new values or objects when called. But Python functions are more flexible and powerful. Python functions are *first-class citizens*, meaning that they are objects with state and behavior. This abstraction is very useful.

A Python function can be

- created both at import time and dynamically at runtime;
- created anonymously with the `lambda` keyword;
- defined inside another function (or other nested scope);
- returned from other functions;
- passed as an argument to other functions;
- called with positional or keyword arguments;
- defined with default values.

C functions have minimal call overhead, making them orders of magnitude faster than Python functions. A C function

- can be passed as an argument to other functions (but doing so is much more cumbersome than in Python);
- cannot be defined inside another function;
- has a statically assigned name that is not modifiable;
- takes arguments only by position;
- does not support default values for parameters.

All of the power and flexibility of Python functions comes at a cost: Python functions are several orders of magnitude slower than C functions—even functions that take no arguments.

Cython supports both Python and C functions and allows them to call each other in a natural and straightforward way, all in the same source file.

Python Functions in Cython with the def Keyword

Cython supports regular Python functions defined with the `def` keyword, and they work as we would expect. For example, consider a recursive `py_fact` function that recursively computes the factorial of its argument:

```
def py_fact(n):
    """Computes n!"""
    if n <= 1:
        return 1
    return n * py_fact(n - 1)
```

This simple Python function is valid Cython code. In Cython, the n argument is a dynamic Python variable, and py_fact must be passed a Python object when called. py_fact is used the same way regardless of whether it is defined in pure Python or defined in Cython and imported from an extension module.

We can compile the py_fact example using any of the methods described in Chapter 2. If we put the py_fact function in a file named *fact.pyx*, we can easily compile it on the fly using pyximport from an interactive prompt (here, IPython):

```
In [1]: import pyximport

In [2]: pyximport.install()
Out[2]: (None, <pyximport.pyximport.PyxImporter at 0x101c65690>)

In [3]: import fact
```

We can now access and use fact.py_fact:

```
In [4]: fact.py_fact?
Type:       builtin_function_or_method
String Form:<built-in function py_fact>
Docstring:  Computes n!

In [5]: fact.py_fact(20)
Out[5]: 2432902008176640000
```

Let's define a pure-Python version of py_fact in the interpreter for comparison:

```
In [7]: def interpreted_fact(n):
   ...:     """Computes n!"""
   ...:     if n <= 1:
   ...:         return 1
   ...:     return n * interpreted_fact(n - 1)
   ...:
```

We can compare their runtimes with the handy IPython %timeit magic:

```
In [8]: %timeit interpreted_fact(20)
100000 loops, best of 3: 4.24 µs per loop

In [9]: %timeit fact.py_fact(20)
1000000 loops, best of 3: 1.78 µs per loop
```

The py_fact function runs approximately two times faster with Cython for small input values on this system, although the speedup depends on a number of factors. The source of the speedup is the removal of interpretation overhead and the reduced function call overhead in Cython.

With respect to *usage*, `interpreted_fact` and the Cython-compiled `py_fact` are identical. With respect to *implementation*, these two functions have some important differences. The Python version has type `function`, while the Cython version has type `builtin_function_or_method`. The Python version has several attributes available to it—such as `__name__`—that are modifiable, while the Cython version is not modifiable. The Python version, when called, executes bytecodes with the Python interpreter, while the Cython version runs compiled C code that calls into the Python/C API, bypassing bytecode interpretation entirely.

Factorials grow very quickly. One nice feature of Python integers is that they can represent arbitrarily large values (memory constraints), and can therefore represent values that C integral types cannot. These large integers are very convenient, but that convenience comes at the cost of performance.

We can tell Cython to type `n` as a C integral type and possibly gain a performance improvement, with the understanding that we are now working with limited-precision integers that may overflow (more on handling overflow later).

Let's define a new function, `typed_fact`, inside our *fact.pyx* file:

```
def typed_fact(long n):
    """Computes n!"""
    if n <= 1:
        return 1
    return n * typed_fact(n - 1)
```

Here, we statically type `n`. Because `n` is a function argument, we omit the `cdef` keyword. When we call `typed_fact` from Python, Cython will convert the Python object argument to a C `long`, raising an appropriate exception (`TypeError` or `OverflowError`) if it cannot.

When defining any function in Cython, we may mix dynamically typed Python object arguments with statically typed arguments. Cython allows statically typed arguments to have default values, and statically typed arguments can be passed positionally or by keyword.

In this case, statically typing `typed_fact`'s argument does not improve performance over `py_fact`. Because `typed_fact` is a Python function, its return value is a Python integer object, *not* a statically typed C `long`. When computing `n * typed_fact(n - 1)`, Cython has to generate lots of code to extract the underlying C `long` from the Python integer returned from `typed_fact`, multiply it by the statically typed `n`, and pack that result into a new Python integer, which is then returned. All this packing and unpacking leads to essentially the same code paths taken by the `py_fact` function we saw earlier.

So how do we improve performance? We could translate this into a loop rather than a recursive function, but we will hold off on that for now. What we would like to do is tell

Cython, "Here is a C `long`; compute its factorial *without creating any Python integers*, and I'll make a Python integer out of that result to return." Essentially, we want a pure C function to do all the hard work using only C function calls and statically typed C data. We can then trivially convert the result to a Python integer and return that. This is a perfect fit for Cython's `cdef` function.

C Functions in Cython with the cdef Keyword

When used to define a function, the `cdef` keyword creates a function with C-calling semantics. A `cdef` function's arguments and return type are typically statically typed, and they can work with C pointer objects, structs, and other C types that cannot be automatically coerced to Python types. It is helpful to think of a `cdef` function as a *C function* that is defined with Cython's Python-like syntax.

A `cdef` version of the factorial function would look something like:

```
cdef long c_fact(long n):
    """Computes n!"""
    if n <= 1:
        return 1
    return n * c_fact(n - 1)
```

Its definition is very similar to `typed_fact`, the primary difference being the `long` return type.

Careful inspection of `c_fact` in the preceding example reveals that the argument type and return type are statically declared, and *no Python objects are used*; hence, no conversions from Python types to C types are necessary. Calling the `c_fact` function is as efficient as calling a pure-C function, so the function call overhead is minimal. Nothing prevents us from declaring and using Python objects and dynamic variables in `cdef` functions, or accepting them as arguments. But `cdef` functions are typically used when we want to get as close to C as possible without writing C code directly.

Cython allows `cdef` functions to be defined alongside Python `def` functions in the same Cython source file. The optional return type of a `cdef` function can be any static type we have seen, including pointers, structs, C arrays, and static Python types like `list` or `dict`. We can also have a return type of `void`. If the return type is omitted, then it defaults to `object`.

A function declared with `cdef` can be called by any other function—`def` or `cdef`—inside the same Cython source file (we will see in Chapter 6 how to relax this constraint). However, Cython does not allow a `cdef` function to be called from external Python code. Because of this restriction, `cdef` functions are typically used as fast auxiliary functions to help `def` functions do their job.

If we want to use `c_fact` from Python code outside this extension module, we need a minimal `def` function that calls `c_fact` internally:

```
def wrap_c_fact(n):
    """Computes n!"""
    return c_fact(n)
```

We get a nice speedup for our efforts: `wrap_c_fact(20)` is about 10 times faster than `typed_fact(20)` and `py_fact(20)`, both of which have significant Python overhead.

Unfortunately, the `wrap_c_fact` function comes with some limitations. One limitation is that `wrap_c_fact` and its underlying `c_fact` are restricted to C integral types only, and do not have the benefit of Python's unlimited-precision integers. In practice, this means that `wrap_c_fact` gives erroneous results for arguments larger than some small value, depending on how large an `unsigned long` is on our system. For typical 8-byte C `longs`, `wrap_c_fact(21)` yields invalid results. One option to partially address this limitation while maintaining Cython's performance would be to use `doubles` rather than integral types.

This is a general issue when we are working with Python and C, and is not specific to Cython: Python objects and C types do not always map to each other perfectly, and we have to be aware of C's limitations.

Combining def and cdef Functions with cpdef

There is a third kind of function, declared with the `cpdef` keyword, that is a hybrid of `def` and `cdef`. A `cpdef` function combines features from both of the other kinds of functions and addresses many of their limitations. In the previous section we made the `cdef` function `c_fact` available to Python by writing a `def` wrapper function, `wrap_c_fact`, that simply forwards its arguments on to `c_fact` and returns its result. A single `cpdef` function gives us these two functions automatically: we get a C-only version of the function and a Python wrapper for it, both with the same name. When we call the function from Cython, we call the C-only version; when we call the function from Python, the wrapper is called. In this way, `cpdef` functions combine the accessibility of `def` functions with the performance of `cdef` functions.

To continue with our example, let us define a `cpdef` function `cp_fact` to see how we can clean up the `wrap_c_fact` and `c_fact` combo:

```
cpdef long cp_fact(long n):
    """Computes n!"""
    if n <= 1:
        return 1
    return n * cp_fact(n - 1)
```

Our `cp_fact` provides the speed of `c_fact` and the Python accessibility of `py_fact`, all in one place. Its performance is identical to that of `wrap_c_fact`; that is, about 10 times faster than `py_fact`.

---

inline cdef and cpdef Functions

C and C++ support an optional `inline` keyword to *suggest* that the compiler replace the so-declared function with its body wherever it is called, thereby further removing call overhead. The compiler is free to ignore `inline`.

Cython supports the `inline` keyword for `cdef` and `cpdef` functions—we simply place `inline` after the `cdef` or `cpdef` keyword:

```
cdef inline long c_fact(long a):
    # ...
```

Cython passes this modifier through to the generated C or C++ code.

The `inline` modifier, when judiciously used, can yield performance improvements, especially for small inlined functions called in deeply nested loops, for example.

A `cpdef` function has one limitation, due to the fact that it does double duty as both a Python and a C function: its arguments and return types have to be compatible with both Python and C types. Any Python object can be represented at the C level (e.g., by using a dynamically typed argument, or by statically typing a built-in type), but not all C types can be represented in Python. So, we cannot use `void`, C pointers, or C arrays indiscriminately as the argument types or return type of `cpdef` functions. Table 3-2 may be useful here.

Functions and Exception Handling

A `def` function always returns some sort of `PyObject` pointer at the C level. This invariant allows Cython to correctly propagate exceptions from `def` functions without issue. Cython's other two function types—`cdef` and `cpdef`—may return a non-Python type, which makes some other exception-indicating mechanism necessary.

For example, suppose we have a `cpdef` function that divides integers, and therefore must consider what to do when the denominator is zero:

```
cpdef int divide_ints(int i, int j):
    return i / j
```

If we call `divide_ints` with `j=0`, a `ZeroDivisionError` exception will be set, but there is no way for `divide_ints` to communicate this to its caller:

```
In [1]: import pyximport; pyximport.install()
Out[1]: (None, <pyximport.pyximport.PyxImporter at 0x101c7d650>)

In [2]: from division import divide_ints

In [3]: divide_ints(1, 1)
Out[3]: 1

In [4]: divide_ints(1, 0)
Exception ZeroDivisionError: 'integer division or modulo by zero'
    in 'division.divide_ints' ignored
Out[4]: 0
```

Note that even though Python detects the `ZeroDivisionError`, the warning message indicates that it was ignored, and the call to `divide_ints(1, 0)` returns an erroneous value of 0.

To correctly propagate this exception, Cython provides an `except` clause to allow a `cdef` or `cpdef` function to communicate to its caller that a Python exception has or may have occurred during its execution:

```
cpdef int divide_ints(int i, int j) except? -1:
    return i / j
```

Because we modified the Cython source, we must restart the Python (or IPython) interpreter; otherwise, we cannot access our modified version of `divide_ints`:

```
In [1]: import pyximport; pyximport.install()
Out[1]: (None, <pyximport.pyximport.PyxImporter at 0x101c67690>)

In [2]: from division import divide_ints

In [3]: divide_ints(1, 0)
Traceback (most recent call last):
File "<ipython-input-3-27c79d4283e7>", line 1, in <module>
  divide_ints(1, 0)
File "division.pyx", line 1, in division.divide_ints (...)
  cpdef int divide_ints(int i, int j) except? -1:
File "division.pyx", line 2, in division.divide_ints (...)
  return i / j
ZeroDivisionError: integer division or modulo by zero
```

We see that the exception is now correctly propagated and is no longer ignored.

The `except? -1` clause allows the return value -1 to act as a possible sentinel that an exception has occurred. If `divide_ints` ever returns -1, Cython checks if the global exception state has been set, and if so, starts unwinding the stack. We do not have to set the return value to -1 ourselves when an exception occurs; Cython does this for us automatically. The value -1 here is arbitrary: we could have used a different integer literal that is within the range of values for the return type.

In this example we use a question mark in the except clause because -1 might be a valid result from divide_ints, in which case no exception state will be set. If there is a return value that always indicates an error has occurred without ambiguity, then the question mark can be omitted. Alternatively, to have Cython check if an exception has been raised regardless of return value, we can use the except * clause instead. This will incur some overhead.

Functions and the embedsignature Compiler Directive

When working with a pure-Python function, we can easily see its signature when using IPython's introspection:

```
In [11]: interpreted_fact?
Type:       function
String Form:<function interpreted_fact at 0x101c711b8>
File:       [...]
Definition: interpreted_fact(n)
Docstring:  Computes n!
```

IPython calls the signature of interpreted_fact the *definition*.

Cython-compiled def and cpdef functions do have a standard docstring, but do not include a signature by default:

```
In [12]: fact.py_fact?
Type:       builtin_function_or_method
String Form:<built-in function py_fact>
Docstring:  Computes n!
```

We can instruct Cython to inject the compiled function's Python signature into the docstring with the embedsignature compiler directive (see "Compiler Directives" on page 28).

When embedsignature is set to True, we see the signature for py_fact in the output:

```
In [3]: fact.py_fact?
Type:       builtin_function_or_method
String Form:<built-in function py_fact>
Docstring:
py_fact(n)
Computes n!
```

This can be helpful to know the argument names, their default values, the order in which arguments are passed in, and more.

Generated C Code

The cython compiler outputs either a C or a C++ source file. The generated code is highly optimized, and the variable names are modified from the original. For these reasons, it is not particularly easy to read.

For a very simple Cython function called mult, defined in *mult.pyx*, let's see a little bit of the generated source. Let's first compile a fully dynamic version:

```
def mult(a, b):
    return a * b
```

We place this function in *mult.pyx* and call cython to generate *mult.c*:

```
$ cython mult.pyx
```

Looking at *mult.c*, we see it is several thousand lines long. Some of this is extension module boilerplate, and most is support code that is not actually used for trivial functions like this. Cython generates embedded comments to indicate what C code corresponds to each line of the original Cython source.

Let's look at the generated C code that computes a + b:

```
/* "mult.pyx":3
 *
 * def mult(a, b):
 *     return a * b         # <<<<<<<<<<<<<<
 */
  __pyx_t_1 = PyNumber_Multiply(__pyx_v_a, __pyx_v_b);
  if (unlikely(!__pyx_t_1)) {
    __pyx_filename = __pyx_f[0];
    __pyx_lineno = 3;
    __pyx_clineno = __LINE__;
    goto __pyx_L1_error;
  }
```

We see that the generated code is calling the PyNumber_Multiply function from the Python/C API, which is the most general way to multiply any two objects in Python (not just numbers, despite the name). The types of the __pyx_v_a and __pyx_v_b variables are PyObject*. This code will work for any objects that support multiplication, and will raise an exception otherwise.

Let's add static typing to mult:

```
def mult(int a, int b):
    return a * b
```

The generated source code now does C-level multiplication of C integers, which will have much better performance:

```
    /* "mult.pyx":3
    *
    * def mult(int a, int b):
    *     return a * b                 # <<<<<<<<<<<<<<
    */
    __pyx_t_1 = __Pyx_PyInt_From_int((__pyx_v_a * __pyx_v_b));
    /* etc. */
```

The __pyx_v_a and __pyx_v_b variables are now declared as ints, as we would expect with our changed declaration, and Cython now computes the product of a and b by generating a call to __Pyx_PyInt_From_int, which is a thin wrapper around the Python/C API function PyInt_FromLong.

A more convenient way to check the generated code is found in Chapter 9, which covers compile-time options that generate an annotated source file. These annotated files help us determine in a high-level way whether Cython is generating the fastest possible code.

Type Coercion and Casting

Both C and Python have well-defined rules for coercion between numeric types. Because statically typed numeric types in Cython are C types, C coercion rules apply here as well.

Explicit casting between types is common in C, especially when we're dealing with C pointers. Cython provides a casting operator that is very similar to C's casting operator, except that it replaces parentheses with angle brackets. A simple cast from a void * to an int * would look like:

```
cdef int *ptr_i = <int*>v
```

For this example, the cython compiler generates the C equivalent:

```
int *ptr_i = (int*)v;
```

Explicit casting in C is not checked, providing total control over type representation. For example, it is possible—but not recommended—to create a function print_address that prints the memory address of a Python object, which should be equivalent to the object's identity as returned by the id built-in function:

```
def print_address(a):
    cdef void *v = <void*>a
    cdef long addr = <long>v
    print "Cython address:", addr
    print "Python id     :", id(a)
```

We can try out print_address on systems where sizeof(void*) equals sizeof(long):

```
In [1]: import pyximport; pyximport.install()
Out[1]: (None, <pyximport.pyximport.PyxImporter at 0x101c64290>)

In [2]: import casting
```

```
In [3]: casting.print_address(1)
Cython address: 4298191640
Python id    : 4298191640
```

We can use casting with Python extension types, either built-in or types that we define ourselves (Chapter 5). A somewhat contrived example:

```
def cast_to_list(a):
    cdef list cast_list = <list>a
    print type(a)
    print type(cast_list)
    cast_list.append(1)
```

In this example, we take a Python object of any type and cast it to a static `list`. Cython will treat `cast_list` as a list at the C level, and will call either `PyList_SET_ITEM` or `PyList_Append` on it for the last line. This will succeed as long as the argument is a `list` or a subtype, and will raise a nasty `SystemError` exception otherwise. Such bare casts are appropriate only when we are *certain* that the object being cast has a compatible type.

When we are less than certain and want Cython to check the type before casting, we can use the *checked casting operator* instead:

```
def safe_cast_to_list(a):
    cdef list cast_list = <list?>a
    print type(a)
    print type(cast_list)
    cast_list.append(1)
```

This version of the function will raise a saner `TypeError` when `a` is not a `list` or a subtype at casting time.

Casting also comes into play when we are working with base and derived classes in an extension type hierarchy. See Chapter 5 for more on extension types with Cython.

Declaring and Using structs, unions, and enums

Cython also understands how to declare, create, and manipulate C structs, unions, and enums. For the un-typedefed C `struct` or `union` declaration:

```
struct mycpx {
    int a;
    float b;
};

union uu {
    int a;
    short b, c;
};
```

the equivalent Cython declarations are:

```
cdef struct mycpx:
    float real
    float imag

cdef union uu:
    int a
    short b, c
```

Cython's syntax for `struct` and `union` declarations uses `cdef` and an indented block for the `struct` or `union` members. This is another case where Cython blends Python with C: it uses Python-like blocks to define C-level constructs.

We can combine `struct` and `union` declarations with `ctypedef`, which creates a new type alias for the `struct` or `union`:

```
ctypedef struct mycpx:
    float real
    float imag

ctypedef union uu:
    int a
    short b, c
```

To declare a variable with the `struct` type, simply use `cdef`, and use the `struct` type as you would any other type:

```
cdef mycpx zz
```

The declaration of `zz` is the same whether the struct was declared with `cdef` or `ctypedef`.

We can initialize a struct in three ways:

- We can use struct literals:

```
cdef mycpx a = mycpx(3.1415, -1.0)
cdef mycpx b = mycpx(real=2.718, imag=1.618034)
```

Note the use of function-like syntax, including keyword-like argument support. This is another instance where Cython blends Python and C++ constructs.

- The struct fields can be assigned by name individually:

```
cdef mycpx zz
zz.real = 3.1415
zz.imag = -1.0
```

For initialization, struct literals are more convenient, but direct assignment can be used to update an individual field.

- Lastly, structs can be assigned from a Python dictionary:

```
cdef mycpx zz = {'real': 3.1415, 'imag': -1.0}
```

This uses Cython's automatic conversion to do the individual assignments automatically. Note that this involves more Python overhead.

Nested and anonymous inner `struct` or `union` declarations are not supported. It is necessary to un-nest the declarations and to provide dummy names when necessary. For example, this nested C `struct` declaration:

```
struct nested {
    int outer_a;
    struct _inner {
        int inner_a;
        } inner;
};
```

can be declared in Cython like this:

```
cdef struct _inner:
    int inner_a

cdef struct nested:
    int outer_a
    _inner inner
```

We can initialize a nested struct on a field-by-field basis or by assigning to a nested dictionary that matches the structure of `nested`:

```
cdef nested n = {'outer_a': 1, 'inner': {'inner_a': 2}}
```

To define an `enum`, we can define the members on separate lines, or on one line separated with commas:

```
cdef enum PRIMARIES:
    RED = 1
    YELLOW = 3
    BLUE = 5

cdef enum SECONDARIES:
    ORANGE, GREEN, PURPLE
```

An `enum` can be declared with either `ctypedef` or `cdef`, as in the preceding examples, like a `struct` or `union`.

Anonymous enums are useful to declare global integer constants:

```
cdef enum:
    GLOBAL_SEED = 37
```

Structs, unions, and enums will be used more frequently when we interface with external code in Chapters 7 and 8.

Type Aliasing with ctypedef

Another C feature that Cython supports is type aliasing with the `ctypedef` keyword. This is used in a similar way to C's `typedef` statement, and is essential when interfacing with external code that uses `typedef` aliases. We will see more of `ctypedef` in Chapters 7 and 8.

Here's a simple example:

```
ctypedef double real
ctypedef long integral

def displacement(real d0, real v0, real a, real t):
    """Calculates displacement under constant acceleration."""
    cdef real d = d0 + (v0 * t) + (0.5 * a * t**2)
    return d
```

In this example, the `ctypedef` aliases allow us to switch the precision of the calculation from double precision to single precision by changing a single line of the program. Cython is able to convert between Python numeric types and these `ctypedef` type aliases without difficulty.

The `ctypedef` feature is particularly useful for C++, when `typedef` aliases can significantly shorten long templated types. A `ctypedef` statement must occur at file scope, and cannot be used inside a function (or other local) scope to declare a local type name. The `typedef` is passed through to the generated source code.

Fused Types and Generic Programming

Cython has a novel typing feature, known as *fused types*, that allows us to refer to several related types with a single type definition. As of this writing, fused types are experimental, and their syntax and semantics may change in future releases. We will therefore cover just the basics here. We will also mention them where relevant in later chapters.

Cython provides three built-in fused types that we can use directly: `integral`, `floating`, and `numeric`. All are accessed via the special `cython` namespace, which must be `cimported` (see Chapter 6).

The `integral` fused type groups together the C `short`, `int`, and `long` scalar types. The `floating` fused type groups the `float` and `double` C types, and `numeric`—the most general—groups all `integral` and `floating` types along with `float complex` and `double complex`. Let's look at an example to make fused types more concrete.

Consider the following implementation of `max` for integral values:

```
from cython cimport integral

cpdef integral integral_max(integral a, integral b):
    return a if a >= b else b
```

Because we've used `cython.integral` as the argument and return type, Cython creates three versions of `integral_max`: one for a and b both `shorts`, one for them both `ints`, and one for them both `longs`. Cython will use the `long` version when we call `integral_max` from Python. When we call `integral_max` from other Cython code, Cython checks the argument types at compile time to determine which version of `integral_max` to use.

For example, these three uses of `integral_max` from Cython are allowed:

```
cdef allowed():
    print integral_max(<short>1, <short>2)
    print integral_max(<int>1, <int>2)
    print integral_max(<long>5, <long>10)
```

But we cannot mix specializations for the same fused type from other Cython code; doing so generates a compile-time error, as Cython does not have a version of `integral_max` to dispatch:

```
cdef not_allowed():
    print integral_max(<short>1, <int>2)
    print integral_max(<int>1, <long>2)
```

Trying to pass in a `float` or `double` to `integral_max` will result in a compile-time error if we're doing so from Cython, and will result in a `TypeError` if we're doing so from Python.

It would be nice to generalize `integral_max` to support `floats` and `doubles` as well. We cannot use the `cython.numeric` fused type to do so, because complex numbers are not comparable. But we can create our own fused type to group the `integral` and `floating` C types. This uses the `ctypedef fused` statement:

```
cimport cython

ctypedef fused integral_or_floating:
    cython.short
    cython.int
    cython.long
    cython.float
    cython.double

cpdef integral_or_floating generic_max(integral_or_floating a,
                                       integral_or_floating b):
    return a if a >= b else b
```

The `generic_max` function now has five specializations, one for each C type included in the `ctypedef fused` block, and can therefore handle `floating` arguments as well as `integral` arguments.

If a function or method uses a fused type, at least one of its arguments must be declared with that fused type, to allow Cython to determine the actual function specialization to dispatch to at compile time or runtime. Provided at least one argument has a fused type, the function or method can have local variables of the fused type as well.

Fused types—and their associated generic functions—have several other features, some of which we will point out in Chapters 8 and 10. Currently the most significant limitation of fused types is that they cannot be used for extension type attributes (Chapter 5). We do not go into full depth on fused types because this feature is still in its infancy. Please refer to Cython's online documentation for the most up-to-date material (*http:// docs.cython.org/src/userguide/fusedtypes.html*) on fused types.

Cython for Loops and while Loops

Python `for` and `while` loops are flexible and high level; their syntax is natural and reads like pseudocode. Cython supports `for` and `while` loops without modification. Because loops, by nature, often occupy the majority of a program's runtime, it is worth keeping in mind some pointers to ensure Cython can translate Python looping constructs into efficient C analogues.

Consider the common Python `for` loop over a `range`:

```
n = 100
# ...
for i in range(n):
    # ...
```

If the index variable `i` and `range` argument `n` are dynamically typed, Cython may not be able to generate a fast C `for` loop. We can easily fix that by typing `i` and `n`:

```
cdef unsigned int i, n = 100
for i in range(n):
    # ...
```

The static typing ensures Cython generates efficient C code:

```
for (i=0; i<n; ++i) {
    /* ... */
}
```

Cython is often able to infer types and generate fast loops automatically, but not always. The following guidelines will help Cython generate efficient loops.

Guidelines for Efficient Loops

When looping over a `range` call, we should type the `range` argument as a C integer:

```
cdef int N
# ...
for i in range(N):
    # ...
```

Cython will automatically type the loop index variable i as an `int` as well, *provided we do not use the index in an expression in the loop body*. If we do use i in an expression, Cython cannot automatically infer whether the operation will overflow, and conservatively refuses to infer a C integer type.

If we are certain the expression will not cause integer overflow, we should statically type the index variable as well:

```
cdef int i, N
for i in range(N):
    a[i] = i + 1
```

When looping over a container (`list`, `tuple`, `dict`, etc.), statically typing the loop indexing variable may introduce *more* overhead, depending on the situation. For efficient loops over containers, consider converting the container to a C++ equivalent container (Chapter 8) or using typed memoryviews (Chapter 10) instead.

These guidelines will likely reduce loop overhead. We will learn more about optimizing loop bodies we cover Cython's NumPy support and typed memoryviews in Chapter 10.

To ensure efficient `while` loops, we must make the loop condition expression efficient. This may involve using typed variables and `cdef` functions. Simple `while True` loops with an internal `break` are efficiently translated to C automatically.

Loop Example

Say we want to smooth a one-dimensional array by updating each element with the average of that point with its immediate neighbors. A Python version (ignoring endpoints) would be:

```
n = len(a) - 1
# "a" is a list or array of Python floats.
for i in range(1, n):
    a[i] = (a[i-1] + a[i] + a[i+1]) / 3.0
```

Because we have to access the i-1 and i+1 elements on each iteration, we cannot iterate through a directly. This example is *almost* in a Cython-friendly format. We only need to add some minimal typing information for Cython to generate a fast loop:

```
cdef unsigned int i, n = len(a) - 1
for i in range(1, n):
    a[i] = (a[i-1] + a[i] + a[i+1]) / 3.0
```

Peeking at the generated source, we find that the `for` statement in the preceding example is translated into:

```
for (i = 1; i < n; i += 1) {
    /* ... */
}
```

In this case, because we use i in indexing expressions, it is essential that we statically type the indexing variable. Typing n is, however, optional; the following version is just as efficient (but perhaps slightly more difficult to read):

```
cdef unsigned int i
for i in range(1, len(a) - 1):
    a[i] = (a[i-1] + a[i] + a[i+1]) / 3.0
```

Performance-wise, the Cython code with the extra typing information is consistently two to three times faster than the untyped equivalent.

The Cython Preprocessor

Cython has a DEF keyword that creates a *macro*, which is a compile-time symbolic constant akin to #define C preprocessor symbolic macros. These can be useful for giving meaningful names to *magic numbers*, allowing them to be updated and changed in a single location. They are textually substituted with their value at compile time.

For example:

```
DEF E = 2.718281828459045
DEF PI = 3.141592653589793

def feynmans_jewel():
    """Returns e**(i*pi) + 1.  Should be ~0.0"""
    return E ** (1j * PI) + 1.0
```

DEF constants must resolve at compile time and are restricted to simple types. They can be made up of literal integrals, floating-point numbers, strings, predefined DEF variables, calls to a set of predefined functions, or expressions involving these types and other DEF variables.

The set of predefined compile-time names, listed in Table 3-3, corresponds to what is returned by os.uname.

Table 3-3. Predefined compile-time names

Predefined DEF variable	Meaning
UNAME_SYSNAME	Operating system name
UNAME_RELEASE	Operating system release
UNAME_VERSION	Operating system version
UNAME_MACHINE	Machine hardware name
UNAME_NODENAME	Name on network

The constants, functions, and types available for defining a DEF constant are summarized in Table 3-4.

Table 3-4. DEF constants, functions, and types

Kind	Options
Constants	`None`, `True`, `False`
Built-in functions	`abs`, `chr`, `cmp`, `divmod`, `enumerate`, `hash`, `hex`, `len`, `map`, `max`, `min`, `oct`, `ord`, `pow`, `range`, `reduce`, `repr`, `round`, `sum`, `xrange`, `zip`
Built-in types	`bool`, `complex`, `dict`, `float`, `int`, `list`, `long`, `slice`, `str`, `tuple`

Remember that the righthand side of a `DEF` declaration must ultimately evaluate to an `int`, `float`, or string object. The `cython` compiler will yield an error if it does not.

Like the C preprocessor, `cython` also supports conditional compilation with the all-caps `IF-ELIF-ELSE` compile-time statement. This can appear anywhere a normal Python statement or declaration can, and it can use any value that is valid in that context. `IF` statements can be nested. The types they use are not restricted like `DEF` constants, and they determine truth and falsehood according to Python semantics.

Taking an example from Cython's documentation, say we want to branch based on the OS we are on:

```
IF UNAME_SYSNAME == "Windows":
    # ...Windows-specific code...
ELIF UNAME_SYSNAME == "Darwin":
    # ...Mac-specific code...
ELIF UNAME_SYSNAME == "Linux":
    # ...Linux-specific code...
ELSE:
    # ...other OS...
```

The last area to cover is Cython's support for Python 2 and Python 3.

Bridging the Python 2 and Python 3 Divide

As we learned in Chapter 2, `cython` generates a C source file that is compiled into an extension module with a specific version of Python. Conveniently, we can write our Cython *.pyx* file using either Python 2 or Python 3 syntax. *The generated C source file is compatible with either Python 2 or Python 3*. This means any Cython code can be compiled for either Python 2 or Python 3 runtimes.

Python 3 changed both the Python language and the C API in nontrivial ways. Python 2 extension modules can be particularly difficult to port to Python 3, given the language (C) and the lack of automatic conversion tools. Cython's ability to generate a single extension module that can be compiled, unmodified, for either Python 2 or Python 3 can remove much of the pain and tedium of porting version 2 extension code to version 3.

By default, Cython assumes the *source* language version (the version of Python in the *.pyx* or *.py* file) uses Python 2 syntax and semantics. This can be set explicitly with the -2 and -3 flags at compile time, the latter changing the default behavior to Python 3 syntax and semantics.

For example, in Python 2 `print` is a statement, whereas in Python 3 it is a function. If we have the following file named *einstein.pyx*:

```
import sys
print("If facts don't fit the theory, change the facts.", file=sys.stderr)
```

it will not compile assuming Python 2 syntax. So, we must pass in the -3 flag to set Python 3 syntax:

```
$ cython -3 einstein.pyx
```

The -2 and -3 cython compiler flags are necessary only if a language construct has different semantics in the respective language version.

The resulting *einstein.c* file can be compiled against the Python 2 or Python 3 runtime. With Python 2, the resulting extension module will run as if the `print` function were instead the Python 2 `print` *statement*. This feature allows us to use a specific Python version for the *.pyx* source, and distribute the extension module source file to anyone, regardless of the version of Python being used to run the extension module.

Cython decouples the *.pyx* language version from the runtime version, nicely managing the Python 2 and Python 3 language divide for us.

Besides decoupling the source and runtime language versions, Cython supports the `unicode_literals`, `print_function`, and `division` imports from `__future__` to bring Python 3 semantics into Python 2.

String types were significantly changed in Python 3, and deserve special mention. Cython has several features to manage string types in a version-agnostic way.

str, unicode, bytes, and All That

Python 2 and Python 3 handle strings and string types differently. Both have a string type that represents a sequence of 8-bit characters, and both have a string type that represents a sequence of variable-width characters. They are named differently in each implementation.

Because Cython straddles the Python 2 and Python 3 divide, it handles strings and string types in a way that allows it to generate code that is compatible with Python 2 or Python 3. This means that Cython string types differ from Python 2 strings and Python 3 strings. Several points of note:

- The `bytes` type is the same for all versions, and Cython supports `bytes` as is.
- Cython's `str` type is equivalent to `bytes` when run with Python 2, and is equivalent to the Unicode `str` type when run with Python 3.
- The Cython `unicode` type is identical to the `unicode` type when run with Python 2, and is equivalent to the `str` type when run with Python 3.
- The Cython `basestring` type is a base type for all string types on both versions, useful for type checking with `isinstance`.
- By default, Cython does not allow implicit conversion between `unicode` strings and data buffers; it requires setting a compiler directive (see next points) or explicit encoding and decoding to convert between the different types.
- Cython provides the global `c_string_type` compiler directive to set the type of an implicit conversion from `char *` (or from `std::string` in C++). The directive can take the value `bytes`, `str`, or `unicode`.
- Cython also provides the global `c_string_encoding` compiler directive to control the encoding used when implicitly converting `char *` or `std::string` to a `unicode` object. The directive can take the name of any valid Unicode encoding (`ascii`, `utf-8`, etc.). It can also take the value `default`, which is `utf-8` in Python 3 and `ascii` in Python 2. The only allowed encoding to convert a `unicode` object to `char *` is `default` or `ascii`.
- Dynamically typed string variables typically just work, and the `cython` compiler will notify us when an explicit encoding or decoding operation is required.
- Statically typed Cython `str` variables can be difficult to use without the `c_string_type` and `c_string_encoding` directives, since `str` in Cython can be equivalent to *either* `bytes` in Python 2 *or* `unicode` in Python 3. The `cython` compiler will yield errors or warnings when assigning to a statically typed `str` object without

explicitly encoding the righthand side. It is often better to statically type strings in Cython with the unambiguous `bytes` and `unicode` types.

- The C `char *` type and the C++ `string` type are automatically compatible with the `bytes` type.

More information on working with string types in Cython can be found in Cython's included documentation.

Summary

This chapter covers the core Cython language features in depth; we will build on these features in future chapters. Because these features are fundamental to Cython, many online examples of their usage can be found via straightforward searches.

Cython's Adoption

Given that Cython is in some sense an auxiliary language, it is rare to have a project entirely or even primarily written in it. Nevertheless, it is a full-fledged language with its own syntax and idioms. Searching GitHub for all Cython files, we found approximately 15,000 source files spread over thousands of repositories as of mid-2014.

Cython's use is so pervasive that a complete catalog of all projects using it would be impossible. But we can survey several foundational projects in the Python ecosystem that use Cython. Some of these projects use it in an auxiliary fashion, to bring in an external random number generation library or speed up a small performance-critical component. Others, like Sage (*http://www.sagemath.org/*), have Cython at their core.

Some prominent projects that use Cython, and their respective lines of Cython code as of September 2014, are summarized in Table 3-5.

Table 3-5. Cython's SLOC in foundational Python projects

Project	Lines of Cython
Sage	477,000
NumPy	5,000
SciPy	24,000
Pandas	27,000
scikit-learn	15,000
scikit-image	11,000
MPI4Py	12,000
PETSc4Py	18,000
lxml	22,000
yt	18,000

Given the pervasiveness of projects like NumPy, SciPy, Pandas, scikit-learn, and scikit-image, Cython code is used directly or indirectly by millions of end users, developers, analysts, engineers, and scientists.[3]

If the Pareto principle is to be believed, then roughly 80 percent of the runtime in a library is due to just 20 percent of the code. For a Python project to see major performance improvements, it need only convert a small fraction of its code base from Python to Cython.

It is no accident that the most active Cython projects have a data analysis and scientific computing bent. Cython shines in these domains for several reasons:

- Cython can wrap existing C, C++, and Fortran libraries efficiently and easily, providing access to existing functionality that is already optimized and debugged.
- Memory- and CPU-bound Python computations perform much better when translated into a statically typed language.
- When dealing with large data sets, having control over the precise data types and data structures at a low level can yield efficient storage and improved performance when compared to Python's built-in data structures.
- Cython can share homogeneous and contiguous arrays with C, C++, and Fortran libraries and make them easily accessible to Python via NumPy arrays.

But Cython is not a one-trick pony. It can speed up general Python code, including data structure–intensive algorithms. For example, lxml, a widely used high-performance XML parser, uses Cython extensively. It is not under the scientific computing umbrella, but Cython works just as well here.

Cython allows us to choose exactly where on the high level Python–to–low level C spectrum we would like to program.

---

3. Cython itself has approximately 100,000 monthly PyPI downloads, and together, NumPy, SciPy, Pandas, and lxml have more than 1 million monthly PyPI downloads. NumPy alone has several million direct downloads per year (not accounting for installations via prepackaged distributions).

## CHAPTER 4

Cython in Practice: N-Body Simulation

> *The programmer, like the poet, works only slightly removed from pure thought-*
> *stuff. He builds his castles in the air, from air, creating by exertion of the imag-*
> *ination. Few media of creation are so flexible, so easy to polish and rework, so*
> *readily capable of realizing grand conceptual structures.*
>
> — F. Brooks

This chapter applies the Cython fundamentals discussed in Chapter 3 to a straightforward but nontrivial example using what we have covered so far. The example starts with a pure-Python N-body simulator to model the solar system, and converts the performance-critical components to use Cython constructs. It comes from the widely known computer language benchmarks game (*http://benchmarksgame.alioth.debian.org/*), allowing comparison between the pure-Python, Cython, and C implementations of the same program.

This chapter will give us a better understanding of how Cython is used in practice. The pure-C, pure-Python, and converted Cython versions can be found in the example code repository (*https://github.com/cythonbook/examples*). Interested readers can follow along with the entire example using this resource.

Overview of the N-Body Python Code

The Python N-body code evolves the positions and velocities of the four Jovian planets in a heliocentric coordinate system. Such a system is chaotic, meaning that the long-term evolution of the system is very sensitive to the initial positions and velocities of all bodies. Small perturbations in the initial conditions lead to arbitrarily diverging results, making prediction difficult. When we are simulating a chaotic system, it is important that the algorithm, or *integrator*, be highly accurate. For this reason the N-body code uses a *symplectic integrator*, which is a fancy term for a time-stepping scheme that does a really good job of computing the right trajectories.

The time step and the initial positions, velocities, and masses of the Jovian planets are given. By passing in a command-line argument, we can vary the number of time steps the integrator takes.

The main routine is straightforward. It takes the number of steps to integrate (n) the initial conditions of the celestial bodies to integrate, and a reference body (in this case, the Sun):

```
def main(n, bodies=BODIES, ref='sun'):
    # ...
```

It first gets a list of all the bodies and makes pairs of all of them for convenience, as many functions need to iterate over all unique pairs:

```
# ...
system = list(bodies.values())
pairs = combinations(system)
```

It then calls `offset_momentum` to correct the Sun's momentum so that it stays at the system's center of mass:

```
# ...
offset_momentum(bodies[ref], system)
```

Before running the integrator, `main` first calls `report_energy` to compute and print the system's total energy:

```
# ...
report_energy(system, pairs)
```

Symplectic integrators are very good at conserving energy, and we will use energy conservation as a way to test the accuracy of the integrator.

After getting the initial energy, we then call `advance`, the core of the computation, and pass in the time step, the number of steps to take, and the sequence of paired bodies:

```
# ...
advance(0.01, n, system, pairs)
```

For this simulation, the unit of time is the mean solar day, the unit of distance is one astronomical unit, and the unit of mass is the solar mass.

After advancing the system, we output the total energy again:

```
# ...
report_energy(system, pairs)
```

Its value should be close to the total energy computed before `advance` was called.

Let's try it out from the command line:

```
$ time python nbody.py 500000
-0.169075164
-0.169096567
python nbody.py 500000  13.21s user 0.04s system 99% cpu 13.286 total
```

The energy before and after match to nearly five decimal places.

This pure-Python version requires about 13 seconds to advance 500,000 steps. When all is said and done, Cython will improve performance by nearly two orders of magnitude, approaching the performance of a pure-C version of the same algorithm.

Converting to Cython

Let's first run our pure-Python version under cProfile to quantify where the runtime is spent:

```
$ ipython --no-banner

In [1]: %run -p nbody.py 500000
       71 function calls in 13.897 seconds

Ordered by: internal time

ncalls  tottime  percall  cumtime  percall filename:lineno(function)
     1   13.880   13.880   13.896   13.896 nbody.py:59(advance)
     2    0.015    0.008    0.015    0.008 {range}
     1    0.001    0.001   13.897   13.897 {execfile}
     2    0.000    0.000    0.000    0.000 nbody.py:82(report_energy)
   ...
```

It is not surprising to find that advance consumes 99.9 percent of the runtime. Converting it to use static types and more efficient data structures is the right approach. The rest of the code can remain as is.

Before we begin converting our code to Cython, we first copy the *nbody.py* file to *nbody.pyx*, which allows us to use Cython-specific declarations and constructs.

Let's compile and run the Cython version to ensure the program works correctly. To compile, we use a simple distuils script named *setup.py*:

```
from distutils.core import setup
from Cython.Build import cythonize

setup(name="nbody",
      ext_modules=cythonize("nbody.pyx"))
```

We need a *run_nbody.py* driver script to run the main function inside our nbody extension module:

```
import sys
from nbody import main

main(int(sys.argv[1]))
```

Building our extension is straightforward:

```
$ python setup.py build_ext -i
```

(Consult Chapter 2 for platform-specific compilation instructions.)

After compiling our extension, we can test that we obtain the same results as before:

```
$ time python run_nbody.py 500000
-0.169075164
-0.169096567
python run_nbody.py 500000  4.78s user 0.03s system 99% cpu 4.821 total
```

The output is identical to the pure-Python version's, and the performance already improved by a factor of 2.8. Cython provides this performance improvement essentially for free.

With our compilation infrastructure in place, we can turn our attention to improving performance further still.

Python Data Structures and Organization

In Python, each celestial body is represented as a tuple with three elements: two three-element lists for the position and velocity, and a float value for the mass. For example, the Sun's initial condition is represented by the following three-element tuple:

```
([0.0, 0.0, 0.0], # position
 [0.0, 0.0, 0.0], # velocity
 SOLAR_MASS # mass
 )
```

And Jupiter's is:

```
([ 4.84143144246472090e+00,
  -1.16032004402742839e+00,
  -1.03622044471123109e-01],
 [ 1.66007664274403694e-03 * DAYS_PER_YEAR,
   7.69901118419740425e-03 * DAYS_PER_YEAR,
  -6.90460016972063023e-05 * DAYS_PER_YEAR],
 9.54791938424326609e-04 * SOLAR_MASS),
```

The global constants DAYS_PER_YEAR and SOLAR_MASS are defined normalization parameters.

The system variable is a list of these tuples, and pairs is a list of all pairs of these tuples. The simulation will access and update the positions and velocities of all planets frequently, so optimizing their representation is essential.

The `advance` function loops over all steps, and for each step, loops over all pairs of bodies:

```
def advance(dt, n, bodies, pairs):
    for i in range(n):
        for (([x1, y1, z1], v1, m1),
             ([x2, y2, z2], v2, m2)) in pairs:
                # ...update velocities...
```

Here we use tuple unpacking to extract the positions (x1, x2, y1, y2, etc.), the velocity lists v1 and v2, and the masses m1 and m2 from each pair in `pairs`. The body of the loop updates the velocities according to the symplectic integration algorithm.

Once the velocities are updated, we update the positions:

```
for (r, [vx, vy, vz], m) in bodies:
    r[0] += dt * vx
    r[1] += dt * vy
    r[2] += dt * vz
```

The `bodies` and `pairs` sequences are set up to refer to the same objects, so updating the velocities in the first loop allows us to update the positions in the second, even though we are looping over different sequences.

Converting Data Structures to structs

Our strategy to improve performance is to convert the pure-Python list-of-tuples-of-lists-of-floats into a C array of C `structs`. With the C version, accessing and updating the planet's data will have much better performance, as these operations will use fast C iteration and optimized lookups, rather than the general (and slow) iteration and lookups we know to expect from the Python interpreter.

Let's define a struct, `body_t`, that has two `double` arrays for the body's position and velocity, and a single `double` for its mass:

```
cdef struct body_t:
    double x[3]
    double v[3]
    double m
```

We place this struct definition toward the top of *nbody.pyx*.

Another goal is to leave most of the *nbody.py* code unmodified, and use our `body_t` struct only where performance matters.

The `advance` function needs to convert the Python list of tuples of celestial body data into a C array of `body_t` elements. Let's make a `cdef` function pair to convert between Python and C data types.

First, `make_cbodies` converts a Python list of tuples into a C array of `body_t` structs. It takes a `bodies` Python list and a preallocated C array of `body_t`s:

```
cdef void make_cbodies(list bodies, body_t *cbodies)
```

The implementation simply loops over the `bodies` list and initializes the preallocated `cbodies` array with the Python list's data:

```
cdef void make_cbodies(list bodies, body_t *cbodies, int num_cbodies):
    cdef body_t *cbody
    for i, body in enumerate(bodies):
        if i >= num_cbodies:
            break
        (x, v, m) = body
        cbody = &cbodies[i]
        cbody.x[0], cbody.x[1], cbody.x[2] = x
        cbody.v[0], cbody.v[1], cbody.v[2] = v
        cbodies[i].m = m
```

Its complement, `make_pybodies`, converts a `body_t` array into a Python list of tuples:

```
cdef list make_pybodies(body_t *cbodies, int num_cbodies):
    pybodies = []
    for i in range(num_cbodies):
        x = [cbodies[i].x[0], cbodies[i].x[1], cbodies[i].x[2]]
        v = [cbodies[i].v[0], cbodies[i].v[1], cbodies[i].v[2]]
        pybodies.append((x, v, cbodies[i].m))
    return pybodies
```

Now we are ready to convert the `for` loops in `advance` to use static types. First, consider the original loop body:

```
def advance(dt, n, bodies, pairs):
    # ...
    for (([x1, y1, z1], v1, m1),
         ([x2, y2, z2], v2, m2)) in pairs:
        dx = x1 - x2
        dy = y1 - y2
        dz = z1 - z2
        mag = dt * ((dx * dx + dy * dy + dz * dz) ** (-1.5))
        b1m = m1 * mag
        b2m = m2 * mag
        v1[0] -= dx * b2m
        v1[1] -= dy * b2m
        v1[2] -= dz * b2m
        v2[0] += dx * b1m
        v2[1] += dy * b1m
        v2[2] += dz * b1m
```

The Cython version is as follows:

```
def advance(double dt, int n, bodies):
    cdef:
        int i, ii, jj
```

```
        double dx, dy, dz, mag, b1m, b2m
        body_t *body1
        body_t *body2
        body_t cbodies[NBODIES]

    make_cbodies(bodies, cbodies, NBODIES)

    for i in range(n):
        for ii in range(NBODIES-1):
            body1 = &cbodies[ii]
            for jj in range(ii+1, NBODIES):
                body2 = &cbodies[jj]
                dx = body1.x[0] - body2.x[0]
                dy = body1.x[1] - body2.x[1]
                dz = body1.x[2] - body2.x[2]
                mag = dt * ((dx * dx + dy * dy + dz * dz) ** (-1.5))
                b1m = body1.m * mag
                b2m = body2.m * mag
                body1.v[0] -= dx * b2m
                body1.v[1] -= dy * b2m
                body1.v[2] -= dz * b2m
                body2.v[0] += dx * b1m
                body2.v[1] += dy * b1m
                body2.v[2] += dz * b1m
        for ii in range(NBODIES):
            body2 = &cbodies[ii]
            body2.x[0] += dt * body2.v[0]
            body2.x[1] += dt * body2.v[1]
            body2.x[2] += dt * body2.v[2]

    return make_pybodies(cbodies, NBODIES)
```

We convert the `for` loop over `pairs` into nested `for` loops over indices into the C array of `body_t` structs. We use two `body_t` pointers to refer to the current bodies in the pair.

We removed the `pairs` argument to `advance`, so we need to update `main` to reflect this change, but we will not show the modification here.

Running the Cythonized Version

After recompiling our code, we can run our latest Cython version and see how it compares to the Python version:

```
$ time python run_nbody.py 500000
-0.169075164
-0.169096567
python run_nbody.py 500000  0.54s user 0.01s system 99% cpu 0.550 total
```

Our Cython version takes about 0.4 seconds to run, and the energy values are in agreement. This is about 25 times faster than the pure Python version.

We can compare this to the runtime of a serial hand-written C version obtained from the computer language benchmarks game, which we compile with equivalent optimization flags:

```
$ time ./nbody.x 500000
-0.169075164
-0.169096567
./nbody.x 500000  0.14s user 0.00s system 97% cpu 0.150 total
```

Our performance thus far is within a factor of four of the C version.

A quick comparison of the C version's `advance` function and our version reveals one important difference when the distance is computed—the C version uses `sqrt`:

```
double inv_distance = 1.0 / sqrt(dx * dx + dy * dy + dz * dz);
double mag = inv_distance * inv_distance * inv_distance;
```

while our version uses the ** operator, which Cython translates to `pow`:

```
mag = dt * ((dx * dx + dy * dy + dz * dz) ** (-1.5))
```

It is straightforward to convert our version to use `sqrt`:

```
ds = dx * dx + dy * dy + dz * dz
mag = dt / (ds * sqrt(ds))
```

This requires that we type `ds` as a `double` and add a `cimport` line at the top of the file (Chapter 6):

```
from libc.math cimport sqrt
```

With this minor syntactic change, we see another significant performance boost:

```
$ time python ./run_nbody.py 500000
-0.169075164
-0.169096567
python ./run_nbody.py 500000  0.15s user 0.01s system 99% cpu 0.159 total
```

This last improvement yields code that is a factor of 3.6 faster than the previous version, is a factor of 90 faster than the pure-Python version, and brings us within a factor of 1.25 of the pure-C version's performance.

Summary

This chapter demonstrates how to take numeric-heavy Python code and convert it to Cython, achieving a factor-of-90 boost in performance. The approach we used is straightforward and ensures that we get the most payoff for our efforts.

The steps we followed are:

1. Profile the pure-Python version (using the cProfile module or IPython's %run -p magic command) to determine where the code spends its time. In this example, nearly all the runtime is spent in the loop-heavy advance function.

2. Inspect the hotspots for nested for loops, numeric-heavy operations, and nested Python containers, all of which can be easily converted with Cython to use more efficient C-level constructs. This example happens to have all of the above.

3. Use Cython to declare C data structures equivalent to the Python data structures identified above. Create converters (if necessary) to transform Python data to C data. In the N-body simulation, we created a body_t struct to represent the nested list-of-tuples-of-lists-of-floats Python data in C, which has better data locality and significantly more efficient access. We also created two converters, make_cbodies and make_pybodies, to convert Python to C and C to Python, respectively. Sometimes these converters are not necessary if Cython can convert the data automatically.

4. Convert the hotspots to use our C-level data structures. Remove Python data structures from nested loops to the extent possible. Ensure all variables used in nested loops (including the loop variables themselves) are statically typed. Our make_pybodies and make_cbodies converters, coupled with plenty of cdef declarations, were sufficient in this example.

5. Test the code to ensure the modifications have not changed the semantics. Profile again. If performance is not satisfactory, use Cython profiling tools (Chapter 9) to draw attention to inefficient code.

6. Repeat as necessary.

Another goal of this chapter was to show *how* to use the components covered in Chapter 3 in a realistic setting. Remembering the Pareto principle (or the *80/20 rule*) is useful: we need only use Cython in the 20 percent of the code that occupies 80 percent (or more) of the runtime. The other 80 percent of the code can (and should) remain unmodified.

Studying this example end-to-end is a good exercise for the Cython newcomer; understanding it fully will solidify many core concepts and techniques useful for any Cython project.

## CHAPTER 5

Cython and Extension Types

Make everything as simple as possible, but not simpler.

— A. Einstein

In Chapter 3, we covered the fundamentals of what Cython adds to the Python language, and the power and control those additions provide. That chapter focused on basic data types and functions. Cython can enhance Python classes as well. Before we learn the specifics, we must first review the difference between Python classes and extension types, which will help us understand the what and why of Cython's approach.

Comparing Python Classes and Extension Types

In Python *everything is an object*. What does that mean, specifically? At its most basic level, an object has three things: identity, value, and type. An object's *identity* distinguishes it from all others and is provided by the `id` built-in function. An object's *value* is simply the data associated with it, accessible via dot notation. Typically Python places an object's data inside an internal *instance dictionary* named `__dict__`. The third essential attribute of any object is its *type*, which specifies the behaviors that an object of that type exhibits. These behaviors are accessible via special functions, called *methods*. A type is responsible for creating and destroying its objects, initializing them, and updating their values when methods are called on the object. Python allows us to create new types, in Python code, with the `class` statement.

We will see in this chapter how Cython allows low-level C access to an object's data and methods, and what benefits that access provides.

The built-in types—`object`, `list`, `dict`, `file`, `int`, `float`, and so on—are implemented at the C level via the Python/C API and are incorporated into the Python runtime.

Usage-wise, built-in types behave just like regular Python classes defined with the `class` statement, and the Python type system treats built-in types just like regular classes.

We can also create our own types at the C level directly using the Python/C API; these are known as *extension types*. They fold into the type system along with regular Python classes and built-in types, and are therefore transparent to the end user. When we call methods on extension type instances, we are running compiled and statically typed code. In particular, the extension type has fast C-level access to the type's methods and the instance's data. As discussed in Chapter 3, this fast C-level access can lead to significant performance improvements. Implementation-wise, defining an extension type's methods and working with a type's instances is very different from defining new classes in pure Python. Implementing an extension type directly in C requires expertise in the Python/C API and is not for the uninitiated.

This is where Cython comes in: Cython makes creating and using extension types as straightforward as working with pure-Python classes. Extension types are created in Cython with the `cdef class` statement, and have much in common with regular Python classes.

Despite the syntactic similarities, it is important to remember that a `cdef` class has fast C-level access to all methods and data. This feature is the most significant difference between an extension type and a plain Python class defined in a *.py* module.

Let's see an example.

Extension Types in Cython

Consider a simple class meant to model particles. Each particle has a mass, an x position, and a velocity. A simple `Particle` class in Python would look something like:[1]

```
class Particle(object):
    """Simple Particle type."""
    def __init__(self, m, p, v):
        self.mass = m
        self.position = p
        self.velocity = v
    def get_momentum(self):
        return self.mass * self.velocity
```

This class can be defined in pure Python at the interpreted level, or it can be compiled by Cython. In both cases, the result is essentially the same. An instance of `Particle` has a `mass`, a `position`, and a `velocity`, and users can call its `get_momentum` method. All attributes are readable and writeable, and users are free to assign other attributes to `Particle` objects outside the class body.

---

1. To follow along with the examples in this chapter, please see *https://github.com/cythonbook/examples*.

When we compile the `Particle` class to C with `cython`, the resulting class is just a regular Python class, not an extension type. When Cython compiles it to C, it is still implemented with general Python objects using dynamic dispatch for all operations. The generated code uses the Python/C API heavily and makes the same calls that the interpreter would if this class were defined in pure Python. Because the interpreter overhead is removed, the Cython version of `Particle` will have a small performance boost. But it does not benefit from any static typing, so the Cython code still has to fall back on dynamic dispatch to resolve types at runtime.

It is trivial to convert the `Particle` class into an extension type:

```
cdef class Particle:
    """Simple Particle extension type."""
    cdef double mass, position, velocity
    # ...
```

There are two additions: `cdef` is added before the `class` statement, and static `cdef` declarations are added in the class body after the docstring, one for each instance attribute assigned to in `__init__`. The `__init__` and `get_momentum` methods remain unchanged.

The `cdef class` statement tells Cython to make an extension type rather than a regular Python class. The `cdef` type declarations in the class body are not, despite appearances, class-level attributes. They are C-level instance attributes; this style of attribute declaration is similar to languages like C++ and Java. All instance attributes must be declared with `cdef` at the class level in this way for extension types. If we did not declare all three of `mass`, `position`, and `velocity` in our `Particle` extension type, we would get a runtime exception inside `__init__` when we tried to assign to an undeclared attribute.

Let's kick the tires. We'll put our `cdef class Particle` in a file *cython_particle.pyx*, and the regular `class Particle` in a file *python_particle.py*. Then, from IPython:

```
In [1]: import pyximport; pyximport.install()
Out[1]: (None, <pyximport.pyximport.PyxImporter at 0x101c64290>)

In [2]: import cython_particle

In [3]: import python_particle
```

Here we use `pyximport` to compile the *cython_particle.pyx* file automatically at import time. We can inspect the two `Particle` types:

```
In [4]: python_particle.Particle?
Type:       type
String Form:<class 'python_particle.Particle'>
File:       [...]/python_particle.py
Docstring:  Simple Particle type.
Constructor information:
 Definition:python_particle.Particle(self, m, p, v)
```

```
In [5]: cython_particle.Particle?
Type:       type
String Form:<type 'cython_particle.Particle'>
File:       [...]/cython_particle.so
Docstring:  Simple Particle extension type.
```

And we see that, besides the fact that the Cython version comes from a compiled library, they are very similar.

The two types have identical initializers, so creation is the same:

```
In [6]: py_particle = python_particle.Particle(1.0, 2.0, 3.0)

In [7]: cy_particle = cython_particle.Particle(1.0, 2.0, 3.0)
```

Calling their get_momentum methods is as we would expect:

```
In [8]: py_particle.get_momentum()
Out[8]: 3.0

In [9]: cy_particle.get_momentum()
Out[9]: 3.0
```

We can access all of the py_particle's attributes:

```
In [10]: py_particle.mass, py_particle.position, py_particle.velocity
Out[10]: (1.0, 2.0, 3.0)
```

but none of cy_particle's:

```
In [11]: cy_particle.mass, cy_particle.position, cy_particle.velocity
Traceback (most recent call last)
[...]
AttributeError: 'cython_particle.Particle' object has no attribute 'mass'
```

Furthermore, we can add new attributes to py_particle on the fly, but cy_particle is locked down:

```
In [13]: py_particle.charge = 12.0

In [14]: cy_particle.charge = 12.0
Traceback (most recent call last)
[...]
AttributeError: 'cython_particle.Particle' object has no attribute 'charge'
```

This seems strange—why are the instance attributes in the extension type not accessible from Python? Why can we add new attributes for py_particle and not cy_particle? And why do we have to declare them with cdef in the first place?

When an extension type like cython_particle.Particle is instantiated, a C struct is allocated and initialized. These steps require that the size and fields of that struct be known *at compile time*, hence the need to declare all attributes with cdef.

In contrast, when `python_particle.Particle` is instantiated, a Python dictionary is created and assigned to the instance's `__dict__` attribute, and all other attributes are stored here with their associated values:

```
In [15]: py_particle.__dict__
Out[15]: {'charge': 12.0, 'mass': 1.0, 'position': 2.0, 'velocity': 3.0}
```

C structs are fixed and not open to new members, so no new attributes can be set on an extension type instance. For an object of a regular Python class, its underlying dictionary is modifiable and open to new key/value pairs, as we can see with the `"charge": 12.0` key/value pair in the preceding IPython output.

Extension type attributes are private by default, and are accessible by the methods of the class. We saw how `get_momentum` was able to return the right value in both cases. An instance of a regular class is wide open—anything can access and modify its attributes.

Type Attributes and Access Control

In the pure-Python `Particle` class, attribute access like `self.mass` goes through a general lookup process that works for any attribute, whether it is an instance attribute, a method, or a method or data attribute inside a base class. In our example the process will eventually find the `mass` key inside the instance's `__dict__` and return its associated value without much effort. But it is possible for the attribute lookup machinery to go through several levels of indirection to find its target. As always, this generality comes with performance overhead.

Methods defined in `cdef class` extension types have full access to all instance attributes. Furthermore, `cython` will translate any accesses like `self.mass` or `self.velocity` into low-level accesses to C-struct fields. This bypasses the general lookup process for pure-Python classes, and can lead to significant performance improvements.

But what if we want to be able to access instance attributes of extension types? It is straightforward to have Cython make instance attributes read-only, or readable and writeable.

First, let's see an example with read-only attributes. We include the `readonly` declaration along with the instance attributes, like this:

```
cdef class Particle:
    """Simple Particle extension type."""
    cdef readonly double mass, position, velocity
    # ...
```

If we wanted just the `mass` attribute to be accessible from Python, but `position` and `velocity` to remain private, we would say:

```
cdef class Particle:
    """Simple Particle extension type."""
    cdef readonly double mass
    cdef double position, velocity
    # ...
```

After making these changes, we have to recompile the extension module, which means reimporting it from a new interpreter session with pyximport:

```
In [1]: import pyximport; pyximport.install()
Out[1]: (None, <pyximport.pyximport.PyxImporter at 0x101c64290>)

In [2]: import cython_particle
```

The mass attribute is now accessible from Python:

```
In [3]: cy_particle = cython_particle.Particle(1.0, 2.0, 3.0)

In [4]: cy_particle.mass
Out[4]: 1.0
```

But it is not modifiable:

```
In [5]: cy_particle.mass = -3.0
Traceback (most recent call last)
[...]
AttributeError: attribute 'mass' of 'cython_particle.Particle'
    objects is not writable
```

If we want to make an attribute both readable and writeable from Python, we can use the public attribute:

```
cdef class Particle:
    """Simple Particle extension type."""
    cdef public double mass
    cdef readonly double position
    cdef double velocity
    # ...
```

Here we have made mass readable and writeable with public, position read-only, and velocity private.

After recompiling via pyximport, we see that we can now access both the mass and position attributes:

```
In [3]: cy_particle = cython_particle.Particle(1.0, 2.0, 3.0)

In [4]: cy_particle.mass
Out[4]: 1.0

In [5]: cy_particle.mass, cy_particle.position
Out[5]: (1.0, 2.0)
```

and we can modify the mass as well:

```
In [6]: cy_particle.mass = 1e-6
```

When calling the `get_momentum` method, Cython still uses fast C-level direct access, and extension type methods essentially ignore the `readonly` and `public` declarations. These exist only to allow and control access from Python.

C-Level Initialization and Finalization

The fact that we have a C struct behind every extension type instance has other implications, particularly for object creation and initialization. When Python calls `__init__`, the `self` argument is required to be a valid instance of that extension type. When `__init__` is called, it typically initializes the attributes on the `self` argument. At the C level, before `__init__` is called, the instance's struct must be allocated, and all struct fields must be in a valid state, ready to accept initial values.

Cython adds a special method named `__cinit__` whose responsibility is to perform C-level allocation and initialization. For the `Particle` extension type declared earlier, `__init__` can take on this role, because the fields are all `double` scalars and require no C-level allocations. But it is possible, depending on how an extension type is subclassed or if there are alternative constructors, for `__init__` to be called multiple times during object creation, and there are other situations where `__init__` is bypassed entirely. Cython guarantees that `__cinit__` is called exactly once and that it is called before `__init__`, `__new__`, or alternative Python-level constructors (e.g., `classmethod` constructors). Cython passes any initialization arguments into `__cinit__`.

For example, say we have an extension type whose instances have an internal C array, dynamically allocated:

```
cdef class Matrix:
    cdef:
        unsigned int nrows, ncols
        double *_matrix
```

The correct place to put `self._matrix`'s dynamic allocation is in a `__cinit__` method:

```
cdef class Matrix:
    cdef:
        unsigned int nrows, ncols
        double *_matrix
    def __cinit__(self, nr, nc):
        self.nrows = nr
        self.ncols = nc
        self._matrix = <double*>malloc(nr * nc * sizeof(double))
        if self._matrix == NULL:
            raise MemoryError()
```

If `self._matrix` were allocated inside `__init__` instead, and `__init__` were never called—which can occur with an alternate `classmethod` constructor, for instance—then any method using self._matrix would lead to ugly segmentation faults. Conversely, if __init__ were called twice—perhaps due to inconsistent use of super in a class hierarchy—then a memory leak would result (and would be particularly difficult to track down).

What about cleanup? Cython also supports C-level finalization through the __dealloc__ special method. This method's responsibility is to undo what __cinit__ did during creation. For our Matrix extension type, we should add a __dealloc__ that frees the self._matrix array:

```
cdef class Matrix:
    cdef:
        unsigned int nrows, ncols
        double *_matrix
    def __cinit__(self, nr, nc):
        self.nrows = nr
        self.ncols = nc
        self._matrix = <double*>malloc(nr * nc * sizeof(double))
        if self._matrix == NULL:
            raise MemoryError()
    def __dealloc__(self):
        if self._matrix != NULL:
            free(self._matrix)
```

If defined, Cython ensures that __dealloc__ is called once during finalization. In this example __dealloc__ need only check that self._matrix is non-null and free it to ensure no memory leaks.

Now that we have covered the essential pieces for creation and finalization of extension type instances, let's focus on extension type methods. Cython's cdef and cpdef declarations work there as well.

cdef and cpdef Methods

The concepts we learned in Chapter 3 about def, cdef, and cpdef *functions* also apply to *extension type methods*. Note that we cannot use cdef and cpdef to define methods on non-cdef classes; doing so is a compile-time error.

A cdef method has C calling semantics, just as cdef functions do: all arguments are passed in as is, so no type mapping from Python to C occurs. This provides cdef methods with a performance boost over their def counterparts, which always have to accept and return Python objects of one type or another. This also means that a cdef method is accessible only from other Cython code and cannot be called from Python.

A cpdef method is particularly useful. As we can infer from what we know about cpdef functions, a cpdef method is callable both from external Python code and from other Cython code. When it is called from Cython, no marshalling to and from Python objects takes place, so it is as efficient as can be. However, the argument and return types have to be automatically convertible from and to Python objects, respectively, which restricts the allowed types somewhat (no pointer types, for example).

For example, we can declare the `get_momentum` method on the `Particle` extension type to be a `cpdef` method instead:

```
cdef class Particle:
    """Simple Particle extension type."""
    cdef double mass, position, velocity
    # ...
    cpdef double get_momentum(self):
        return self.mass * self.velocity
```

Say we have a function `add_momentums`:

```
def add_momentums(particles):
    """Returns the sum of the particle momentums."""
    total_mom = 0.0
    for particle in particles:
        total_mom += particle.get_momentum()
    return total_mom
```

This could be defined in interpreted Python, or it could be compiled and run by Cython— in either case, the call to `get_momentum` is a fully general Python attribute lookup and call, because Cython does not know that `particles` is a list of `Particle` objects.

Calling `add_momentums` in the preceding example on a list of 1,000 `Particle` objects takes approximately 65 microseconds.

When Python calls `get_momentum` on a `Particle` object, the `get_momentum` Python wrapper is used, and the correct packing and unpacking from Python object to underlying `Particle` struct occurs automatically.

If we add typing information, then Cython will be able to generate faster code:

```
def add_momentums_typed(list particles):
    """Returns the sum of the particle momentums."""
    cdef:
        double total_mom = 0.0
        Particle particle
    for particle in particles:
        total_mom += particle.get_momentum()
    return total_mom
```

Note that we typed the `particles` argument as a `list`, `total_mom` as a `double`, and, crucially, the loop indexing variable `particle` as a `Particle`.

Because `particle` is a statically typed `Particle` and `get_momentum` is a `cpdef` method, when `get_momentum` is called in `add_momentums_typed`, no Python objects are involved.

Even the in-place sum is a C-only operation, because `total_mom` is a statically typed C `double`.

This typed version takes about 7 microseconds to run on the same list as before, indicating a tenfold speedup over the untyped version. To see the effect of the `cpdef` over the `def` method, we can remove the `Particle particle` declaration, forcing Cython to use Python calling semantics on `particle.get_momentum()`. The result isn't pretty: 71 microseconds, which is slower than the all-Python version! Typing the `particle` loop variable here yields the most significant performance improvement; typing `particles` and `total_mom` has less of an effect.

There is one last comparison to make: what if we make `get_momentum` a `cdef` method? To keep things separate, we will define another method, `get_momentum_c`:

```
cdef class Particle:
    """Simple Particle extension type."""
    cdef double mass, position, velocity
    # ...
    cpdef double get_momentum(self):
        return self.mass * self.velocity
    cdef double get_momentum_c(self):
        return self.mass * self.velocity
```

We will have to modify `add_momentums_typed` as well; we will call the new version `add_momentums_typed_c` for clarity:

```
def add_momentums_typed_c(list particles):
    """Returns the sum of the particle momentums."""
    cdef:
        double total_mom = 0.0
        Particle particle
    for particle in particles:
        total_mom += particle.get_momentum_c()
    return total_mom
```

This version has the best performance: approximately 4.6 microseconds, another 40 percent boost over the `add_momentums_typed` version. The downside is that `get_momentum_c` is not callable from Python code, only Cython.[2]

What explains this additional performance improvement? To answer that, we will have to understand the basics of inheritance, subclassing, and polymorphism with extension types.

---

2. Because both the `get_momentum` and `get_momentum_c` methods are trivial, these performance measures are skewed heavily toward function call overhead. For methods that perform more significant calculations, the performance difference between the `cdef` and `cpdef` versions will be insignificant, and the flexibility that `cpdef` provides becomes a more relevant consideration.

Inheritance and Subclassing

An extension type can subclass a single base type, and that base type must itself be a type implemented in C—either a built-in type or another extension type. If the base type is a regular Python class, or if the extension type attempts to inherit from multiple base types, a cython compile-time error will result.

For example, consider a subclass of Particle, called CParticle, that stores the particle's momentum rather than computing it on the fly. We do not want to duplicate work done in Particle, so we subclass it:[3]

```
cdef class CParticle(Particle):
    cdef double momentum
    def __init__(self, m, p, v):
        super(CParticle, self).__init__(m, p, v)
        self.momentum = self.mass * self.velocity
    cpdef double get_momentum(self):
        return self.momentum
```

Because a CParticle is a (more specific) Particle, everywhere we use a Particle, we should be able to substitute in a CParticle without any modification to the code, all while we revel in the Platonic beauty of polymorphism. In our add_momentums or add_momentums_typed functions defined in the preceding examples, we can pass in a list of CParticles instead. The add_momentums function does everything with dynamic Python variables, so everything follows Python semantics there. But add_momentums_typed expects the elements of the list to be Particle instances. When CParticles are passed in, the right version of get_momentum is resolved, bypassing the Python/C API.

We can subclass Particle in pure Python as well. Consider PyParticle:

```
class PyParticle(Particle):
    def __init__(self, m, p, v):
        super(PyParticle, self).__init__(m, p, v)
    def get_momentum(self):
        return super(PyParticle, self).get_momentum()
```

The PyParticle class cannot access any private C-level attributes or cdef methods. It can override def and cpdef methods defined on Particle, as we have done with get_momentum. We can pass add_momentums_typed a list of PyParticles as well; doing so takes about 340 microseconds per call, making it about five times slower than using Particle objects. Crossing the Cython/Python language boundary polymorphically is nice, but it does have overhead.

---

3. Note that we use the Python 2 syntax for calling super here, but Cython will generate code that is compatible with either Python 2 or Python 3.

Because a cdef method is not accessible or overrideable from Python, it does not have to cross the language boundary, so it has less call overhead than a cpdef equivalent. This is a relevant concern only for small functions where call overhead is non-negligible. For methods that perform significant calculations, the performance difference between cdef and cpdef is less a concern.

Casting and Subclasses

When working with a dynamically typed object, Cython cannot access any C-level data or methods on it. All attribute lookup must be done via the Python/C API, which is slow. If we know the dynamic variable is or may possibly be an instance of a built-in type or an extension type, then it is worth casting to the static type. Doing so allows Cython to access C-level attributes and methods, and it can do so more efficiently. Further, Cython can also access Python-level attributes and cpdef methods directly without going through the Python/C API.

There are two ways to perform this casting: either by creating a statically typed variable of the desired type and assigning the dynamic variable to it, or by using Cython's casting operator, covered briefly in Chapter 3.

For example, say we are working with an object p that might be an instance of Particle or one of its subclasses. All Cython knows about p is that it is a Python object. We can call get_momentum on it, which will work if p has such a method and fail with an At tributeError otherwise. Because p is a dynamic variable, Cython will access get_momentum by looking it up in a Python dictionary, and if successful, PyOb ject_Call will execute the method. But if we cast it to a Particle explicitly, the call to get_momentum will be much faster:

```
cdef Particle static_p = p
print static_p.get_momentum()
print static_p.velocity
```

The assignment to static_p will raise a TypeError exception if p is not an instance of Particle or its subclasses, so this is safe. The call static_p.get_momentum will use direct access to the get_momentum cpdef method. It also allows access to the private velocity attribute, which is not available via p.

 Cython uses general Python method lookups on dynamically typed objects. This will fail with an AttributeError if the method is declared cdef. To ensure fast access to cpdef methods, or to allow any access to cdef methods, we must provide static type information for the object.

Cython also supports the casting operator, and we can use it to achieve the same result:

```
print (<Particle>p).get_momentum()
print (<Particle>p).velocity
```

This removes the need to create a temporary variable as in the previous example. The cast is enclosed in parentheses due to Cython's precedence rules. Because we use a raw cast to a Particle object in this example, no type checking is performed for performance reasons. It is unsafe if p is not an instance of Particle, which may lead to a segmentation fault. If there is a possibility that p is not a Particle, then using the checked cast is safer:

```
print (<Particle?>p).get_momentum()
print (<Particle?>p).velocity
```

If p is not a Particle, this example will raise a TypeError. The tradeoff is that a checked cast calls into the Python/C API and incurs runtime overhead, trading performance for safety.

Extension Type Objects and None

Consider a simple function dispatch:

```
def dispatch(Particle p):
    print p.get_momentum()
    print p.velocity
```

If we call dispatch and pass a non-Particle object, then we would expect to get a TypeError. Usually, this is the case:

```
dispatch(Particle(1, 2, 3))   # OK
dispatch(CParticle(1, 2, 3))  # OK
dispatch(PyParticle(1, 2, 3)) # OK
dispatch(object())            # TypeError
```

However, Cython treats None specially—even though it is not an instance of Particle, Cython allows it to be passed in as if it were. This is analogous to the NULL pointer in C: it is allowed wherever a C pointer is expected, but doing anything other than checking whether it is NULL will result in a segmentation fault or worse.

Calling dispatch with None does *not* result in a TypeError:

```
dispatch(None) # Segmentation fault!
```

The reason for the segmentation fault when None is passed to dispatch is because dispatch (unsafely) accesses the cpdef function get_momentum and the private attribute velocity, both of which are part of Particle's C interface. Python's None object essentially *has no C interface*, so trying to call a method on it or access an attribute is not valid. To make these operations safe, dispatch could check if p is None first:

```
def dispatch(Particle p):
    if p is None:
        raise TypeError("...")
```

```
    print p.get_momentum()
    print p.velocity
```

This is such a common operation that Cython provides special syntax for it:

```
def dispatch(Particle p not None):
    print p.get_momentum()
    print p.velocity
```

This version of dispatch will do the right thing when passed None, at the expense of
some up-front type checking. If there is any possibility that a function or method argument might be None, then it is our responsibility to guard against it if accessing any
C-level attributes or methods on the object. Not doing so will result in ugly segmentation
faults or data corruption. If we access only Python-level methods (i.e., def methods)
and Python-level attributes (public or readonly attributes, for example) on the object,
then an exception will be raised, as the Python/C API will handle things for us.

Many see the need for the not None clause as inconvenient; this feature of Cython is
often debated. Fortunately, it is straightforward to write None-safe code with the
not None clause in the function's argument declaration.

Cython also provides a nonecheck compiler directive—off by default for performance
reasons—that makes all function and method calls None-safe. To enable None checking
globally for an extension module, we can either place a directive comment toward the
beginning of the file:

```
# cython: nonecheck=True
```

or set nonecheck to True from the command line during compilation:

```
$ cython --directive nonecheck=True source.pyx
```

Extension Type Properties in Cython

Python properties are handy and very powerful, allowing precise control over attribute
access and on-the-fly computation.

All this time, the Particle extension type has had a get_momentum method, but any
Python programmer would berate us for having a getter method like that; the right way
to do it is to either expose momentum directly or make a property instead. Doing so in
pure Python is simple with the property built-in function:

```
class Particle(object):
    # ...
    def _get_momentum(self):
        return self.mass * self.velocity
    momentum = property(_get_momentum)
```

Accessing p.momentum (no parentheses!) on a Particle instance p calls _get_momentum automatically. It is not possible to set or delete p.momentum because no setter or deleter was passed to property when the momentum property was defined.

Cython has different syntax for extension type properties, but it achieves the same end:

```
cdef class Particle:
    """Simple Particle extension type."""
    cdef double mass, position, velocity
    # ...
    property momentum:
        """The momentum Particle property."""
        __get__(self):
            """momentum's getter"""
            return self.mass * self.velocity
```

We can now access p.momentum from either Python code or Cython code; doing so calls the underlying __get__() momentum getter. The property and __get__ docstrings are optional; if present, they can be extracted by automatic documentation generators, and are equivalent to passing in a doc argument to the Python property built-in function. If Cython knows the static type of the object in question, the property access will be efficient and bypass the Python/C API. Like the pure-Python property in the initial example, this is a read-only property.

For the sake of this example, suppose we want to be able to get and set a Particle's momentum. We can add a __set__ property method to do so:

```
cdef class Particle:
    """Simple Particle extension type."""
    # ...
    property momentum:
        """The momentum Particle property."""
        def __get__(self):
            """momentum's getter"""
            return self.mass * self.velocity
        def __set__(self, m):
            """momentum's setter"""
            self.velocity = m / self.mass
```

We arbitrarily decide that setting the momentum will modify the velocity and leave the mass unchanged. This allows p.momentum to be assigned to:

```
In [3]: p = cython_particle.Particle(1, 2, 3)

In [4]: p.momentum
Out[4]: 3.0

In [5]: p.momentum = 4.0

In [6]: p.momentum
Out[6]: 4.0
```

If it makes sense to do so, we can also define a __del__ property method, which controls property deletion. If any one of __get__, __set__, or __del__ is not defined, then that operation is not allowed.

To finish our treatment of extension types in Cython, we should cover how extension type special methods are different from their pure-Python counterparts.

Special Methods Are Even More Special

When providing support for operator overloading with a Cython extension type, we have to define a special method; that is, a method of a specific name with leading and trailing double underscores. We previously covered the __cinit__, __init__, and __dealloc__ special methods and saw how they handle C-level initialization, Python-level initialization, and finalization, respectively. Extension types do not support the __del__ special method; that is the role of __dealloc__.

Arithmetic Methods

To support the in-place + operator for a pure-Python class C, we define an __add__(self, other) method. The operation c + d is transformed into C.__add__(c, d) when c is an instance of the C class. If C does not know how to add itself to the other argument, then it returns NotImplemented. In this case, the Python interpreter then calls type(d).__radd__(d, c) to give d's class a chance to add itself to a C instance.

For extension types, the situation is different.[4] Extension types do not support __radd__; instead, they (effectively) overload __add__ to do the job of both the regular __add__ and __radd__ in one special method. This means that, for a Cython-defined extension type E, __add__ will be called when the expression e + f is evaluated and e is an E instance. In this case, the arguments to __add__ are e and f, in that order. The __add__ method will *also* be called when the expression f + e is evaluated and f's __add__ method returns NotImplemented, indicating that f cannot handle an E instance. In this case, E.__add__ is called with f and e as arguments, *in that order*! So __add__ may be called with an arbitrary type as the first argument, *not an instance of the E class*; because of this possibility, it is misleading to name its first argument self.

Here is the proper implementation of __add__ for a simple Cython extension type that can be added to integers:

```
cdef class E:
    """Extension type that supports addition."""
    cdef int data
```

4. This behavior applies to *all* extension types, not just extension types defined via Cython.

```
        def __init__(self, d):
            self.data = d
        def __add__(x, y):
            # Regular __add__ behavior
            if isinstance(x, E):
                if isinstance(y, int):
                    return (<E>x).data + y
            # __radd__ behavior
            elif isinstance(y, E):
                if isinstance(x, int):
                    return (<E>y).data + x
            else:
                return NotImplemented
```

Cython does not automatically type either argument to __add__, making the isinstance check and cast necessary to access each E instance's internal .data attribute.

Let's place the preceding code block in *special_methods.pyx* and try it out from IPython:

```
In [1]: import pyximport; pyximport.install()
Out[1]: (None, <pyximport.pyximport.PyxImporter at 0x101c65290>)

In [2]: import special_methods

In [3]: e = special_methods.E(100)

In [4]: e + 1
Out[4]: 101

In [5]: 1 + e
Out[5]: 101
```

The first addition takes the first branch of E.__add__, and the second addition takes the second branch. What about the error cases?

```
In [6]: e + 1.0
Traceback (most recent call last):
[...]
TypeError: unsupported operand type(s) for +:
        'special_methods.E' and 'float'
```

For this case, E.__add__ returns NotImplemented, and the built-in float type tries to do an __radd__ with an E instance as the left argument. Not knowing how to add itself to an E object, it again returns NotImplemented, and Python then raises a TypeError.

One more case to consider:

```
In [7]: 1.0 + e
Traceback (most recent call last):
[...]
TypeError: unsupported operand type(s) for +:
        'float' and 'special_methods.E'
```

For this case, float's __add__ was called, realized it did not know how to handle E instances, and returned NotImplemented. Python then called E.__add__(1.0, e) (or the equivalent), which also returned NotImplemented, causing Python to raise the TypeError.

Phew. That rounds it out for __add__. Cython follows the same pattern for all arithmetic special methods, so what we have learned about __add__ here applies elsewhere.

The in-place operations like __iadd__ always take an instance of the class as the first argument, so self is an appropriate name in these cases. The exception to this is __ipow__, which may be called with a different order of arguments, like __add__.

Rich Comparisons

Cython extension types do not support the individual comparison special methods like __eq__, __lt__, and __le__. Instead, Cython provides a single (some would say cryptic) method, __richcmp__(x, y, op), that takes an integer third argument to specify which comparison operation to perform. The correspondence between integer argument and comparison operation is detailed in Table 5-1.

Table 5-1. richcmp comparison operations

Integer argument	Comparison
Py_LT	<
Py_LE	<=
Py_EQ	==
Py_NE	!=
Py_GT	>
Py_GE	>=

In Table 5-1, the integer arguments are compile-time constants declared in the Python runtime *object.h* header. We can access these constants via a cimport statement, the details of which are covered in Chapter 6.

For example, to support comparisons with an extension type, we would do the following:

```
from cpython.object cimport Py_LT, Py_LE, Py_EQ, Py_GE, Py_GT, Py_NE

cdef class R:
    """Extension type that supports rich comparisons."""
    cdef double data
    def __init__(self, d):
        self.data = d

    def __richcmp__(x, y, int op):
        cdef:
```

```
        R r
        double data

        # Make r always refer to the R instance.
        r, y = (x, y) if isinstance(x, R) else (y, x)

        data = r.data
        if op == Py_LT:
            return data < y
        elif op == Py_LE:
            return data <= y
        elif op == Py_EQ:
            return data == y
        elif op == Py_NE:
            return data != y
        elif op == Py_GT:
            return data > y
        elif op == Py_GE:
            return data >= y
        else:
            assert False
```

The behavior is as expected:

```
In [1]: import pyximport; pyximport.install()
Out[1]: (None, <pyximport.pyximport.PyxImporter at 0x101c7d290>)

In [2]: from special_methods import R

In [3]: r = R(10)

In [4]: r < 20 and 20 > r
Out[4]: True

In [5]: r > 20 and 20 < r
Out[5]: False

In [6]: 0 <= r <= 100
Out[6]: True

In [7]: r == 10
Out[7]: True

In [8]: r != 10
Out[8]: False

In [9]: r == 20
Out[9]: False

In [10]: 20 == r
Out[10]: False
```

Note that if a type supports rich comparisons, then chained comparisons like 0 <= r <= 100 are automatically supported as well.

One last major difference between regular Python and Cython extension types is iterator support.

Iterator Support

To make an extension type iterable, we define __iter__ on it, just as in regular Python. To make an extension type an *iterator*, we define a __next__ special method on it, as we would in Python 3. This is different from a pure-Python object, where we would define a next method instead. Cython will expose __next__ as next to Python.

A (perhaps contrived) example:

```
cdef class I:
    cdef:
        list data
        int i
    def __init__(self):
        self.data = range(100)
        self.i = 0
    def __iter__(self):
        return self
    def __next__(self):
        if self.i >= len(self.data):
            raise StopIteration()
        ret = self.data[self.i]
        self.i += 1
        return ret
```

Because I defines __iter__, instances of I can be used in for loops:

```
In [1]: import pyximport; pyximport.install()
Out[1]: (None, <pyximport.pyximport.PyxImporter at 0x101c7e290>)

In [2]: from special_methods import I

In [3]: i = I()

In [4]: s = 0

In [5]: for x in i:
   ...:     s += x
   ...:

In [6]: s
Out[6]: 4950
```

Because I defines __next__, instances can be used where an *iterator* is required:

```
In [15]: it = iter(I())

In [16]: it.next()
Out[16]: 0

In [17]: next(it)
Out[17]: 1
```

This covers the primary differences between Cython special methods and their usual semantics in Python. For a full list of special methods, please refer to the relevant sections in Cython's online documentation (*http://docs.cython.org/*).

Summary

The easiest way to create Python extension types, without exception, is through Cython. Trying to do so in straight C via the Python/C API is a useful exercise, but it requires a certain facility with the Python object model and C API that is hard to come by.

Extension types are another instance where Cython melds C-level performance with a Python-like look and feel. A Cython-defined extension type

- allows easy and efficient access to an instance's C-level data and methods;
- is memory efficient;
- allows control over attribute visibility;
- can be subclassed from Python;
- works with existing built-in types and other extension types.

In future chapters we will make use of extension types liberally. In particular, we will cover in Chapters 7 and 8 how to use extension types to wrap C structs, functions, and C++ classes to provide nice object-oriented interfaces to external libraries.

## CHAPTER 6

Organizing Cython Code

Namespaces are one honking great idea—let's do more of those!

— T. Peters
"The Zen of Python"

Python provides *modules* and *packages* to help organize a project. This allows us to group functions, classes, and variables into logical units, making a project easier to understand and navigate. Modules and packages also make it easier to reuse code. In Python, we use the `import` statement to access functions, objects, and classes inside other modules and packages.

Cython also allows us to break up our project into several modules. It fully supports the `import` statement, which has the same meaning as in Python. This allows us, at runtime, to access Python objects defined in external pure-Python modules or Python-accessible objects defined in other extension modules.

If that were the end of the story, it would not allow two Cython modules to access each other's `cdef` or `cpdef` functions, `ctypedef`s, or structs, and it would not allow C-level access to other extension types.

To address this, Cython provides three file types that help organize the Cython-specific and C-level parts of a project. Until now we have been working with Cython source files with a *.pyx* extension, known as *implementation files*. Here we will see how these files work with a new Cython file type called *definition files*, which have a *.pxd* extension. We will also look at the third Cython file type, with a *.pxi* extension; these are called *include files*.

In addition to the three file types, Cython has a `cimport` statement that provides *compile-time* access to *C-level* constructs, and it looks for these constructs' declarations inside definition (*.pxd*) files.

This chapter covers the details of the `cimport` statement; the interrelationship between *.pyx* files, *.pxd* files, and *.pxi* files; and how to use them all to structure larger Cython projects. With the `cimport` statement and the three file types, we have the tools to effectively organize our Cython projects without compromising performance.

Cython Implementation (.pyx) and Declaration (.pxd) Files

We have been working with implementation files all along. As noted earlier, an implementation file typically has the extension *.pyx*, although we can treat a pure-Python file with the extension *.py* as an implementation file as well. If we have a small Cython project and no other code needs to access C-level constructs in it, then a single implementation file is sufficient. But as soon as we want to share its C-level constructs, we need to create a definition file.

Suppose we have an implementation file, *simulator.pyx*, meant to run some sort of physical simulation—we keep the details intentionally vague. Inside *simulator.pyx* we find the following:

- A `ctypedef`
- A `cdef` class named `State` to hold the simulation state
- Two `def` functions, `setup` and `output`, to initialize the simulation and to report or visualize the results
- Two `cpdef` functions, `run` and `step`, to drive the simulation and to advance one time step

An outline of our implementation file is:[1]

```
ctypedef double real_t

cdef class State:
    cdef:
        unsigned int n_particles
        real_t *x
        real_t *vx

    def __cinit__(...):
        # ...
    def __dealloc__(...):
        # ...
    cpdef real_t momentum(self):
        # ...

def setup(input_fname):
```

---

1. To follow along with the examples in this chapter, please see *https://github.com/cythonbook/examples*.

```
    # ...

cpdef run(State st):
    # ...calls step function repeatedly...

cpdef int step(State st, real_t timestep):
    # ...advance st one time step...

def output(State st):
    # ...
```

The `State` extension type has the regular `__cinit__` and `__dealloc__` methods for allocation and deallocation, a `cpdef` method called `momentum`, and perhaps other `def` methods not listed here.

Because everything is in one file, all functions have access to the C-level attributes of the simulation state, so there is no Python overhead when we are accessing or manipulating it. Because `step` is a `cpdef` function, when `run` calls it, it can access its fast C implementation, bypassing its slower Python wrapper.

As we develop the simulation, the *simulator.pyx* extension module gains more functionality and becomes harder to maintain. To make it modular, we need to break it up into logical subcomponents.

To do so, first we need to create a *simulator.pxd* definition file. In it we place the *declarations* of C-level constructs that we wish to share:

```
ctypedef double real_t

cdef class State:
    cdef:
        unsigned int n_particles
        real_t *x
        real_t *vx

    cpdef real_t momentum(self)

cpdef run(State st)

cpdef int step(State st, real_t timestep)
```

Because definition files are meant for compile-time access, note that we put only C-level declarations in it. No Python-only declarations—like `def` functions—are allowed, and it is a compile-time error to put them here. These functions are accessible at runtime, so they are just declared and defined inside the implementation file.

Our implementation file, *simulator.pyx*, also needs to change. The *simulator.pxd* and *simulator.pyx* files, because they have the same base name, are treated as one namespace by Cython. We cannot repeat any of the *simulator.pxd* declarations in the implementation file, as doing so would be a compilation error.

Declarations and Definitions

What makes something a Cython *declaration* as opposed to a Cython *definition*? Syntactically, a declaration for a function or method includes everything for the function or method's signature: the declaration type (`cdef` or `cpdef`); the function or method's name; and everything in the argument list, including the parentheses. It does not include the terminating colon. For a `cdef` class, the declaration includes the `cdef class` line (colon included) as well as the extension type's name, all attribute declarations, and all method declarations.

A Cython *definition* is everything required for that construct's implementation. The definition for a function or method repeats the declaration as part of the definition (i.e., the implementation); the definition for a `cdef` class does not redeclare the attribute declarations.

Our implementation file is now:

```
cdef class State:

    def __cinit__(...):
        # ...
    def __dealloc__(...):
        # ...
    cpdef real_t momentum(self):
        # ...

def setup(input_fname):
    # ...

cpdef run(State st):
    # ...calls step function repeatedly...

cpdef int step(State st, real_t timestep):
    # ...advance st one time step...

def output(State st):
    # ...
```

The `ctypedef` and the `State` type's attributes have been moved to the definition file, so they are removed from the implementation file. The definitions of all objects, whether C level or Python level, go inside the implementation file. The `def` functions and methods remain. When compiling *simulator.pyx*, the cython compiler will automatically detect the *simulator.pxd* definition file and use its declarations.

What belongs inside a definition file? Essentially, anything that is meant to be publicly accessible to other Cython modules at the C level. This includes:

- C type declarations—ctypedef, struct, union, or enum (Chapter 7)
- Declarations for external C or C++ libraries (i.e., cdef extern blocks—Chapters 7 and 8)
- Declarations for cdef and cpdef module-level functions
- Declarations for cdef class extension types
- The cdef attributes of extension types
- Declarations for cdef and cpdef methods
- The implementation of C-level inline functions and methods

A definition file cannot contain:

- Implementations of Python or non-inline C functions or methods
- Python class definitions (i.e., regular classes)
- Executable Python code outside of IF or DEF macros

What functionality does our *.pxd* file provide? Now an external implementation file can access all C-level constructs inside *simulator.pyx* via the cimport statement.

The cimport Statement

Suppose another version of the simulation—in a separate *improved_simulator.pyx* implementation file—wants to work with our simulator, using the same setup and step functions but a different run function, and needs to subclass our State extension type:

```
from simulator cimport State, step, real_t
from simulator import setup as sim_setup

cdef class NewState(State):
    cdef:
        # ...extra attributes...
    def __cinit__(self, ...):
        # ...
    def __dealloc__(self):
        # ...

def setup(fname):
    # ...call sim_setup and tweak things slightly...

cpdef run(State st):
    # ...improved run that uses simulator.step...
```

Inside *improved_simulator.pyx*, the first line uses the cimport statement to access the State extension type, the step cpdef function, and the real_t ctypedef. This access is at the C level and occurs at compile time. The `cimport` statement looks for the *simulator.pxd* definition file, and only the declarations there are `cimport`able. This is in contrast to the second line in the file, which uses the `import` statement to access the `setup def` function from the `simulator` extension module. The `import` statement works at the Python level and the import occurs at runtime.

The `cimport` statement has the same syntax as the `import` statement. We can `cimport` the *.pxd* filename and use it as a module-like namespace:

```
cimport simulator

# ...
cdef simulator.State st = simulator.State(params)
cdef simulator.real_t dt = 0.01
simulator.step(st, dt)
```

We can provide an alias when `cimport`ing the definition file:

```
cimport simulator as sim

# ...
cdef sim.State st = sim.State(params)
cdef sim.real_t dt = 0.01
sim.step(st, dt)
```

We can also provide an alias to specific `cimport`ed declarations with the `as` clause:

```
from simulator cimport State as sim_state, step as sim_step
```

All of these forms of `cimport` should be familiar from Python's `import` statement.

It is a compile-time error to `cimport` a Python-level object like the `setup` function. Conversely, it is a compile-time error to `import` a C-only declaration like `real_t`. We *are* allowed to `import` or `cimport` the `State` extension type or the `step` `cpdef` function, although `cimport` is recommended. If we were to `import` rather than `cimport` extension types or `cpdef` functions, we would have Python-only access. This blocks access to any private attributes or `cdef` methods, and `cpdef` methods and functions use the slower Python wrapper.

A definition file can contain `cdef extern` blocks. It is useful to group such declarations inside their own *.pxd* files for use elsewhere. Doing so provides a useful namespace to help disambiguate where a function is declared.

For example, the Mersenne Twister random-number generator (RNG) header file has a few functions that we can declare inside a *_mersenne_twister.pxd* definition file:

```
cdef extern from "mt19937ar.h":
    # initializes mt[N] with a seed
    void init_genrand(unsigned long s)

    # generates a random number on [0,0xffffffff]-interval
```

```
unsigned long genrand_int32()

# generates a random number on [0,0x7fffffff]-interval
long genrand_int31()

# generates a random number on [0,1]-real-interval
double genrand_real1()

# generates a random number on [0,1)-real-interval
double genrand_real2()

# generates a random number on (0,1)-real-interval
double genrand_real3()

# generates a random number on [0,1) with 53-bit resolution
double genrand_res53()
```

Now any implementation file can simply `cimport` the necessary function:

```
from _mersenne_twister cimport init_genrand, genrand_real3
```

or, using an alias:

```
cimport _mersenne_twister as mt

mt.init_genrand(42)
for i in range(len(x)):
    x[i] = mt.genrand_real1()
```

Several definition files come packaged with Cython itself.

Predefined Definition Files

Conveniently, Cython comes with several predefined definition files for often-used C, C++, and Python header files. These are grouped into definition file packages and are located in the *Includes* directory underneath the main *Cython* source directory. There is a package for the C standard library, named `libc`, that contains *.pxd* files for the *stdlib*, *stdio*, *math*, *string*, and *stdint* header files, among others. There is also a `libcpp` declaration package with *.pxd* files for common C++ standard template library (STL) containers such as `string`, `vector`, `list`, `map`, `pair`, and `set`. Python-side, the `cpython` declaration package has *.pxd* files for the C header files found in the CPython source distribution, providing easy access to Python/C API functions from Cython. The last declaration package we will mention here is `numpy`, which provides access to the NumPy/C API. It is covered in Chapter 10.

Common patterns using `cimport` and their effects are described next.

Using cimport with a module in a package

```
from libc cimport math
math.sin(3.14)
```

The `from ... cimport ...` pattern used here imports the module-like `math` namespace from the `libc` package, and allows dotted access to C functions declared in the *math.h* C standard library.

Using cimport with an object from a dotted module name

```
from libc.math cimport sin
sin(3.14)
```

This form allows `cimport`ing the C `sin` function from `libc.math` in a Python-like way, but it is important to remember that the call to `sin` will call the fast C version.

Multiple named cimports

```
from libc.stdlib cimport rand, srand, qsort, malloc, free
cdef int *a = <int*>malloc(10 * sizeof(int))
```

This imports multiple C functions from C's *stdlib.h* standard library header.

Using cimport with an alias

```
from libc.string cimport memcpy as c_memcpy
```

In this form, we can use `c_memcpy` as an alias for `memcpy`.

Using cimport with C++ STL template classes

```
from libcpp.vector cimport vector
cdef vector[int] *vi = new vector[int](10)
```

Cython supports `cimport`ing C++ classes from the C++ STL.

If we `import` and `cimport` different functions with the same name, Cython will issue a compile-time error. For example, the following is not valid:

```
from libc.math cimport sin
from math import sin
```

It is simple to fix with an alias, however:

```
from libc.math cimport sin as csin
from math import sin as pysin
```

It is possible to `import` and `cimport` namespace-like objects (modules or Cython packages) that have the same name, although this is not recommended, for sanity's sake. So, Cython allows the following:

```
# compile-time access to functions from math.h
from libc cimport math
# runtime access to the math module
import math

def call_sin(x):
```

```
    # which `sin()` does this call?
    return math.sin(x)
```

In the preceding example, it is not immediately obvious that `call_sin` will call the `sin` function from the C standard library, and *not* the `sin` function from Python's `math` built-in module. It is better to rename one of the imports to make explicit which `math` namespace is intended:

```
from libc cimport math as cmath
import math as pymath

def call_csin(x):
    return cmath.sin(x)

def call_pysin(x):
    return pymath.sin(x)
```

Definition files have some similarities to C (and C++) header files:

- They both declare C-level constructs for use by external code.
- They both allow us to break up what would be one large file into several components.
- They both declare the public C-level interface for an implementation.

C and C++ access header files via the `#include` preprocessor command, which essentially does a dumb source-level inclusion of the named header file. Cython's `cimport` statement is more intelligent and less error prone: we can think of it as a compile-time `import` statement that works with namespaces.

Cython's predecessor, Pyrex, did not have the `cimport` statement, and instead had an `include` statement for source-level inclusion of an external include file. Cython also supports the `include` statement and include files, which are used in several Cython projects.

Include Files and the include Statement

Suppose we have an extension type that we want available on all major platforms, but it must be implemented differently on different platforms. This scenario may arise due to, for example, filesystem incompatibilities, or wrapping different APIs in a consistent way. Our goal is to abstract away these differences and to provide a consistent interface in a transparent way. Include files and the `include` statement provide one way to accomplish our nice platform-independent design goals.

We place three different implementations of the extension type in three *.pxi* files: *linux.pxi*, *darwin.pxi*, and *windows.pxi*. One of the three will be selected and used at compile time. To pull everything together, inside *interface.pyx* we have the following code, using the `IF` compile-time statement:

```
IF UNAME_SYSNAME == "Linux":
    include "linux.pxi"
ELIF UNAME_SYSNAME == "Darwin":
    include "darwin.pxi"
ELIF UNAME_SYSNAME == "Windows":
    include "windows.pxi"
```

This example does a source-level inclusion of one of the *.pxi* files.

 Using include twice with the same source file may lead to compilation errors due to duplicated definitions or implementations, so take care to use include correctly.

Even though the include statement is indented inside the IF block, the inserted code will not retain this extra indentation level. The include statement can appear in any scope and the indentation level will be adjusted accordingly.

Some older Cython projects use include in place of cimport. For new code, it is recommended to use cimport with definition files rather than include with include files, except when source-level inclusion is what is desired.

With definition files, include files, and implementation files at our command, we can adapt Cython as needed to any Python or C code base.

Organizing and Compiling Cython Modules Inside Python Packages

A great feature of Cython is that it allows us to incrementally convert Python code to Cython code as performance and profiling dictate. This approach allows the external interface to remain unchanged while the overall performance significantly improves.

Let's take a different approach to our simulation example. Suppose we start with a Python package pysimulator with the following structure:

```
pysimulator
├── __init__.py
├── main.py
├── core
│   ├── __init__.py
│   ├── core.py
│   └── sim_state.py
├── plugins
│   ├── __init__.py
│   ├── plugin0.py
│   └── plugin1.py
└── utils
```

```
├── __init__.py
├── config.py
└── output.py
```

The focus for this example is not the internal details of the pysimulator modules; it's how Cython modules can access compile-time declarations and work easily within the framework of a Python project.

Suppose we have profiled the simulator and determined that the *core.py*, *sim_state.py*, and *plugin0.py* modules need to be converted into Cython extension modules for performance. All other modules can remain pure Python for flexibility.

The *sim_state.py* module contains the State class that we will convert into an extension type. The *core.py* module contains two functions, run and step, that we will convert to cpdef functions. The *plugin0.py* module contains a run function that we will also convert to a cpdef function.

The first step is to convert the *.py* modules into implementation files and extract their public Cython declarations into definition files. Because components are spread out in different packages and subpackages, we must remember to use the proper qualified names for importing.

The *sim_state.pxd* file contains just the declarations for a ctypedef and the cdef class State:

```
ctypedef double real_t

cdef class State:
    cdef:
        unsigned int n_particles
        real_t *x
        real_t *vx

    cpdef real_t momentum(self)
```

All cpdef functions will take a State instance, and they need C-level access. So, all modules will have to cimport the State declaration from the appropriate definition file.

The *core.pxd* file declares the run and step cpdef functions:

```
from simulator.core.sim_state cimport State, real_t

cpdef int run(State, list plugins=None)
cpdef step(State st, real_t dt)
```

The cimport is absolute, using the fully qualified name to access the sim_state definition file for clarity.

Lastly, the *plugin0.pxd* file declares its own run cpdef function that takes a State instance:

```
from simulator.core.sim_state cimport State

cpdef run(State st)
```

The *main.py* file—still pure Python, like everything inside the utils subpackage—pulls everything together:

```
from simulator.utils.config import setup_params
from simulator.utils.output import output_state
from simulator.core.sim_state import State
from simulator.core.core import run
from simulator.plugins import plugin0

def main(fname):
    params = setup_params(fname)
    state = State(params)
    output_state(state)
    run(state, plugins=[plugin0.run])
    output_state(state)
```

The *main.py* module remains unchanged after our conversion to Cython, as do any other pure-Python modules in the project. Cython allows us to surgically replace individual components with extension modules, and the rest of a project remains as is.

To run this simulation, we first have to compile the Cython source into extension modules. We can use pyximport for on-the-fly compilation during development and testing:

```
In [1]: import pyximport; pyximport.install()
Out[1]: (None, <pyximport.pyximport.PyxImporter at 0x101c67650>)

In [2]: from simulator.main import main
```

The import statement here imported all extension modules, and pyximport compiled them for us automatically. We now call main, passing in a parameter file:

```
In [3]: main("params.txt")

simulator.utils.config.setup_params('dummy.params')
simulator.utils.output.output(State(n_particles=100000))
        state.momentum() == 0.0

running simulator.core.run(State(n_particles=100000))
simulator.plugins.plugin0.run(State(n_particles=100000))
simulator.utils.output.output(State(n_particles=100000))
        state.momentum() == 300000.0
```

The output is simply indicating that everything is running as it should. We see output for the simulation setup, for the initial state, and for running the core.run function, which in turn calls the plugin's run function and the step function. Lastly, the final simulation state is output.

Using `pyximport` here to compile our simulator on the fly is fine for quick development. To create a distributable compiled package, we will want to use a `distutils` script or another build system to manage the compilation and packaging for us.

For a package like `simulator`, the `cythonize` function from the `Cython.Build` package can handle all the details for us. A minimal *setup.py* script for `simulator` is:

```
from distutils.core import setup
from Cython.Build import cythonize

setup(name="simulator",
      packages=["simulator", "simulator.core",
                "simulator.utils", "simulator.plugins"],
      ext_modules=cythonize("**/*.pyx"),
      )
```

We call `cythonize` with a glob pattern to recursively search all directories for *.pyx* implementation files and compile them as needed. Using `cythonize` with `distutils` in this way is flexible and powerful—it will automatically detect when a *.pyx* file has changed and recompile as needed. Further, it will detect interdependencies between implementation and definition files and recompile all dependent implementation files.

Summary

Cython's three file types, in conjunction with the `cimport` and `include` statements, allow us to organize Cython code into separate modules and packages, without sacrificing performance. This allows Cython to expand beyond speeding up isolated extension modules, and allows it to scale to full-fledged projects. We can use the techniques in this chapter to speed up select Python modules after profiling indicates the need, or we can use them to design and organize an entire project that uses Cython as the primary language.

## CHAPTER 7

Wrapping C Libraries with Cython

Controlling complexity is the essence of computer programming.

— B. Kernighan

We have seen how Cython can take Python code and improve its performance with ahead-of-time compilation. This chapter will focus on the inverse: starting with a C library, how do we make it accessible to Python? Such a task is typically the domain of specialized tools like SWIG, SIP, Boost.Python, `ctypes`, `cffi`, or others. Cython, while not automating the process like some, provides the capability to wrap external libraries in a straightforward way. Cython also makes C-level Cython constructs available to external C code, which can be useful when we are embedding Python in a C application, for instance.

Because Cython understands both the C and Python languages, it allows full control over all aspects during interfacing. It accomplishes this feat while remaining Python-like, making Cython interfacing code easier to understand and debug. When wrapping C libraries in Cython, we are not restricted to a domain-specific wrapping language—we can bring to bear all of the Python language, its standard library, and any third-party libraries to help us, along with all the Cython constructs we have learned about in previous chapters.

When done well, Cython-wrapped libraries have C-level performance, minimal wrapper overhead, and a Python-friendly interface. End users need never suspect they are working with wrapped code.

Declaring External C Code in Cython

To wrap a C library with Cython, we must first declare in Cython the interface of the C components we wish to use. To this end, Cython provides the `extern` block statement.

These declaration blocks are meant to tell Cython what C constructs we wish to use from a specified C header file. Their syntax is:[1]

```
cdef extern from "header_name":
    indented declarations from header file
```

The *header_name* goes inside a single- or double-quoted string.

Including the `extern` block has the following effects:

- The `cython` compiler generates an `#include` *"header_name"* line inside the generated source file.
- The types, functions, and other declarations made in the block body are accessible from Cython code.
- Cython will check at compile time that the C declarations are used in a *type-correct manner*, and will produce a compilation error if they are not.

The declarations inside the `extern` block have a straightforward C-like syntax for variables and functions. They use the Cython-specific syntax for declaring `structs` and `unions` covered briefly in Chapter 3.

Bare extern Declarations

Cython supports the `extern` keyword, which can be added to any C declaration in conjunction with `cdef`:

```
cdef extern external_declaration
```

When we use `extern` in this manner, Cython will place the declaration—which can be a function signature, variable, `struct`, `union`, or other such C declaration—in the generated source code with an `extern` modifier. The Cython `extern` declaration must match the C declaration.

This style of external declarations is not recommended, as it has the same drawbacks as using `extern` in C directly. The `extern` block is preferred.

If it is necessary to have an `#include` preprocessor directive for a specific header file, but no declarations are required, the declaration block can be empty:

```
cdef extern from "header.h":
    pass
```

---

1. To follow along with the examples in this chapter, please see *https://github.com/cythonbook/examples*.

Conversely, if the name of the header file is not necessary (perhaps it is already included by another header file that has its own `extern` block), but we would like to interface with external code, we can suppress `#include` statement generation with `from *`:

```
cdef extern from *:
    declarations
```

Before we go into the details of the declaration block, it is important to realize what `extern` blocks do *not* do.

Cython Does Not Automate Wrapping

The purpose of the `extern` block is straightforward, but can be misleading at first glance. In Cython, `extern` blocks (and `extern` declarations) exist to ensure we are calling and using the declared C functions, variables, and structs in a type-correct manner. The `extern` block does *not* automatically generate wrappers for the declared objects. As mentioned, the only C code that is generated for the *entire extern block* is a single `#include "header.h"` line. We still have to write `def` and `cpdef` (and possibly `cdef`) functions that call the C functions declared in the `extern` block. If we do not, then the external C functions declared in the `extern` block cannot be accessed from Python code. Cython does not parse C files and automate wrapping C libraries.

It would be nice if Cython automatically wrapped everything declared in an `extern` block (and there is an active project (*http://xdress.org/index.html*) that builds on Cython to do the equivalent). Using Cython to wrap large C libraries with hundreds of functions, structs, and other constructs is a significant undertaking. Brave souls have successfully done just this for the MPI (MPI4Py), PETSc (PETSc4Py), and HDF5 (h5py) libraries, for example. They chose Cython as their wrapping tool over other options (which can automatically wrap libraries) for various reasons:

- Cython's generated wrapper code is highly optimized and generates wrappers that are up to an order of magnitude faster than those of other wrapping tools.
- Often the goal is to customize, improve, simplify, or otherwise Pythonize the interface as it is wrapped, so an automated wrapping tool would not provide much gain.
- The Cython language is a high-level, Python-like language and not limited to domain-specific interfacing commands, making complicated wrapping tasks easier.

Now that we realize what an `extern` block does and does not do, let's look at the declarations in the `extern` block in more detail.

Declaring External C Functions and typedefs

The most common declarations placed inside an `extern` block are C functions and `typedefs`. These declarations translate almost directly from their C equivalents. Typically the only modifications necessary are to:

- change `typedef` to `ctypedef`;
- remove unnecessary and unsupported keywords such as `restrict` and `volatile`;
- ensure the function's return type and name are declared on a single line;
- remove line-terminating semicolons.

It is possible to break up a long function declaration over several lines after the opening parenthesis of the argument list, as in Python.

For example, consider these simple C declarations and macros in the file *header.h*:

```
#define M_PI 3.1415926
#define MAX(a, b) ((a) >= (b) ? (a) : (b))

double hypot(double, double);

typedef int integral;
typedef double real;

void func(integral, integral, real);

real *func_arrays(integral[], integral[][10], real **);
```

The Cython declarations for them are, except for the macros, nearly copy and paste:

```
cdef extern from "header.h":

    double M_PI
    float MAX(float a, float b)

    double hypot(double x, double y)

    ctypedef int integral
    ctypedef double real

    void func(integral a, integral b, real c)

    real *func_arrays(integral[] i, integral[][10] j, real **k)
```

Note that when declaring the `M_PI` macro, we declare it as if it were a global variable of type `double`. Similarly, when declaring the `MAX` function-like macro, we declare it in Cython as if it were a regular C function named `MAX` that takes two `float` arguments and returns a `float`.

In the preceding `extern` block we added variable names for the function arguments. This is recommended but not mandatory: doing so allows us to call these functions with keyword arguments and, if the argument names are meaningful, helps document the interface. This is impossible if argument names are omitted.

Cython supports the full range of C declarations, even the function-pointer-returning-array-of-function-pointers variety. Of course, simple type declarations—scalars of built-in numeric types, arrays, pointers, `void`, and the like—form the backbone of most C declarations and compose the majority of C header files. Most of the time, we can cut and paste straightforward C function declarations into the body of the `extern` block, remove the semicolons, and be on our way.

As an example of a more complicated declaration that Cython handles without difficulty, consider a header file, *header.h*, containing a function named `signal` that takes a function pointer and returns a function pointer. The `extern` block would look like:

```
cdef extern from "header.h":
    void (*signal(void(*)(int)))(int)
```

Because Cython uses `extern` blocks only to check type correctness, we can add a helper `ctypedef` to this `extern` block to make `signal`'s declaration easier to understand:

```
cdef extern from "header.h":
    ctypedef void (*void_int_fptr)(int)
    void_int_fptr signal(void_int_fptr)
```

The second declaration is equivalent to the first but markedly easier to understand. Because Cython does not declare the `void_int_ptr` typedef in generated code, we can use it to help make the C declarations more straightforward. The `void_int_fptr` ctypedef is only a Cython declaration convenience; there is no corresponding typedef in the header file.

Declaring and Wrapping C structs, unions, and enums

To declare an external `struct`, `union`, or `enum` in an `extern` block, we use the same syntax as described in "Declaring and Using structs, unions, and enums" on page 56, but we can omit the `cdef`, as that is implied:

```
cdef extern from "header_name":

    struct struct_name:
        struct_members

    union union_name:
        union_members

    enum enum_name:
        enum_members
```

These match the following C declarations:

```
struct struct_name {
    struct_members
};

union union_name {
    union_members
};

enum enum_name {
    enum_members
};
```

Cython generates `struct struct_name` declarations for the struct, and the equivalent for `union` and `enum`.

For the `typedef`ed version of these:

```
typedef struct struct_name {
    struct_members
} struct_alias;

typedef union union_name {
    union_members
} union_alias;

typedef enum enum_name {
    enum_members
} enum_alias;
```

simply prefix with `ctypedef` on the Cython side and use the type alias name:

```
cdef extern from "header_name":

    ctypedef struct struct_alias:
        struct_members

    ctypedef union union_alias:
        union_members

    ctypedef enum enum_alias:
        enum_members
```

In this case, Cython will use just the alias type names for declarations and will not generate the `struct`, `union`, or `enum` as part of the declaration, as is proper.

To statically declare a `struct` variable in Cython code, use `cdef` with the struct name or the `typedef` alias name; Cython will generate the right thing for us in either case.

It is only necessary to declare the fields that are *actually used* in the preceding `struct`, `union`, and `enum` declarations in Cython. If no fields are used but it is necessary to use the `struct` as an opaque type, then the body of the `struct` should be the `pass` statement.

Wrapping C Functions

After we have declared the external functions we want to use, we still must wrap them in a def function, a cpdef function, or a cdef class to access them from Python.

For example, say we want to wrap a simple random-number generator (RNG). We will wrap the Mersenne twister (*http://bit.ly/mersenne_twister*), which requires us to expose at least two functions to Python. To initialize the RNG's state we call init_genrand; after doing so we can call genrand_real1 to get a random real number on the closed interval [0, 1]. The init_genrand function takes an unsigned long int as a seed value, and genrand_real1 takes no arguments and returns a double.

Declaring them in Cython is straightforward:

```
cdef extern from "mt19937ar.h":
    void init_genrand(unsigned long s)
    double genrand_real1()
```

We must provide def or cpdef functions so that these declarations can be called from Python:

```
def init_state(unsigned long s):
    init_genrand(s)

def rand():
    return genrand_real1()
```

To compile everything together, we can use a distutils script, which we name *setup.py*. We must be sure to include the *mt19937ar.c* source file in the sources list:

```
from distutils.core import setup, Extension
from Cython.Build import cythonize

ext = Extension("mt_random",
                sources=["mt_random.pyx", "mt19937ar.c"])

setup(
    name="mersenne_random",
    ext_modules = cythonize([ext])
)
```

Compiling is straightforward. Please see Chapter 2 for platform-specific command-line flags:

```
$ python setup.py build_ext --inplace
```

This command will generate several lines of output. If it is successful, Python's distutils will produce an extension module named *mt_random.so* or *mt_random.pyd*, depending on whether we are on Mac OS X, Linux, or Windows.

We can use it from IPython as follows:

```
In [1]: import mt_random

In [2]: mt_random.init_state(42)

In [3]: mt_random.rand()
Out[3]: 0.37454011439684315
```

Note that we cannot call either `init_genrand` or `genrand_real1` from Python:

```
In [4]: mt_random.init_genrand(42)
Traceback (most recent call last):
  File "<ipython-input-2-34528a64a483>", line 1, in <module>
    mt_random.init_genrand(42)
AttributeError: 'module' object has no attribute 'init_genrand'

In [5]: mt_random.genrand_real1()
Traceback (most recent call last):
  File "<ipython-input-3-23619324ba3f>", line 1, in <module>
    mt_random.genrand_real1()
AttributeError: 'module' object has no attribute 'genrand_real1'
```

In about two dozen lines of code, we have wrapped a simple random-number generator with minimal overhead. One downside of the RNG's design is that it uses a static global array to store the RNG's state, allowing only one RNG at a time.

In the next section, we will wrap a version of the RNG API that supports concurrent generators.

Wrapping C structs with Extension Types

The improved API first forward-declares a `struct` typedef in the header file:

```
typedef struct _mt_state mt_state;
```

It then declares creation and destruction functions:

```
mt_state *make_mt(unsigned long s);
void free_mt(mt_state *state);
```

The random-number-generation functions take a pointer to a heap-allocated `mt_state` struct as an argument. We will wrap just one of them:

```
double genrand_real1(mt_state *state);
```

The Cython `extern` declaration for this new interface is, again, mostly copy and paste:

```
cdef extern from "mt19937ar-struct.h":
    ctypedef struct mt_state
    mt_state *make_mt(unsigned long s)
    void free_mt(mt_state *state)
    double genrand_real1(mt_state *state)
```

Because the mt_state struct is opaque and Cython does not need to access any of its internal fields, the preceding ctypedef declaration is sufficient. Essentially, mt_state is a named placeholder.

Again, Cython exposes none of these C extern declarations to Python. In this case, it is nice to wrap this improved version in an extension type named MT. The only attribute this extension type will hold is a private pointer to an mt_state struct:

```
cdef class MT:
    cdef mt_state *_thisptr
```

Because creating an mt_state heap-allocated struct must happen at the C level before an MT object is initialized, the proper place to do it is in a __cinit__ method:

```
cdef class MT:
    cdef mt_state *_thisptr
    def __cinit__(self, unsigned long s):
        self._thisptr = make_mt(s)
        if self._thisptr == NULL:
            msg = "Insufficient memory."
            raise MemoryError(msg)
```

The corresponding __dealloc__ just forwards its work to free_mt:

```
cdef class MT:
    # ...
    def __dealloc__(self):
        if self._thisptr != NULL:
            free_mt(self._thisptr)
```

These Cython methods allow us to properly create, initialize, and finalize an MT object. To generate random numbers, we simply define def or cpdef methods that call the corresponding C functions:

```
cdef class MT:
    # ...
    cpdef double rand(self):
        return genrand_real1(self._thisptr)
```

Declaring and interfacing the remaining generation functions is straightforward and is left as an exercise for the reader.

To try out our extension type wrapper, we must first compile it into an extension module. We compile the *mt_random_type.pyx* file together with the *mt19937ar-struct.c* source using distutils. A script named *setup_mt_type.py* to take care of the gory details would look something like the following:

```
from distutils.core import setup, Extension
from Cython.Build import cythonize

ext_type = Extension("mt_random_type",
                     sources=["mt_random_type.pyx",
```

```
                    "mt19937ar-struct.c"])

    setup(
        name="mersenne_random",
        ext_modules = cythonize([ext_type])
    )
```

As in the previous section, we compile it with the standard `distutils` invocation:

```
$ python setup_mt_type.py build_ext --inplace
```

This generates an extension module that we can import as `mt_random_type` from Python:

```
In [1]: from mt_random_type import MT

In [2]: mt1, mt2 = MT(0), MT(0)
```

Here we have created two separate random-number generators with the same seed to verify that each has separate state:

```
In [3]: mt1.rand() == mt2.rand()
Out[3]: True

In [4]: for i in range(1000):
   ...:         assert mt1.rand() == mt2.rand()
   ...:

In [5]:
```

If they were using the same state, the `MT` objects would modify the same state array each time `rand` is called, leading to inconsistent results and failed assertions.

The entire *mt_random_type.pyx* file is just 22 lines, and it is easily extensible to cover the remaining RNG functions. It provides a Pythonic interface to a useful RNG library that is familiar to anyone who has used Python classes before. Its performance is likely as efficient as a hand-coded C extension type while requiring a fraction of the effort and no manual reference counting.

For wrapping C structs in Cython, the pattern used in this example is common and recommended. The internal `struct` pointer is kept private and used only internally. The `struct` is allocated and initialized in `__cinit__` and automatically deallocated in `__dealloc__`. Declaring methods `cpdef` when possible allows them to be called by external Python code, and efficiently from other Cython code. It also allows these methods to be overridden in Python subclasses.

Now that we have covered the basics of wrapping a C interface with Cython, let's focus on some of the customization features that provide greater control.

Constants, Other Modifiers, and Controlling What Cython Generates

As mentioned in Chapter 3, the Cython language understands the const keyword, but it is not useful in cdef declarations. It *is* used in specific instances within cdef extern blocks to ensure Cython generates const-correct code.

The const keyword is *not* necessary for declaring function arguments, and can be included or omitted without effect. It may be required when we are declaring a typedef that uses const, or when a function return value is declared const:

```
typedef const int * const_int_ptr;
const double *returns_ptr_to_const(const_int_ptr);
```

We can carry these declarations over into Cython and use them as required:

```
cdef extern from "header.h":
    ctypedef const int * const_int_ptr
    const double *returns_ptr_to_const(const_int_ptr)
```

Other C-level modifiers, such as volatile and restrict, should be removed in Cython extern blocks; leaving them in results in a compile-time error.

Occasionally it is useful to use an alias for a function, struct, or typedef name in Cython. This allows us to refer to a C-level object with a name in Cython that is different from its actual name in C. This feature also provides a lot of control over exactly what is declared at the C level.

For instance, suppose we want to wrap a C function named print. We cannot use the name print in Cython, because it is a reserved keyword in Python 2 and it clashes with the print function in Python 3. To give such a function an alias, we can use the following declaration:

```
cdef extern from "printer.h":
    void _print "print"(fmt_str, arg)
```

The function is called _print in Cython, but it is called print in generated C. This also works for typedefs, structs, unions, and enums:

```
cdef extern from "pathological.h":

    # typedef void * class
    ctypedef void * klass "class"

    # int finally(void) function
    int _finally "finally"()

    # struct del { int a, b; };
    struct _del "del":
        int a, b
```

```
# enum yield { ALOT; SOME; ALITTLE; };
enum _yield "yield":
    ALOT
    SOME
    ALITTLE
```

In all cases, the string in quotes is the name of the object in generated C code. Cython does no checking on the contents of this string, so this feature can be used (or abused) to control the C-level declaration.

Exposing Cython Code to C

As we saw in Chapter 3, Cython allows us to declare *C-level* functions, variables, and structs with the cdef keyword, and we saw how we can use these C-level constructs directly from Cython code. Suppose, for instance, that it would be useful to call a cdef Cython function from an external C function in an application, essentially wrapping Python in C. This use case is less frequent than wrapping a C library in Python, but it does arise. Cython provides two mechanisms to support this scenario.

The first mechanism is via the public keyword. We already saw public in the context of declaring the external visibility of extension type attributes; here we use it for a different purpose.

If we add the public keyword to a C-level type, variable, or function declared with cdef, then these constructs are made accessible to C code that is compiled or linked with the extension module.

For instance, suppose we have a file named *transcendentals.pyx* that uses the public keyword for a cdef variable and function:

```
cdef public double PI = 3.1415926

cdef public double get_e():
    print "calling get_e()"
    return 2.718281828
```

When we generate an extension module from *transcendentals.pyx*, the public declarations cause the cython compiler to output a *transcendentals.h* header in addition to *transcendentals.c*. This header declares the public C interface for the Cython source. It must be included in external C code that wants to call get_e or that wants to use PI.

External C code that calls into our Cython code must also be sure both to initialize the Python interpreter with Py_Initialize and to initialize the module with inittranscendentals before using any public declarations:

```
#include "Python.h"
#include "transcendentals.h"
#include <math.h>
```

```
#include <stdio.h>

int main(int argc, char **argv)
{
    Py_Initialize();
    inittranscendentals();
    printf("pi**e: %f\n", pow(PI, get_e()));
    Py_Finalize();
    return 0;
}
```

After generating *transcendentals.c*:

```
$ cython transcendentals.pyx
```

we can then compile our *main.c* source file with the *transcendental.c* source:

```
$ gcc $(python-config --cflags) \
      $(python-config --ldflags) \
      transcendentals.c main.c
```

and run the result:

```
$ ./a.out
calling get_e()
pi**e: 22.459157
```

The second mechanism uses the api keyword, which can be attached to C-level functions and extension types only:

```
cdef api double get_e():
    print "calling get_e()"
    return 2.718281828
```

Both api and public modifiers can be applied to the same object.

In a similar way to the public keyword, the api keyword causes cython to generate *transcendentals_api.h*. It can be used by external C code to call into the api-declared functions and methods in Cython. This method is more flexible in that it uses Python's import mechanism to bring in the api-declared functions dynamically without explicitly compiling with the extension module source or linking against the dynamic library.

The one requirement is that import_transcendentals be called before we use get_e:

```
#include "transcendentals_api.h"
#include <stdio.h>

int main(int argc, char **argv)
{
    import_transcendentals();
    printf("e: %f\n", get_e());
    return 0;
}
```

Note that we cannot access PI via this method—to access it using api, we would have to create an api function that returns PI, as the api method can work only with functions and extension types. This is the tradeoff for the flexibility the api mechanism provides via dynamic runtime importing.

Error Checking and Raising Exceptions

It is common for an external C function to communicate error states via return codes or error flags. To properly wrap these functions, we must test for these cases in the wrapper function and, when an error is signaled, explicitly raise a Python exception. It is tempting to use an except clause (see "Functions and Exception Handling" on page 51) to automatically convert a C error return code into a Python exception, but doing so will not work; this is not the purpose of the except clause. Cython cannot automatically detect when an external C function sets a C error state.

The except clause *can* be used in conjunction with cdef callbacks, however. We will see an example of this in the next section.

Callbacks

As we saw previously, Cython supports C function pointers. Using this capability, we can wrap C functions that take function pointer callbacks. The callback can be a pure-C function that does not call the Python/C API, or it can call arbitrary Python code, depending on the use case. This powerful feature allows us to pass in a Python function created at runtime to control the behavior of the underlying C function.

Working with callbacks across language boundaries can get complicated, especially when it comes to proper exception handling.

To get started, suppose we want to wrap the qsort function from the C standard library. It is declared in *stdlib.h*:

```
cdef extern from "stdlib.h":
    void qsort(void *array, size_t count, size_t size,
               int (*compare)(const void *, const void *))
```

The first void pointer is to an array with count elements, and each element occupies size bytes. The compare function pointer callback takes two void pointers, a and b, into array. It must return a negative integer if a < b, 0 if a == b, and a positive integer if a > b.

For the sake of this example, we will create a function named pyqsort to sort a Python list of integers using C's qsort with varying comparison functions.

The function proceeds in four steps:

1. Allocate a C array of integers of the proper size.

2. Convert the list of Python integers into the C `int` array.

3. Call qsort with the proper `compare` function.

4. Convert the sorted values back to Python and return.

The function definition looks like this:

```
cdef extern from "stdlib.h":
    void *malloc(size_t size)
    void free(void *ptr)

def pyqsort(list x):
    cdef:
        int *array
        int i, N

    # Allocate the C array.
    N = len(x)
    array = <int*>malloc(sizeof(int) * N)
    if array == NULL:
        raise MemoryError("Unable to allocate array.")

    # Fill the C array with the Python integers.
    for i in range(N):
        array[i] = x[i]

    # qsort the array...

    # Convert back to Python and free the C array.
    for i in range(N):
        x[i] = array[i]
    free(array)
```

To actually sort the array, we need to set up a `compare` callback. To do a standard sort, we can use a `cdef` function:

```
cdef int int_compare(const void *a, const void *b):
    cdef int ia, ib
    ia = (<int*>a)[0]
    ib = (<int*>b)[0]
    return ia - ib
```

In `int_compare`, we convert the `void` pointer arguments into C integers. We learned in Chapter 3 that to dereference a pointer in Cython we index into it with index 0. If `ia < ib`, then `ia - ib` will return the correctly signed value for qsort.

We now have all the pieces we need to call qsort in pyqsort:

```
    # qsort the array...
    qsort(<void*>array, <size_t>N, sizeof(int), int_compare)
```

This version of the function works, but is fairly static. One way to expand its capability is to allow reverse-sorting the array by negating the return value of int_compare:

```
cdef int reverse_int_compare(const void *a, const void *b):
    return -int_compare(a, b)
```

By providing the optional reverse argument, the user can exert some control over sorting. Let's also add a ctypedef to make working with the callback easier:

```
ctypedef int (*qsort_cmp)(const void *, const void *)

def pyqsort(list x, reverse=False):
    # ...
    cdef qsort_cmp cmp_callback

    # Select the appropriate callback.
    if reverse:
        cmp_callback = reverse_int_compare
    else:
        cmp_callback = int_compare

    # qsort the array...
    qsort(<void*>array, <size_t>N, sizeof(int), cmp_callback)

    # ...
```

Let's try out our routine. First, we compile on the fly with pyximport and import the pyqsort function:

```
In [1]: import pyximport; pyximport.install()
Out[1]: (None, <pyximport.pyximport.PyxImporter at 0x101c7c650>)

In [2]: from pyqsort import pyqsort

In [3]: pyqsort?
Type:       builtin_function_or_method
String Form:<built-in function pyqsort>
Docstring:  <no docstring>
```

To test our function, we need a mixed-up list of integers:

```
In [4]: from random import shuffle

In [5]: intlist = range(10)

In [6]: shuffle(intlist)

In [7]: print intlist
[2, 1, 3, 7, 6, 4, 0, 9, 5, 8]
```

Calling pyqsort should sort the list in place:

```
In [8]: pyqsort(intlist)

In [9]: print intlist
[0, 1, 2, 3, 4, 5, 6, 7, 8, 9]
```

And passing in `reverse=True` should reverse-sort:

```
In [10]: pyqsort(intlist, reverse=True)

In [11]: print intlist
[9, 8, 7, 6, 5, 4, 3, 2, 1, 0]
```

Our basic functionality is looking good.

For full control over the sorting, let's allow users to pass in their own Python comparison function. For this to work, the C callback has to call the Python callback, converting arguments between C types and Python types.

We will use a module-global Python object, `py_cmp`, to store the Python comparison function. This allows us to set the Python callback at runtime, and the C callback wrapper can access it when needed:

```
cdef object py_cmp = None
```

Because `qsort` expects a C comparison function, we have to create a callback wrapper `cdef` function that matches the `compare` function pointer signature and that calls our `py_cmp` Python function:

```
cdef int py_cmp_wrapper(const void *a, const void *b):
    cdef int ia, ib
    ia = (<int*>a)[0]
    ib = (<int*>b)[0]
    return py_cmp(ia, ib)
```

Inside `py_cmp_wrapper`, we must cast the `void` pointer arguments to `int` pointers, dereference them to extract the underlying integers, and pass these integers to `py_cmp`. Because `py_cmp` is a Python function, Cython will automatically convert the C integers to Python integers for us. The return value from `py_cmp` will be converted to a C integer.

We can define a `reverse_py_cmp_wrapper` to invert the values to support reverse sorting:

```
cdef int reverse_py_cmp_wrapper(const void *a, const void *b):
    return -py_cmp_wrapper(a, b)
```

We now have four callbacks: `int_compare` and `reverse_int_compare`, which are in pure C; and `py_cmp_wrapper` and `reverse_py_cmp_wrapper`, which call a user-provided Python callback.

The logic to select the right callback looks something like the following:

```
def pyqsort(list x, cmp=None, reverse=False):
    global py_cmp
    # ...

    # Set up comparison callback.
    if cmp and reverse:
        py_cmp = cmp
        cmp_callback = reverse_py_cmp_wrapper
    elif cmp and not reverse:
        py_cmp = cmp
        cmp_callback = py_cmp_wrapper
    elif reverse:
        cmp_callback = reverse_int_compare
    else:
        cmp_callback = int_compare

    # qsort the array...
    qsort(<void*>array, <size_t>N, sizeof(int), cmp_callback)
```

There are four cases to consider: cmp is provided or left as None, and reverse is True or
False. Each case results in cmp_callback being set to a different cdef function. If cmp
is provided, then the global py_cmp is set to it so that the callback wrapper can access it.

Let's try out the new functionality. First we import, using pyximport to recompile, and
create a random array of positive and negative values:

```
In [13]: import pyximport; pyximport.install()
Out[13]: (None, <pyximport.pyximport.PyxImporter at 0x101c7c650>)

In [14]: from pyqsort import pyqsort

In [15]: from random import shuffle

In [16]: a = range(-10, 10)

In [17]: shuffle(a)

In [18]: print a
[-8, 3, -10, 5, -3, 8, 7, -6, 4, -4, -2, 2, -7, 0, -5, -1, 6, -9, 9, 1]
```

Suppose we want to sort a according to absolute value. We can create a Python comparison function for that, and call pyqsort with it:

```
In [19]: def cmp(a, b):
    ....:     return abs(a) - abs(b)
    ....:

In [20]: pyqsort(a, cmp=cmp)

In [21]: print a
[0, 1, -1, -2, 2, 3, -3, 4, -4, -5, 5, 6, -6, -7, 7, -8, 8, 9, -9, -10]
```

Reversing the result works as well:

```
In [22]: pyqsort(a, cmp=cmp, reverse=True)

In [23]: print a
[-10, 9, -9, 8, -8, 7, -7, -6, 6, 5, -5, -4, 4, -3, 3, -2, 2, 1, -1, 0]
```

What about error handling? For that, we can make use of the except * clause with our cdef callbacks.

Callbacks and Exception Propagation

Thus far, any Python exception raised in cmp is ignored. To address this limitation, we can use the except * clause when declaring our cdef callbacks. The except * clause is part of the function's declaration, so we must update the qsort declaration as well to allow it to be exception-friendly:

```
cdef extern from "stdlib.h":
    void qsort(void *array, size_t count, size_t size,
               int (*compare)(const void *, const void *) except *)
```

We also add the except * clause to the qsort_cmp ctypedef, and to each of our four cdef callbacks:

```
ctypedef int (*qsort_cmp)(const void *, const void *) except *

cdef int int_compare(const void *a, const void *b) except *:
    # ...

cdef int reverse_int_compare(const void *a, const void *b) except *:
    # ...

cdef int py_cmp_wrapper(const void *a, const void *b) except *:
    # ...

cdef int reverse_py_cmp_wrapper(const void *a, const void *b) except *:
    # ...
```

With these trivial modifications, Cython now checks for an exception every time our callbacks are called, and properly unwinds the call stack. Let's see it in action:

```
$ ipython --no-banner

In [1]: import pyximport; pyximport.install()
Out[1]: (None, <pyximport.pyximport.PyxImporter at 0x101c68710>)

In [2]: from pyqsort import pyqsort

In [3]: def cmp(a, b):
   ...:     raise Exception("Not very interesting.")
   ...:

In [4]: ll = range(10)
```

```
In [5]: pyqsort(ll, cmp=cmp)
Traceback (most recent call last):
  File "pyqsort.pyx", line 68, in pyqsort.py_cmp_wrapper (...)
    return py_cmp((<int*>a)[0], (<int*>b)[0])
  File "<ipython-input-3-747656ee32db>", line 2, in cmp
    raise Exception("Not very interesting.")
Exception: Not very interesting.
```

Because we use the except * clause, the callbacks check for an exception after every call. This means there is some overhead associated with this functionality. However, the improved error handling may be more than worth the small performance cost.

Exception propagation with cdef callbacks goes a long way toward providing a Pythonic interface to a pure-C library.

Summary

Compiling Python to C and wrapping C in Python are the *yin* and *yang* of Cython. There is no strict separation between the two: once a C function is declared in an extern block, it can be used and called as if it were a regular cdef function defined in Cython itself. All of the Python-specific parts can be used to help wrap C libraries. To the outside Python world, no one has to know whether we laboriously implemented an algorithm on our own or simply called out to a preexisting implementation defined elsewhere.

The concepts, techniques, and examples in this chapter cover basic and intermediate usage of Cython's interfacing features. We will use these basics in the next chapter, where we cover interfacing with C++.

## CHAPTER 8

Wrapping C++ Libraries with Cython

> *There are only two kinds of languages: the ones*
> *people complain about and the ones nobody uses.*
>
> — B. Stroustrup

Using Cython to wrap C++ has much in common with using it to wrap C: we must declare the C or C++ interface we want to wrap in an `extern` block; we must define Python-accessible functions and extension types that wrap the library; and we must convert Python types to and from C or C++ types when Cython cannot apply automatic conversions.

But C++ is a much larger and more complex language than C. To deal with this added complexity and the additional language constructs, Cython has C++-specific syntax to help.

In this chapter, we will cover all of Cython's C++ wrapping features. Using them, we will learn how to wrap most C++ constructs in Python.

To get an overview, let's wrap a simple C++ class from end to end.

Simple Example: MT_RNG Class

To extend our example in Chapter 7, suppose we reimplement our random-number generator in a simple C++ class with the following interface:[1]

```
namespace mtrandom {

const static unsigned int N = 624;
```

---

1. To follow along with the examples in this chapter, please see *https://github.com/cythonbook/examples*.

```
class MT_RNG {
  public:
    MT_RNG();
    MT_RNG(unsigned long s);
    MT_RNG(unsigned long init_key[], int key_length);

    // initializes RNG state, called by constructors
    void init_genrand(unsigned long s);

    // generates a random number on [0,0xffffffff]-interval
    unsigned long genrand_int32();

    // generates a random number on [0,1]-real-interval
    double genrand_real1();

  private:
    unsigned long mt[N];
    int mti;
}; // class MT_RNG
} // namespace mtrandom
```

Cython can only wrap public methods and members; any private or protected methods or members are not accessible, and thus not wrappable.

To declare this class interface for use in Cython, we use an extern block as before. This extern block requires three additional elements to handle C++-isms:

- Declaring the C++ namespace with the Cython namespace clause
- Using the cppclass keyword to declare a C++ class interface block
- Declaring the class's interface in this block

Because MT_RNG is declared in the mtrandom namespace, we must declare the namespace to Cython in a namepace clause with the cdef extern statement:

```
cdef extern from "mt19937.h" namespace "mtrandom":
    # ...
```

Inside the extern block, we declare the namespace-level constant integer N, and we use the cppclass keyword to declare the MT_RNG C++ class:

```
cdef extern from "mt19937.h" namespace "mtrandom":
    unsigned int N
    cdef cppclass MT_RNG:
        # ...
```

Lastly, inside the MT_RNG class's declaration we place all public constructors, methods, and data that we wish to access from Cython:

```
# ...
    cdef cppclass MT_RNG:
```

```
MT_RNG(unsigned long s)
MT_RNG(unsigned long init_key[], int key_length)
void init_genrand(unsigned long s)
unsigned long genrand_int32()
double genrand_real1()
```

If there is no namespace, the namespace clause can be omitted. If there are several nested namespaces, we can declare them to Cython as namespace "*ns_outer::ns_inner*".

> There can be many cdef extern blocks for each C++ namespace, but only one C++ namespace per cdef extern block. All C++ constructs inside a cdef extern block with a namespace clause must be declared inside that C++ namespace. The namespace clause is required to ensure that Cython generates the proper fully qualified names in the extension module. We do not use the C++ namespace in Cython code.

This suffices to *declare* the MT_RNG class, allowing us to instantiate it and call its methods from Cython code. To access it from *Python*, we still need to write Python-accessible functions and extension types that wrap MT_RNG.

The Wrapper Extension Type

The conventional way to wrap a C++ class in Cython is with an extension type. We name it RNG to avoid clashing with the MT_RNG name, although there are ways to allow them to have the same name (see Chapter 6). Typically, a wrapper extension type has a pointer to a heap-allocated instance of the C++ class it is wrapping:

```
cdef class RNG:
    cdef MT_RNG *_thisptr
    # ...
```

> Storing a pointer to a heap-allocated C++ object in an extension type works in all instances. If the C++ class provides a nullary (no-argument) constructor, we can store a stack-allocated object directly —that is, no pointer indirection required. This removes the need to allocate and delete the instance, and there are efficiency gains as well.

In order for the RNG object to be in a valid state, we need to create and initialize a valid MT_RNG object, requiring a __cinit__ method. Inside it, we use the new operator to create a heap-allocated MT_RNG object:

```
cdef class RNG:
    cdef MT_RNG *_thisptr
    def __cinit__(self, unsigned long s):
        self._thisptr = new MT_RNG(s)
```

Cython passes the new operator through to the generated C++ code. The new operator can be used only with C++ classes; the cython compiler will issue a compile-time error if it's used incorrectly. (We could check for a NULL result, but Cython can automatically convert C++ exceptions; see "C++ Exceptions" on page 144.) The __cinit__ call here uses the first overloaded MT_RNG constructor.

Because every call to new must be matched by a call to delete, we need a __dealloc__ method. Inside it, we call del on self._thisptr, which Cython translates to the C++ delete operator in the generated code:

```
cdef class RNG:
    # ...
    def __dealloc__(self):
        if self._thisptr != NULL:
            del self._thisptr
```

As we learned in Chapters 5 and 7, __dealloc__ is called once at finalization, when no more references to an RNG instance remain.

That takes care of basic creation, initialization, and finalization. To generate random numbers from Python, we can create simple forwarding cpdef methods for the genrand_int32 and genrand_real1 methods:

```
cdef class RNG:
    # ...
    cpdef unsigned long randint(self):
        return self._thisptr.genrand_int32()
    cpdef double rand(self):
        return self._thisptr.genrand_real1()
```

With these in place, our basic wrapper class is complete.

Compiling with C++

When compiling a C++ project, we need to specify that we are using C++ rather than C, and we need to include all C++ source files for compilation. To do this with a distu tils script, we:

- Add a language = "c++" argument to the Extension instance.
- Include all C++ source files in the sources list argument.

For example, a minimal *setup.py* distutils script to compile our *RNG.pyx* example would look like:

```
from distutils.core import setup, Extension
from Cython.Build import cythonize

ext = Extension("RNG",
                sources=["RNG.pyx", "mt19937.cpp"],
```

```
                            language="c++")

    setup(name="RNG",
          ext_modules=cythonize(ext))
```

If we use compiler directives inside *RNG.pyx* (see Chapter 2), we can simplify the `distutils` script. At the top of *RNG.pyx*, we add the following directive comments:

```
# distutils: language = c++
# distutils: sources = mt19937.cpp
```

With these directives in place, the `cythonize` command can extract the necessary information automatically to correctly build the extension. The *setup.py* script then simplifies to:

```
from distutils.core import setup
from Cython.Build import cythonize

setup(name="RNG",
      ext_modules=cythonize("RNG.pyx"))
```

To compile our extension, we can use the usual command-line invocation:

```
$ python setup.py build_ext -i
```

See Chapter 2 for platform-specific details when invoking the compilation step.

We can also use `pyximport` to compile this extension module. It necessitates creating an *RNG.pyxbld* file—not shown here—to instruct `pyximport` that we are compiling for C++ and tell it which C++ source files to include.

After compiling, we can try out our RNG class from Python.

Using Our Wrapper from Python

We can import the RNG extension module from the default Python interpreter or from IPython:

```
In [1]: from RNG import RNG
```

and we can instantiate the RNG class and use its methods:

```
In [2]: r = RNG(42)

In [3]: r.randint()
Out[3]: 1608637542L

In [4]: r.randint()
Out[4]: 3421126067L

In [5]: r.rand()
Out[5]: 0.9507143117838339
```

```
In [6]: r.rand()
Out[6]: 0.1834347877147223
```

We see that using our random-number generator is high level and straightforward. Using __cinit__ and __dealloc__ in our RNG extension type allows Cython to properly tie allocation and finalization to Python's reference counting.

This covers the basics of wrapping our Mersenne twister C++ class in Cython. Going deeper, we can also wrap C++-specific features with Cython, starting with function overloading.

Overloaded Methods and Functions

The MT_RNG class has an alternate constructor that takes an array of unsigned longs to initialize the random-number generator's state. How can we call this from Python?

Because Python does not support overloading methods, it is up to us to emulate overloading by checking argument types and dispatching to the proper C++ constructor inside __cinit__. To call MT_RNG's alternate constructor, we need to supply an array of unsigned longs and its length. To help with this, we can use the array built-in type from the Python standard library. An array instance has a similar interface to a list, but it requires that all contained elements have the same scalar C type. Cython knows how to work with array objects at both the Python and the C level. In particular, we can grab a pointer to an array's underlying C array to pass to our C++ MT_RNG class constructor.[2]

To access the built-in array type at the C level, we must use the cimport statement, which is covered in depth in Chapter 6. We first need to add the proper cimport to *RNG.pyx*:

```
from cpython.array cimport array
```

We then modify RNG's __cinit__ to take either a Python integer or a Python sequence. If the user creates an RNG with an integer argument, we want __cinit__ to call the original constructor:

```
# ...
    def __cinit__(self, seed_or_state):
        if isinstance(seed_or_state, int):
            self._thisptr = new MT_RNG(seed_or_state)
```

If a sequence is passed instead, we want to call the second constructor. Before doing so, we must convert the argument to an array:

---

2. We could use a NumPy array rather than the built-in array type. We choose the array type here because it is simple to use and does not introduce an external dependency. Cython's support for NumPy arrays is covered in Chapter 10.

```
# ...
    def __cinit__(self, seed_or_state):
        cdef array state_arr
        if isinstance(seed_or_state, int):
            self._thisptr = new MT_RNG(seed_or_state)
        else:
            state_arr = array("L", seed_or_state)
```

This converts the `seed_or_state` argument into a Python array of `unsigned longs` and fails with a runtime exception if the conversion is not possible.

Because we have C-level access to the `array` object, we can extract its underlying C array of `unsigned long` integers by using `state_arr.data.as_ulongs`. Putting it all together, this allows us to dispatch to the second constructor:

```
# ...
    def __cinit__(self, seed_or_state):
        # ...
        else:
            state_arr = array("L", seed_or_state)
            self._thisptr = new MT_RNG(state_arr.data.as_ulongs,
                                       len(state_arr))
```

After recompiling with this improved `__cinit__`, we can now create an RNG object by passing in either an integer or a sequence of integers:

```
In [36]: from RNG import RNG

In [37]: r = RNG(42)

In [38]: r.rand()
Out[38]: 0.37454011439684315

In [39]: r2 = RNG(range(30, 40))

In [40]: r2.rand()
Out[40]: 0.04691027990703245

In [41]: r2.randint()
Out[41]: 2626217183L
```

To wrap overloaded C++ functions, we use a similar pattern. Either we can provide several differently named functions in Python, each calling a different version of the overloaded C++ function, or we can provide a single Python function that does the dispatching, as we did with `__cinit__`.

The other form of overloading, *operator overloading*, is also supported by Cython. Because Python also supports overloaded operators, exposing them to Python is much more straightforward.

Operator Overloading

Cython supports most C++ operator overloads. This includes the binary and unary arithmetic operators, the bitwise operators, the Boolean comparison operators, the pre- and post-increment and -decrement operators, the indexing operator (square brackets), and the function call operator (parentheses). Currently, the in-place operators (+=, -=, etc.) are not supported. Some operators are incompatible with Python's syntax, so Cython provides a special `cython.operators` magic module to allow Python-compatible access. Table 8-1 gives the full details.

Table 8-1. C++ operators

Operator type	C++ syntax	Notes

Unary and binary arithmetic operators	`operator+`
	`operator-`
	`operator*`
	`operator/`
	`operator%`
		Unary form takes no arguments; binary form takes an `rhs`. In-place operators not currently supported.

Pre- and post-increment, pre- and post-decrement	`operator++()`
	`operator--()`
	`operator++(int)`
	`operator--(int)`
		No arg indicates pre, `int` arg indicates post. Must use `cython.operator.preincrement` to call.

Bitwise operators	`operator|`
	`operator&`
	`operator^`
	`operator~`
	`operator<<`
	`operator>>`
		Bitshift operators often overloaded for input/output.

Dereferencing, comma operators	`operator,` `operator*()`	Must use `cython.operator.comma` and `cython.operator.dereference` to access.

Boolean operators	`operator==`
	`operator!`
	`operator!=`
	`operator>=`
	`operator<=`
	`operator>`
	`operator<`	

Indexing, call operators	`operator[]` `operator()`	

Cython provides no way to declare the assignment operator `operator=`; assignment by value is assumed.

Suppose our `MT_RNG` class implements the function call operator, `operator`. By calling an `MT_RNG` instance we get back a random `double` on the closed `[0,1]` interval, essentially forwarding to the `genrand_real1` method.

We only have to add a single declaration to our `cppclass` block for `MT_RNG`:

```
# ...
    cdef cppclass MT_RNG:
        # ...
        double operator()()
```

Python, of course, has its own operator overloading syntax. To support calling `RNG` instances in Python, we implement the `__call__` magic method on our `RNG` extension type:

```
cdef class RNG:
    # ...
    def __call__(self):
        return self._thisptr[0]()
```

We cannot say `self._thisptr` directly, as `_thisptr` is, of course, a *pointer* to an `MT_RNG` object. Cython allows us to use the dot operator on a C or C++ pointer and will automatically convert it to the indirection or *arrow* operator, `->`. Not so for operators: we first dereference the pointer using Cython's Python-compatible pointer-dereferencing-by-indexing-at-zero `[0]` syntax, which allows us to then apply `operator` on it.

Alternatively, we can use the `dereference` Cython operator from the special `cython.operator` module (Chapter 3):

```
from cython.operator cimport dereference as deref
```

```
cdef class RNG:
    # ...
    def __call__(self):
        return deref(self._thisptr)()
```

Using either `self._thisptr[0]` or `deref(self._thisptr)` has equivalent semantics when `_thisptr` is a raw pointer.

After recompiling, we can now use our new operator from Python:

```
In [1]: from RNG import RNG

In [2]: r = RNG(10)

In [3]: r()
Out[3]: 0.7713206433158649

In [4]: [r() for i in range(3)]
Out[4]: [0.02075194661057367, 0.49458992841993227, 0.6336482317730897]
```

In some cases C++ operators are implemented as external functions rather than member methods. For instance, suppose the binary + operator for a C++ class C is implemented as:

```
inline C operator+(C lhs, const C& rhs) {
    // ...
}
```

Cython does not support nonmember `operators`, but we can simply declare the `C operator+(const C& rhs)` as if it were a member-defined operator inside the `cppclass` declaration, in the same way we declared the `operator` previously. Because Cython does not generate any redeclarations inside a `cdef extern` block, this bending of the rules will allow us to work around this limitation. By declaring the operator as a class member, Cython sees that C instances support binary addition, even though that addition is implemented as a nonmember function.

C++ Exceptions

Because C++ supports exceptions, Cython has features to detect when they occur and convert them into corresponding Python exceptions automatically. It is not possible, however, to catch C++ exceptions in a Python `try`/`except` block, nor is it possible to throw C++ exceptions from Cython.

To enable this functionality, we simply add an `except +` clause to the function or method declaration that may raise a C++ exception. For instance, to automatically convert a C++ `bad_alloc` exception into a Python `MemoryError`, we change the `MT_RNG` constructor declarations like so:

```
cdef extern from "mt19937.h" namespace "mtrandom":
    cdef cppclass MT_RNG:
        MT_RNG(unsigned long s) except +
        MT_RNG(unsigned long init_key[], int key_length) except +
```

This removes the need to check whether the result of a `new` allocation is `NULL`; with an `except +` clause, Cython does the check for us automatically and propagates the exception into Python code.

Cython automatically converts most standard C++ exception types into corresponding Python exception types. The currently supported exceptions and their Python counterparts are in Table 8-2; this list of exceptions may expand or be refined in future releases.

Table 8-2. C++-to-Python exception mapping

C++	Python
bad_alloc	MemoryError
bad_cast	TypeError
domain_error	ValueError
invalid_argument	ValueError
ios_base::failure	IOError
out_of_range	IndexError
overflow_error	OverflowError
range_error	ArithmeticError
underflow_error	ArithmeticError
All others	RuntimeError

The error message is set from the C++ exception's what method.

To instruct Cython to raise a particular type of Python exception, we can append the Python exception type to the except + clause:

```
# ...
    cdef cppclass MT_RNG:
        MT_RNG(unsigned long s) except +MemoryError
        MT_RNG(unsigned long init_key[], int key_length) except +MemoryError
        # ...
```

Lastly, a custom exception handler function can be used to do the C++-to-Python exception translation manually. This handler can be defined in C++ or Cython.

To call a cdef function handler whenever a C++ method throws an exception, we would say:

```
cdef int handler():
    # ...

cdef extern from "mt19937.h" namespace "mtrandom":
    cdef cppclass MT_RNG:
        MT_RNG(unsigned long init_key[], int key_length) except +handler
        # ...
```

If handler does not raise a Python exception, a RuntimeError is raised automatically.

Stack and Heap Allocation of C++ Instances

We've already seen how to wrap a simple C++ class in an extension type. This is often the most common use of C++ from Cython, but we can, of course, use the class directly in Cython code without exposing it to Python. For instance, if we need to simply *use* the MT_RNG class without wrapping it, we can stack-allocate an MT_RNG instance, allowing

C++ finalization rules to automatically clean up the stack-allocated instance for us, even in the event of exceptions (i.e., the obscurely named resource-allocation-is-initialization pattern).

To declare and use stack-allocated C++ objects in Cython, we must declare a default constructor for the C++ object in the `cdef cppclass` block:

```
cdef extern from "mt19937.h" namespace "mtrandom":
    cdef cppclass MT_RNG:
        MT_RNG()
        void init_genrand(unsigned long s)
        # ...
```

We can now use an `MT_RNG` object inside a function that makes and returns a list of random values:

```
def make_random_list(unsigned long seed, unsigned int len):
    cdef:
        list randlist = [0] * len
        MT_RNG rng  # calls default constructor
        unsigned int i
    rng.init_genrand(seed)
    for i in range(len):
        randlist[i] = rng.genrand_int32()
    return randlist
```

If there is no nullary constructor, then we cannot use stack-allocated C++ objects in Cython, and we have to use a heap-allocated one. In that case, we need to ensure that we call `del` on the object (likely in a `try/finally` block) to ensure it is `deleted` on the C++ side:

```
def make_random_list(unsigned long seed, unsigned int len):
    cdef:
        # ...
        MT_RNG *rng
    rng = new MT_RNG(seed)
    try:
        # ...
    finally:
        del rng
```

Clearly the stack-allocated version is more convenient, removing the need for the `try/finally` block to ensure the `rng` instance is cleaned up.

Besides allocation patterns, subclassing and class hierarchies are important C++ features, and can require some special handling in Cython.

Working with C++ Class Hierarchies

If we want to wrap an `MT_RNG` subclass named `MT_RNGImproved` with Cython, there are techniques to handle method overriding.

Suppose our MT_RNG class has a virtual method, serialize, that returns a std::string serialization of the MT_RNG state. Because it is virtual, serialize is meant to be overridden by subclasses, which the MT_RNGImproved subclass does. The virtual keyword is not supported or necessary in Cython, so we leave it out of any method declaration. We can simply declare the serialize method in both the MT_RNG and MT_RNGImproved declarations, and Cython will generate the correct code.

Handling the remaining nonvirtual inherited methods requires more work. Cython's cppclass declaration does not support subclassing. To work with this limitation, we can handle nonoverridden inherited methods in two ways. We can redeclare the nonvirtual base class methods in the subclass:

```
cdef extern from "mt19937.h" namespace "mtrandom":
    cdef cppclass MT_RNG:
        # ...

    cdef cppclass MT_RNGImproved:
        MT_RNGImproved()
        unsigned long genrand_int32()
        double genrand_real1()
```

Or we can explicitly cast a subclass pointer to the base class, thereby accessing the base class's nonvirtual methods:

```
cdef MT_RNGImproved *rng = new MT_RNGImproved()
return (<MT_RNG*>rng).genrand_int32()
```

In either case, Cython will allow us to call a method on an object only if that method is declared explicitly in its type's interface.

 When using polymorphism in C++, we must use a pointer to the base class. A pointer to an instance of a subclass can be assigned to the base class's pointer, which can then be used elsewhere.

Besides interfacing—and wrapping—ordinary C++ classes, Cython also supports *templated* C++ functions and classes.

C++ Templates

The C++ standard template library (STL) has several templated functions and classes ready for use. We can wrap and use these functions and classes from Cython.

Templated Functions and Cython's Fused Types

The `<algorithm>` header declares many fundamental templated functions especially designed to be used on ranges of elements. Two of the simpler templated functions are `min` and `max`:

```
template <class T>
const T& min(const T& a, const T& b);

template <class T>
const T& max(const T& a, const T& b);
```

How do we declare and use these in Cython?

Declaration is straightforward: we use a `cdef extern` block as usual. To indicate that these are templated functions, we provide a template parameter name in brackets immediately after the function's name and before the argument list:

```
cdef extern from "<algorithm>" namespace "std":
    const T max[T](T a, T b) except +
    const T min[T](T a, T b) except +
```

Careful readers will notice that the argument types are declared as non-`const` value types, and the return types are declared as `const` values. This code works, since C++ reference variables are passed and returned like values, and reference variables can be assigned to a value-typed variable. Cython currently does not support returning reference types from templated functions, but this support is likely to come in future versions.

Calling `min` and `max` from Cython is straightforward. If the templated types can be inferred from the argument type(s), we can call the templated C++ function as if it were nontemplated, which is frequently the case.

If the argument types are ambiguous, we can add brackets after the function name, filling in the specific type to use for the template parameter or parameters.

The cleanest way to wrap these functions is to declare their interface in a definition file, the details of which are covered in Chapter 6. Supposing we put the previous declarations in a definition file *_algorithm.pxd*, we can access the C++ `min` and `max` via the `_algorithm` Cython namespace.

Fused types (Chapter 3) are ideal for wrapping templated functions such as these:

```
cimport cython
cimport _algorithm

ctypedef fused long_or_double:
    cython.long
    cython.double

def min(long_or_double a, long_or_double b):
    return _algorithm.min(a, b)
```

```
def max(long_or_double a, long_or_double b):
    return _algorithm.max(a, b)
```

By using a `long_or_double` fused type that includes the Python-compatible numeric types of interest, we make `min` and `max` generic templated Cython functions, providing a clean interface. Cython automatically dispatches to the right function specialization when `min` or `max` is called from Python.

This covers the basics of declaring, using, and wrapping templated functions; declaring and using templated classes follows a similar pattern.

Templated Classes

Perhaps the most widely used STL container is `vector`: it is the workhorse container for many C++ algorithms. How do we declare and use it in Cython?

To declare a templated class like `vector`, we use a `cdef extern` block in conjunction with a `cppclass` declaration, as for a nontemplated class. To indicate that the class is templated, we place template parameters in brackets after the class name:

```
cdef extern from "<vector>" namespace "std":
    cdef cppclass vector[T]:
        vector() except +
        vector(vector&) except +
        vector(size_t) except +
        vector(size_t, T&) except +
        T& operator[](size_t)
        void clear()
        void push_back(T&)
```

We use `T` as the template type, and have declared four of `vector`'s constructors along with a few of `vector`'s more common methods. If there is more than one template parameter, we put a comma-separated list of unique parameter names in the brackets.

Suppose we want to declare and use a `vector` of `int`s inside a wrapper function. For templated classes, we are required to instantiate them with a specific templated type in brackets after the templated class name:

```
def wrapper_func(elts):
    cdef vector[int] v
    for elt in elts:
        v.push_back(elt)
    # ...
```

This works for a stack-allocated `vector`, but creating a heap-allocated vector requires the `new` operator:

```
def wrapper_func(elts):
    cdef vector[int] *v = new vector[int]()
    # ...
```

When heap-allocating with new, we need to ensure that we call del on the vector pointer when we're finished using it to prevent memory leaks.

Iterators and Nested Classes

The C++ STL uses the iterator pattern everywhere, and vectors are no exception. To use the vector's iterator from Cython, we declare the vector's internal iterator as an internal cppclass:

```
cdef extern from "<vector>" namespace "std":
    cdef cppclass vector[T]:
        # ...
        cppclass iterator:
            T& operator*()
            iterator operator++()
            iterator operator--()
            iterator operator+(size_t)
            iterator operator-(size_t)
            bint operator==(iterator)
            bint operator!=(iterator)
            bint operator<(iterator)
            bint operator>(iterator)
            bint operator<=(iterator)
            bint operator>=(iterator)
```

Suppose we want to rotate a Python list in place by shifting n elements left and putting the shifted elements on the end. The STL has a rotate templated function declared in <algorithm> for just this purpose. We need to pass an std::vector<T>::iterator to indicate the beginning, middle, and end of the vector to rotate. The element pointed to by the middle iterator is rotated to the front of the resulting list.

First we need to declare std::rotate to Cython:

```
cdef extern from "<algorithm>" namespace "std":
    void rotate[iter](iter first, iter middle, iter last)
```

We place this declaration in our _algorithm.pxd file as before.

Because rotate does not care about the values in the container object being rotated, we can simply create a vector of void pointers that point to the Python list's contents and use that in our call to _algorithm.rotate.

First, the vector initialization:

```
def rotate_list(list ll, int rot):
    cdef vector[void*] vv
    for elt in ll:
        vv.push_back(<void*>elt)
```

We iterate through our Python list and initialize our vv vector, casting each element to a void pointer. Note that both the Python list ll and the C++ vector vv share references to the same underlying Python objects.

The rotate_list function's second argument is the number of elements to rotate by. It can be either positive or negative, and is normalized to a positive value here:

```
def rotate_list(list ll, int rot):
    # ...
    if rot < -len(ll) or rot >= len(ll):
        raise IndexError()
    rot = (rot + len(ll)) % len(ll)
```

For convenience, let's declare a ctypedef to make the iterator type more succinct:

```
ctypedef vector[void*].iterator vvit
```

Now the call to _algorithm.rotate is straightforward:

```
def rotate_list(list ll, int rot):
    # ...
    _algorithm.rotate[vvit](vv.begin(), vv.begin()+rot, vv.end())
```

Lastly, we create a new list out of the vector's contents, casting back to Python objects:

```
def rotate_list(list ll, int rot):
    # ...
    return [<object>o for o in vv]
```

The entire function is only eight lines of code, three of which are declaration and error checking. After compiling, we can try it out from Python:

```
In [1]: import wrap_funcs

In [2]: wrap_funcs.rotate_list(range(10), 5)
Out[2]: [5, 6, 7, 8, 9, 0, 1, 2, 3, 4]
```

It is remarkable that Cython makes possible such a fluid mix of Python and templated C++, all while retaining a Python-like look and feel.

Now that we have some familiarity with interfacing with templated C++ classes and iterators, let's look at interfacing with the STL. Cython makes this particularly easy.

Included STL Container Class Declarations

Cython includes built-in definition files for several STL classes, primarily containers:

- string
- vector
- map
- set
- unordered_map
- unordered_set

- pair
- list
- queue
- priority_queue
- deque
- stack

To access any of these class declarations, we use the `cimport` statement with the `libcpp` package–like Cython namespace, as covered in detail in Chapter 6:

```
from libcpp.vector cimport vector
cdef vector[int] *vec_int = new vector[int](10)
```

The `libcpp` package's contents are located in the *Cython/Includes/libcpp* directory included with the Cython source distribution. If we are using any of these templated classes, it is worthwhile to look at the definition file to know exactly the interface Cython exposes.

For example, we can build up a `std::map` of element names to their atomic numbers in Cython as follows:

```
from libcpp.string cimport string
from libcpp.map cimport map
from libcpp.pair cimport pair

def periodic_table():
    cdef map[string, int] table
    cdef pair[string, int] entry
    # Insert Hydrogen
    entry.first = b"H"; entry.second = 1
    table.insert(entry)
    # Insert Helium
    entry.first = b"He"; entry.second = 2
    table.insert(entry)
    # ...
```

Cython automatically converts `std::map` and other STL containers to and from their Python analogues. We can use this to easily assign a Python `dict` to a `std::map`, for example. It also allows us to return a `std::map` from a `def` function—Cython automatically copies the `std::map`'s contents to a new Python `dict` and returns that. These conversions copy the underlying data, and are triggered when we assign (or cast) from a statically typed Python container to a C++ container type, and vice versa.

Table 8-3 lists all currently supported built-in conversions from Python to C++ containers.

Table 8-3. Python to C++ containers

From Python type	To C++ type(s)
bytes, str, unicode	string
mapping (dict)	map, unordered_map
iterable	set, unordered_set
iterable	vector, list
length two iterable	pair

Table 8-4 lists the allowed conversions from C++ to Python.

Table 8-4. C++ to Python containers

From C++ type	To Python type
string	bytes, str, unicode
map, unordered_map	dict
set, unordered_set	set
vector, list	list
pair	tuple

> The automatic conversions to and from the Python string types—
> bytes, str, and unicode—are influenced by the c_string_type and
> c_string_encoding compiler directives (see Chapters 2 and 3). If
> neither of these directives is set, then only the bytes type is conver-
> tible to and from the std::string type by default.

All conversions are recursive, so a std::map<std::pair<int, int>, std::vector<std::string> > converts to a Python dict with tuple keys of ints and list values of bytes objects.

This powerful feature allows us to return a supported C++ container directly from a def or cpdef function or method, provided the container and its templated type are supported. Cython automatically converts the container's contents to the right Python container.

Previous examples, such as the periodic_table function that inserts elements into a std::map, can be more simply expressed:

```
from libcpp.string cimport string
from libcpp.map cimport map

def periodic_table():
    cdef map[string, int] table
    table = {"H": 1, "He": 2, "Li": 3}
```

```
    # ...use table in C++...
    return table
```

In this example, assigning a dictionary literal to `table` automatically converts all key/value pairs to the corresponding C++ `std::pair` type and stores them in the `std::map` instance. The complement works as well: returning `table` converts the `std::map<string, int>` to a Python dictionary.

Automatic conversions also simplify working with `std::vector` objects: assigning a Python `list` to a statically typed `vector` is much easier than iterating through the `list` and calling `push_back` for each element.

Cython also knows how to use standard C++ container objects when an iterable is required—in `for` loops, list comprehensions, and the like. For this to work, the C++ object must have `begin` and `end` methods that return a pointer-like iterator, which is the case for most STL containers. This removes the need to declare and work with C++ iterators explicitly in many situations, and makes working with C++ containers feel like Python.

For example, calling `std::sort` with the contents of a Python `list` is simple. First we `cimport` from `libcpp.vector` and declare the `std::sort` templated function:

```
from libcpp.vector cimport vector

cdef extern from "<algorithm>" namespace "std":
    void std_sort "std::sort" [iter](iter first, iter last)
```

With this in place, the actual sorting function is just three lines:

```
def sort_list(list ll):
    cdef vector[int] vv = ll
    std_sort[vector[int].iterator](vv.begin(), vv.end())
    return vv
```

This example serves to demonstrate how straightforward Cython makes conversions between Python and C++ containers, and how easy it is to call into a C++ STL function. It is not intended to demonstrate how to sort a `list`: the right way to do that, of course, is to use the `list.sort` method or the `sorted` built-in function.

Memory Management and Smart Pointers

Many C++ libraries use *smart pointers*, for the many advantages they provide beyond C-style raw pointers. They help clarify and enforce pointer ownership semantics, prevent memory and resource leaks, and simplify memory management when we are dealing with C++ exceptions. Of particular relevance to Python is the `shared_ptr` smart pointer, which supports basic reference counting. As we know, CPython (and Cython, by extension) also uses reference counting for the majority of its memory management of Python objects. Can we get C++ shared pointers to work nicely with Python reference counting in Cython? To quote a well-known political figure's campaign slogan, "Yes we can!"

First, let's declare the `smart_ptr` template class interface to Cython. We use the declarations from the Boost C++ library, but the C++11 version is very similar:

```
cdef extern from "boost/smart_ptr/shared_ptr.hpp" namespace "boost":
    cdef cppclass shared_ptr[T]:
        shared_ptr()
        shared_ptr(T *p)
        shared_ptr(const shared_ptr&)
        long use_count()
        T operator*()
```

Here we have declared that `boost::shared_ptr` has a single template parameter, used for the type of object pointed to. It has a default constructor, a single-argument constructor, and a copy constructor. Besides these, we declare the `use_count` method to report the number of reference counts on this shared pointer instance, and `operator*` to allow us to dereference a shared pointer.

To illustrate working with shared pointers, suppose we have an externally defined function, `histogram`, that takes a `std::vector<int>` argument and returns a shared pointer to a vector of integers, which is the number of integers with that value in the input `vector`. This can arise when a library uses shared pointers to allow objects to share ownership of large containers.

Say also that we want to get the average count in the histogram vector from Python. Using our `libcpp.vector` and `shared_ptr` template class declarations, we can define a `def` function, `hist_sum`. First, we need to get our shared pointer to a vector of integers:

```
from libcpp.vector cimport vector

def hist_sum(args):
    cdef:
        shared_ptr[vector[int]] ptr_hist = histogram(args)
    # ...
```

Now that we have our shared pointer, we can dereference it to access the underlying vector. We need to use `cython.operator.dereference` to do so, since the `shared_ptr` does not support indexing with `operator[]`:

```
from cython.operator cimport dereference as deref

def hist_sum(args):
    cdef:
        shared_ptr[vector[int]] ptr_hist = histogram(args)
        vector[int] hist = deref(ptr_hist)
    # ...
```

We now can walk through the `hist` vector to get the average count:

```
def hist_sum(args):
    cdef:
        shared_ptr[vector[int]] ptr_hist = histogram(args)
        vector[int] hist = deref(ptr_hist)
        double weighted_sum = 0.0
        int elt, n_total = 0

    for idx, elt in enumerate(hist):
        weighted_sum += idx * elt
        n_total += elt
    return weighted_sum / n_total
```

The nice part about this function is that we are working with a pointer to a vector, but we do not have to worry about memory leaks or who is responsible for cleaning it up. The shared pointer handles that automatically for us, even if exceptions occur.

We can also use smart pointers as the attributes inside extension types. This is useful if we want to share our C++ objects between Python and other C++ code that uses shared pointers.

For example, suppose we want to wrap a C++ vector of integers in an extension type and make it look like a Python list. First, we declare the vector attribute:

```
cdef class Vector:
    cdef shared_ptr[vector[int]] _thisptr
```

The __cinit__ method just creates an empty vector inside a shared_ptr:

```
cdef class Vector:
    cdef shared_ptr[vector[int]] _thisptr
    def __cinit__(self):
        self._thisptr = shared_ptr[vector[int]](new vector[int]())
```

To make our Vector act like a Python list, we can add some def methods. Every time we want to work with the underlying vector, we need to dereference the _thisptr attribute:

```
from cython.operator cimport dereference as deref

cdef class Vector:
    # ...
    def __len__(self):
        return deref(self._thisptr).size()
    def __getitem__(self, int index):
        return deref(self._thisptr)[index]
    def __setitem__(self, int index, int i):
        return deref(self._thisptr)[index] = i
    def append(self, int i):
        deref(self._thisptr).push_back(i)
    def __repr__(self):
        return repr([i for i in deref(self._thisptr)])
```

We place Vector's definition in *vector.pyx* and compile it into an extension module. It is list-like enough to allow us to shuffle a Vector from Python:

```
from vector import Vector
from random import shuffle

v = Vector()
for i in range(20):
    v.append(i)
shuffle(v)
print v
```

When running our script *test_vector.py*, we see everything hangs together:

```
$ python test_vector.py
[19, 1, 15, 13, 12, 18, 8, 2, 16, 4, 3, 14, 17, 11, 10, 9, 0, 6, 5, 7]
```

To take this example further, we could implement a sort method that uses C++'s std::sort function. Doing so is left as an exercise for the reader.

Because the _thisptr for Vector is a shared pointer, Vector instances can share ownership of the underlying std::vector<int> with C++. This means that Python objects can work with C++ objects in a nice and unobtrusive way, avoiding expensive copies, removing ambiguities regarding pointer ownership, and allowing the two languages' reference counting systems to work together.

Summary

This chapter covered all of Cython's current C++ interfacing features. We learned how to

- declare C++ namespaces, classes, and global constants;
- make an extension type to wrap a C++ class;
- use the new and del operators properly to work with C++ memory management;
- compile C++-based Cython projects;
- work with overloaded constructors, methods, functions, and operators;
- easily propagate C++ exceptions to Python;
- manage stack-allocated C++ objects;
- work with C++ type hierarchies;
- declare and use templated functions and classes;
- use included C++ STL container definition files.

Cython's C++ support is continually improving and stabilizing. It is expected that some of the more manual tasks in this chapter will be better supported in future releases.

## CHAPTER 9

Cython Profiling Tools

I've never been a good estimator of how long things are going to take.

— D. Knuth

If you optimize everything, you will always be unhappy.

— D. Knuth

Cython lets us easily move across the boundary between Python and C. Rather than taking this as license to bring in C code wherever we like, however, we should consider just how much C we want to mix with our Python. When we are wrapping a library, the answer is usually determined for us: we need enough C to wrap our library, and enough Python to make it nice to use. When we're using Cython to speed up a Python module, though, the answer is much less clear. Our goal is to bring in enough C code to get the best results for our efforts, and no more. Cython has tools that can help us find this sweet spot, which we cover in this chapter.

Cython Runtime Profiling

When we are optimizing Cython code, the principles, guidelines, and examples in the rest of this book help us answer the *how*. But sometimes the challenge is determining *what* code needs to change in the first place. I strongly recommend that, rather than looking at code and guessing, we use profiling tools to provide data to quantify our programs' performance.

Python users are spoiled when it comes to profiling tools. The built-in `profile` module (and its faster C implementation, `cProfile`) makes runtime profiling easy. On top of that, the IPython interpreter makes profiling nearly effortless with the `%timeit` and `%run` magic commands, which support profiling small statements and entire programs, respectively.

These profiling tools work without modification on pure-Python code. But when Python code calls into C code in an extension module or in a separate library, these profiling tools cannot cross the language boundary. All profiling information for C-level operations is lost.

Cython addresses this limitation: it can generate C code that plays nicely with these runtime profiling tools, fooling them into thinking that C-level calls are regular Python calls.

For instance, let's start with a pure-Python version of the integration example from Chapter 3:[1]

```python
def integrate(a, b, f, N=2000):
    dx = (b-a)/N
    s = 0.0
    for i in range(N):
        s += f(a+i*dx)
    return s * dx
```

We will use runtime profiling to help improve integrate's performance.

First, we create a *main.py* Python script to drive integrate:

```python
from integrate import integrate
from math import pi, sin

def sin2(x):
    return sin(x)**2

def main():
    a, b = 0.0, 2.0 * pi
    return integrate(a, b, sin2, N=400000)
```

To profile our function, we can use cProfile in the script itself, sorting by the internal time spent in each function:

```python
if __name__ == '__main__':
    import cProfile
    cProfile.run('main()', sort='time')
```

Running our script gives the following output:

```
$ python main.py
        800005 function calls in 0.394 seconds

   Ordered by: internal time
```

---

1. To follow along with the examples in this chapter, please see *https://github.com/cythonbook*.

```
ncalls  tottime  percall  cumtime  percall  filename:lineno(function)
     1    0.189    0.189    0.394    0.394  integrate.py:2(integrate)
400000    0.140    0.000    0.188    0.000  main.py:4(sin2)
400000    0.048    0.000    0.048    0.000  {math.sin}
     1    0.017    0.017    0.017    0.017  {range}
     1    0.000    0.000    0.394    0.394  main.py:7(main)
     1    0.000    0.000    0.394    0.394  <string>:1(<module>)
  ...
```

This output is generated by the cProfile.run call. Each row in the table is the collected runtime data for a function called in the course of running our program. The ncalls column is, unsurprisingly, the number of times that function or method was called. The tottime column is the total time spent in the function, *not including time spent in called functions*. This is the column used to sort the output, and it usually provides the most useful information. The first percall column is tottime divided by ncalls. The cumtime column is the total time spent in this function *including time spent in called functions*, and the second percall column is cumtime divided by ncalls. The last column is the name of the module, the line number, and the function name for the table row.

As expected, most time is spent in the integrate function, followed by our sin2 function.

Let's convert *integrate.py* to an extension module, *integrate.pyx*. For now, we change only the filename without changing the contents. Doing so requires us to compile our extension module before using it in *main.py*.

We can use pyximport to compile at import time; at the top of *main.py*, we add this one line before importing integrate:

```
import pyximport; pyximport.install()
from integrate import integrate
# ...
```

Running our script again compiles the extension module automatically and generates the profiling output for our Cythonized version of integrate:

```
$ python main.py
        800004 function calls in 0.327 seconds

  Ordered by: internal time

ncalls  tottime  percall  cumtime  percall  filename:lineno(function)
     1    0.141    0.141    0.327    0.327  {integrate.integrate}
400000    0.138    0.000    0.185    0.000  main.py:5(sin2)
400000    0.047    0.000    0.047    0.000  {math.sin}
     1    0.000    0.000    0.327    0.327  main.py:8(main)
     1    0.000    0.000    0.327    0.327  <string>:1(<module>)
  ...
```

Just compiling our module gives us an overall 17 percent performance boost, and improves `integrate`'s performance by about 25 percent. We will see just how much faster we can make `integrate` by using more Cython features.

Let's add static type information to `integrate` to generate more efficient code:

```
def integrate(double a, double b, f, int N=2000):
    cdef:
        int i
        double dx = (b-a)/N
        double s = 0.0
    for i in range(N):
        s += f(a+i*dx)
    return s * dx
```

What is the effect on the runtime?

```
$ python main.py
        800004 function calls in 0.275 seconds

   Ordered by: internal time

   ncalls  tottime  percall  cumtime  percall filename:lineno(function)
   400000    0.133    0.000    0.176    0.000 main.py:5(sin2)
        1    0.099    0.099    0.275    0.275 {integrate.integrate}
   400000    0.043    0.000    0.043    0.000 {math.sin}
        1    0.000    0.000    0.275    0.275 main.py:8(main)
        1    0.000    0.000    0.275    0.275 <string>:1(<module>)
   ...
```

Static typing and a faster `for` loop give a modest 16 percent overall additional performance boost.

Let's turn our focus on `sin2`—it is a pure-Python function, but if we put it in our implementation file, it is compiled. This requires us to modify *integrate.pyx*:

```
from math import sin

def sin2(x):
    return sin(x)**2

def integrate(...):
    # ...
```

We must also modify *main.py* to import `sin2` from `integrate`.

As we can see, compiling `sin2` boosts overall performance by more than a factor of two:

```
$ python main.py
        4 function calls in 0.103 seconds

   Ordered by: internal time
```

```
ncalls  tottime  percall  cumtime  percall filename:lineno(function)
     1    0.103    0.103    0.103    0.103 {integrate.integrate}
     1    0.000    0.000    0.103    0.103 main.py:8(main)
     1    0.000    0.000    0.103    0.103 <string>:1(<module>)
   ...
```

Note that now the profiler detects and reports on only 4 function calls, whereas before it detected all 800,000 or so. Because we are compiling sin2 and its contents, as far as the profiler is concerned, integrate is a black box.

We can fix this by directing Cython to support runtime profiling in the generated code. At the top of *integrate.pyx*, we enable the profile compiler directive globally (see "Compiler Directives" on page 28):

```
# cython: profile=True
from math import sin
# ...
```

The next time we run *main.py*, we see sin2 again:

```
$ python main.py
        400005 function calls in 0.180 seconds

   Ordered by: internal time

ncalls  tottime  percall  cumtime  percall filename:lineno(function)
400000    0.096    0.000    0.096    0.000 integrate.pyx:6(sin2)
     1    0.084    0.084    0.180    0.180 integrate.pyx:10(integrate)
     1    0.000    0.000    0.180    0.180 main.py:8(main)
     1    0.000    0.000    0.180    0.180 {integrate.integrate}
     1    0.000    0.000    0.180    0.180 <string>:1(<module>)
```

Runtime increased significantly, but why? In this case, the overhead introduced by the profiler distorts the true runtime of the code being measured. Because sin2 is called inside a loop, when Cython instruments it to be profiled, the profiling overhead is amplified.

We still don't see the call to math.sin, since that is called internally and not exposed to the profiler. Cython cannot profile imported functions, only functions and methods defined in the extension module itself.

We can selectively profile functions as well: we can remove the module-wide profiling directive, cimport the cython magic module, and use the @cython.profile(True) decorator with the functions we want to profile.

The sin2 function requires the most total runtime, so how can we speed it up further? Rather than use Python's math.sin function inside sin2, let's use sin from the C standard library. We only have to change the import to the right cimport in *integrate.pyx* to do so:

```
# cython: profile=True
from libc.math cimport sin
# ...
```

This more than halves `sin2`'s runtime, making `integrate` the slowpoke again:

```
$ python main.py
         400005 function calls in 0.121 seconds

   Ordered by: internal time

   ncalls  tottime  percall  cumtime  percall filename:lineno(function)
        1    0.081    0.081    0.121    0.121 integrate.pyx:11(integrate)
   400000    0.040    0.000    0.040    0.000 integrate.pyx:7(sin2)
        1    0.000    0.000    0.121    0.121 main.py:8(main)
        1    0.000    0.000    0.121    0.121 {integrate.integrate}
        1    0.000    0.000    0.121    0.121 <string>:1(<module>)
```

There is more we can do to remove call overhead inside the `for` loop, but we leave that as an exercise to the reader.

Let's turn off profiling inside *integrate.pyx* and run our script again:

```
$ python main.py
         4 function calls in 0.039 seconds

   Ordered by: internal time

   ncalls  tottime  percall  cumtime  percall filename:lineno(function)
        1    0.039    0.039    0.039    0.039 {integrate.integrate}
        1    0.000    0.000    0.039    0.039 main.py:8(main)
        1    0.000    0.000    0.039    0.039 <string>:1(<module>)
```

We went from a pure-Python version with a 0.4-second runtime to a Cython version that is 10 times faster: not bad. Along the way, we learned how to use the `cProfile` module to help focus our efforts, and we learned how to use the `profile` directive to have Cython instrument our code for us.

Performance Profiling and Annotations

Runtime profiling with `cProfile` and Cython's `profile` directive is the first profiling tool we should use. It directly tells us *what* code to focus on based on runtime performance.

To answer the question of *why* a given function is slow, Cython provides *compile-time annotations*, the topic of this section. Runtime profiling and compile-time annotations together provide complementary views of the performance of our Cython code.

As we learned in Chapter 3, calling into the Python/C API is—more often than not—slow when compared to the equivalent operation implemented in straight-C code. In particular, when manipulating dynamically typed Python objects, Cython must generate code that makes many calls into the C API. Besides performing the intended operation, the generated code must also properly handle object reference counts and perform proper error handling, all of which incurs overhead and, incidentally, requires a lot of logic at the C level.

This suggests a simple heuristic: if a line of Cython code generates many calls into the Python/C API, then it is likely that that line manipulates many Python objects and, more often than not, has poor performance. If a line translates into few lines of C and does not call into the C API, then it does not manipulate Python objects and may very well have good performance.

The cython compiler has an optional --annotate flag (short form: -a) that instructs cython to generate an HTML representation of the Cython source code, known as a *code annotation*. Cython color-codes each line in the annotation file according to the number of calls into the Python/C API: a line that has many C API calls is dark yellow, while a line with no C API calls has no highlighting. Clicking on a line in the annotation file expands that line into its generated C code for easy inspection.

 Keep in mind that using the number of C API calls as a proxy for poor performance is a simplification; some C API calls are significantly faster than others. Also, a function is not guaranteed to be fast simply by virtue of not having a Py_ prefix.

Consider again our pure-Python version of the integration example:

```
def integrate(a, b, f, N=2000):
    dx = (b-a)/N
    s = 0.0
    for i in range(N):
        s += f(a+i*dx)
    return s * dx
```

There is no static typing information in this function, so all operations use the general Python/C API calls.

If we put this code in *integrate.pyx*, we can create a code annotation for it:

```
$ cython --annotate integrate.pyx
```

If no compiler errors result, cython generates a file, *integrate.html*, which we can open in a browser. It should look similar to Figure 9-1.

```
Raw output: integrate.c

1: def integrate(a, b, f, N=2000):
2:     dx = (b-a)/N
3:     s = 0.0
4:     for i in range(N):
5:         s += f(a+i*dx)
6:     return s * dx
7:
```

Figure 9-1. Annotated integrate without static typing

Except for line 3, all lines are a deep shade of yellow.[2] Clicking on line 2 expands it, as shown in Figure 9-2. It is clear why this line is colored yellow; there are calls to `PyNum ber_Subtract` and `__Pyx_PyNumber_Divide` as well as error handling and reference counting routines.

```
Raw output: integrate.c

1: def integrate(a, b, f, N=2000):
2:     dx = (b-a)/N

       __pyx_t_1 = PyNumber_Subtract(__pyx_v_b, __pyx_v_a); if (
       __Pyx_GOTREF(__pyx_t_1);
       __pyx_t_2 = __Pyx_PyNumber_Divide(__pyx_t_1, __pyx_v_N);
       __Pyx_GOTREF(__pyx_t_2);
       __Pyx_DECREF(__pyx_t_1); __pyx_t_1 = 0;
       __pyx_v_dx = __pyx_t_2;
       __pyx_t_2 = 0;

3:     s = 0.0
4:     for i in range(N):
5:         s += f(a+i*dx)
6:     return s * dx
7:
```

Figure 9-2. Expanded line in annotated integrate

Of particular interest is the `for` loop, which we expand in Figure 9-3.

---

2. In this book's print version or on a black-and-white ereader, all figures are rendered grayscale. Please try the examples in this chapter (*https://github.com/cythonbook/examples*) to see the result.

```
Raw output: integrate.c
1: def integrate(a, b, f, N=2000):
2:     dx = (b-a)/N
3:     s = 0.0
4:     for i in range(N):

    __pyx_t_2 = PyTuple_New(1); if (unlikely(!__pyx_t_2)) {
    __Pyx_GOTREF(__pyx_t_2);
    __Pyx_INCREF(__pyx_v_N);
    PyTuple_SET_ITEM(__pyx_t_2, 0, __pyx_v_N);
    __Pyx_GIVEREF(__pyx_v_N);
    __pyx_t_1 = __Pyx_PyObject_Call(__pyx_builtin_range, __]
    __Pyx_GOTREF(__pyx_t_1);
    __Pyx_DECREF(__pyx_t_2); __pyx_t_2 = 0;
    if (PyList_CheckExact(__pyx_t_1) || PyTuple_CheckExact(
    __pyx_t_2 = __pyx_t_1; __Pyx_INCREF(__pyx_t_2); __pyx
    __pyx_t_4 = NULL;
    } else {
    __pyx_t_3 = -1; __pyx_t_2 = PyObject_GetIter(__pyx_t_:
    __Pyx_GOTREF(__pyx_t_2);
    __pyx_t_4 = Py_TYPE(__pyx_t_2)->tp_iternext;
    }
    __Pyx_DECREF(__pyx_t_1); __pyx_t_1 = 0;
    for (;;) {
      if (!__pyx_t_4 && PyList_CheckExact(__pyx_t_2)) {
        if (__pyx_t_3 >= PyList_GET_SIZE(__pyx_t_2)) break;
        #if CYTHON_COMPILING_IN_CPYTHON
        __pyx_t_1 = PyList_GET_ITEM(__pyx_t_2, __pyx_t_3);
        #else
        __pyx_t_1 = PySequence_ITEM(__pyx_t_2, __pyx_t_3);
        #endif
      } else if (!__pyx_t_4 && PyTuple_CheckExact(__pyx_t_2
        if (__pyx_t_3 >= PyTuple_GET_SIZE(__pyx_t_2)) break
        #if CYTHON_COMPILING_IN_CPYTHON
        __pyx_t_1 = PyTuple_GET_ITEM(__pyx_t_2, __pyx_t_3);
        #else
        __pyx_t_1 = PySequence_ITEM(__pyx_t_2, __pyx_t_3);
        #endif
      } else {
        __pyx_t_1 = __pyx_t_4(__pyx_t_2);
        if (unlikely(!__pyx_t_1)) {
          PyObject* exc_type = PyErr_Occurred();
          if (exc_type) {
            if (likely(exc_type == PyExc_StopIteration || P
            else {__pyx_filename = __pyx_f[0]; __pyx_lineno
          }
          break;
        }
        __Pyx_GOTREF(__pyx_t_1);
      }
      __Pyx_XDECREF_SET(__pyx_v_i, __pyx_t_1);
      __pyx_t_1 = 0;
```

Figure 9-3. Expanded annotated for loop

Without typing information, this one line of Python expands into nearly 40 lines of C code! The loop body (line 5) is similar.

Let's add some simple static type declarations:

```
def integrate(double a, double b, f, int N=2000):

    cdef:
        int i
        double dx = (b-a)/N
        double s = 0.0

    for i in range(N):
```

```
        s += f(a+i*dx)
    return s * dx
```

After regenerating our annotated source file, we see in Figure 9-4 a significant difference in the code highlighting.

```
Raw output: integrate.c

1: def integrate(double a, double b, f, int N=2000):
2:
3:     cdef:
4:         int i
5:         double dx = (b-a)/N
6:         double s = 0.0
7:
8:     for i in range(N):
9:         s += f(a+i*dx)
10:    return s * dx
11:
```

Figure 9-4. Annotated integrate with static typing

The for loop on line 8, expanded in Figure 9-5, now has no highlighting and translates to much more efficient code.

```
Raw output: integrate.c

1: def integrate(double a, double b, f, int N=2000):
2:
3:     cdef:
4:         int i
5:         double dx = (b-a)/N
6:         double s = 0.0
7:
8:     for i in range(N):

    __pyx_t_2 = __pyx_v_N;
    for (__pyx_t_3 = 0; __pyx_t_3 < __pyx_t_2; __pyx_t_3+=1) {
        __pyx_v_i = __pyx_t_3;

9:         s += f(a+i*dx)
10:    return s * dx
11:
```

Figure 9-5. Expanded annotated for loop with static typing

Also noteworthy is the loop body, which remains highlighted. A moment's thought reveals why: func is a dynamic Python object that we are calling in each loop iteration. We can see what the C code has to do to call a general Python object by clicking on line 9. Even though we statically typed a, i, dx, and s, we must convert the func argument to a Python object (PyFloat_FromDouble), create an argument tuple with our Python float (PyTuple_New and PyTuple_SET_ITEM), call func with this argument tuple (__Pyx_PyObject_Call), get the resulting Python object, and add it to s in place (PyNumber_InPlaceAdd). All the while, we need to do proper reference counting and error checking.

The line is yellow because the annotation heuristic picks up all the Python/C API calls and highlights accordingly. It makes it easy to see that our loop body is where we should focus our efforts to improve this function's performance. We could, for example, make func an instance of an extension type with a call cpdef method, and inside our for loop, we could call func.call instead. This would allow us to implement compiled versions of our callback function in Cython while providing a way to subclass them in Python.

Often the first and last lines of a function are highlighted a deep shade of yellow even when all operations are C-level and should be fast. This is because the function setup and teardown logic in a def or cpdef function is grouped together during annotation; this often involves several calls into the C API and leads to the highlighting we see here. This serves as a visual indicator of Python's function call overhead. A cdef function does not have this overhead and is not highlighted provided no Python objects are involved.

To see this, let's write a cdef version of integrate called c_integrate. We type func as a C function pointer and turn on the cdivision compiler directive while we're at it:[3]

```
cimport cython

@cython.cdivision(True)
cdef double c_integrate(double a, double b, double (*f)(double), int N=2000):

    cdef:
        int i
        double dx = (b-a)/N
        double s = 0.0

    for i in range(N):
        s += f(a+i*dx)
    return s * dx
```

The annotation for c_integrate (Figure 9-6) is encouraging—the entire function has no highlighting, indicating no C API calls were generated.

---

3. In this example, because no division is taking place inside the for loop, using the cdivision directive has essentially no effect on performance. We use it here to show how it removes all C API calls from the dx initialization. We could remove the cdivision directive without affecting performance.

```
Raw output: integrate.c

1: cimport cython
2:
3: @cython.cdivision(True)
4: cdef double c_integrate(double a, double b, double (*f)(double), int N=2000):
5:
6:     cdef:
7:         int i
8:         double dx = (b-a)/N
9:         double s = 0.0
10:
11:     for i in range(N):
12:         s += f(a+i*dx)
13:     return s * dx
14:
```

Figure 9-6. Annotated integrate without C API calls

This comes with a convenience tradeoff, of course: we lose the ability to call c_integrate from Python, so we have to create other entry points to do so. We can use c_integrate from other Cython code, of course.

Code annotations are a powerful feature to help focus efforts on possible performance bottlenecks. It is up to us to use annotations effectively. If a line of code makes many C API calls but is itself run only once, its overhead is not an important factor. On the other hand, if the code annotation indicates that a line in an inner for loop makes many C API calls, then it is likely worth the effort to improve its performance.

Keep in mind that Cython's annotation feature provides *static*, *compile-time* performance data and uses simple heuristics to suggest which lines of code need attention. Using it in conjunction with Cython's *runtime* profiling tools makes for a powerful combination.

Summary

The cardinal rule of code optimization is *measure, don't guess*. Using annotations and runtime profiling together, we can let Cython tell us what code needs attention rather than guessing ourselves. Runtime profiling, which should always be the first tool we use to acquire quantitative data, tells us *what* routines to focus on. Code annotations can then help us determine *why* specific lines are slow, and can help us remove C API calls from the generated source. We split profiling and annotations into separate sections in this chapter, but in practice, their usage is often finely interleaved.

## CHAPTER 10

Cython, NumPy, and Typed Memoryviews

All problems in computer science can be solved by another level of indirection, except, of course, for the problem of too many indirections.

— D. Wheeler

Two great qualities of Cython are its breadth and maturity: it compiles *nearly* all Python code (and whatever it cannot handle is typically straightforward to address); it brings the power and control of C's type system to Python; and it integrates with external C and C++ code with ease. The task for this chapter is to round out Cython's capabilities and cover Cython's array features—which include support for NumPy arrays—in depth.

We have seen how well Cython supports built-in containers like `list`, `tuple`, `dict`, and `set`. These container objects are very easy to use, can contain any type of Python object, and are highly optimized for object lookup, assignment, and retrieval. The way the `list` type implements storage and retrieval is very different from `dict`, but from an implementation perspective, containers all have one thing in common: *they all store references to Python objects*. If we have a Python list of one million `int`s, every element in that list, at the C level, is a pointer to a boxed-up `PyObject`. Converting such a list to a C array of C `int`s is expensive, requiring us to iterate through the list and convert each `PyObject` to a C `int`, all the while doing proper error checking.

For homogeneous containers (e.g., a `list` containing nothing but `float`s), we can do much better in terms of storage overhead and performance. Large arrays of homogeneous numeric types are common, and not just in numerical programming contexts. Furthermore, CPUs and modern memory hierarchies are optimized to work with such arrays. C has fixed-size and heap-allocated arrays. C++ has the `std::vector` workhorse STL templated type. What we want is a way to represent and work with a homogeneous contiguous array, or *buffer*, of unboxed data types in Python.

Enter Python buffers and the new Python buffer protocol. Buffers allow us to represent contiguous or simply strided unboxed data of a single data type. NumPy arrays—the most widely used array type in Python—support the buffer protocol. It is useful to think of buffers as simplified NumPy arrays.

Using buffers effectively is often the key to obtaining C-level performance from Cython code. Fortunately, Cython makes it particularly easy to work with buffers. It has first-class support for the new buffer protocol and, with it, NumPy arrays.

The Power of the New Buffer Protocol

The new buffer protocol is a C-level protocol.[1] Python objects can implement the protocol, but it does not affect their interface at the Python level. The protocol is supported in all Python 3 versions and has been backported to Python 2.6 and later. It defines a C-level `struct` that has a data buffer and metadata to describe the buffer's layout, data type, and read and write permissions. It also defines the API that an object supporting the protocol must implement.

 The new buffer protocol's most important feature is its ability to represent the same underlying data in different ways. It allows NumPy arrays, several Python built-in types, and Cython-level array-like objects to *share the same data without copying*. With Cython, we can also easily extend the buffer protocol to work with data coming from an external library.

We do not cover the protocol's details here; it is thoroughly documented in Python's C API reference manual (*https://docs.python.org/2/c-api/buffer.html*). Thankfully, Cython allows us to work with buffers without having to know the details of the protocol. It is sufficient to know that, when working with buffers, we can efficiently access their underlying data without copying, reducing overhead.

What types implement the protocol?

NumPy `ndarray`
> The well-known and widely used NumPy package has an `ndarray` object that supports the buffer protocol, making it a valid Python buffer.

Built-in `str` *(Py 2)*
> The built-in string type in Python 2.6 and 2.7 implements the protocol. The Unicode type in Python 2 and the string type in Python 3, however, do not.

---

1. The new buffer protocol is also referred to as *PEP-3118* (*http://legacy.python.org/dev/peps/pep-3118/*), referring to the Python Enhancement Proposal that is the protocol's authoritative source of documentation.

Built-in bytes *and* bytearray *types*

The bytes and bytearray types in all Python versions implement the protocol.

Standard library array.array

The array.array Python standard library type implements a list-like array type that supports the protocol.

Standard library ctypes *arrays*

Arrays in the ctypes package also implement the protocol.

Various third-party types

For instance, the Python Imaging Library (PIL) implements the protocol for various image types.

The memoryview Type

There is another built-in Python type, memoryview, whose sole purpose is to represent a C-level buffer at the Python level. We create a memoryview object by passing the memoryview callable an object that implements the protocol, like a bytes object:

```
$ ipython --no-banner

In [1]: bb = b"These are the times that try men's souls."

In [2]: memv = memoryview(bb)

In [3]: memv
Out[3]: <memory at 0x101955348>
```

Here, memv is an object that *shares* data with the bytes string.

Playing with a memoryview object gives us a feel for what buffers are doing at the C level.

For instance, we can access data from the underlying buffer by indexing:

```
In [4]: memv[0]
Out[4]: 'T'

In [5]: memv[-1]
Out[5]: '.'
```

Slicing returns another memoryview, which also shares the underlying bytes data:

```
In [6]: memv[:10]
Out[6]: <memory at 0x102a223e0>

In [7]: memv[:10][0]
Out[7]: 'T'
```

We can slice a `memoryview` with arbitrary start, stop, and step values, allowing us to efficiently select only the data elements of interest. In this way, `memoryview` objects provide functionality beyond having multiple variables referring to the same object.

Because a `bytes` object is immutable, a `memoryview` of a `bytes` object is `readonly`:

```
In [8]: memv.readonly
Out[8]: True

In [9]: memv[0] = 'F'
...
TypeError: cannot modify read-only memory
```

If, instead, we take a `memoryview` of a mutable buffer like `bytearray`, we can modify its data. First, let's make two `memoryviews` that share an underlying buffer:

```
In [10]: ba = bytearray(b"If the facts don't fit the theory, change the facts.")

In [11]: mutable1 = memoryview(ba)

In [12]: mutable2 = mutable1[:10]
```

Modifying the `mutable1` memoryview modifies it in the original `bytearray` and in `mutable2` as well:

```
In [13]: mutable2[0]
Out[13]: 'I'

In [14]: mutable1[0] = "A"

In [15]: mutable2[0]
Out[15]: 'A'

In [16]: ba[:1]
Out[16]: bytearray(b'A')
```

A `memoryview` has several attributes that query the underlying buffer's metadata. We have already seen the `readonly` attribute. For something a bit more interesting, let's take a `memoryview` of a multidimensional NumPy array:

```
In [17]: import numpy as np

In [18]: np_mv = memoryview(np.ones((10, 20, 30)))
```

We can ask for the number of dimensions using `ndim`:

```
In [19]: np_mv.ndim
Out[19]: 3L
```

And we can see the extent of the `memoryview` in each dimension with the `shape` attribute:

```
In [20]: np_mv.shape
Out[20]: (10L, 20L, 30L)
```

`memoryviews` also have a `strides` attribute, which specifies the number of bytes separating elements in the buffer in that dimension:

```
In [21]: np_mv.strides
Out[21]: (4800L, 240L, 8L)
```

Looking at `strides`, we can tell that the buffer is C contiguous in memory, as the skip in the last dimension is smallest and matches `np_mv.itemsize`.

 The `strides` of an array indicates the number of bytes separating elements in the array in that dimension. A NumPy array also has a `strides` attribute, and more details about `strides` and how it is used can be found in NumPy's `strides` documentation. (*http://bit.ly/ strides_docs*)

The underlying data type comes from the `format` attribute, which gives back a format string:

```
In [22]: np_mv.format
Out[22]: 'd'
```

Structured data types are supported as well. First, let's create a NumPy structured dtype with fields a and b with data types `int8` and `complex128`, respectively:

```
In [23]: dt = np.dtype([('a', np.int8), ('b', np.complex128)])

In [24]: dt
Out[24]: dtype([('a', 'i1'), ('b', '<c16')])
```

We can now make a `memoryview` from an empty NumPy array with our new dtype:

```
In [25]: structured_mv = memoryview(np.empty((10,), dtype=dt))
```

The `memoryview`'s format string comes from the `struct` standard library module's specification, and for structured types is rather cryptic:

```
In [26]: structured_mv.format
Out[26]: 'T{b:a:=Zd:b:}'
```

We leave the details of `memoryview` format strings to the official documentation; thankfully, we do not have to work with them directly. We can rest assured that buffers and `memoryview` objects work with simple scalar types as well as user-defined structured types.

How do `memoryviews` and buffer objects translate to Cython? Given that Cython lives between Python and C, it is ideally suited to work with `memoryview` objects and the buffer protocol at the C level.

Typed Memoryviews

Cython has a C-level type, the *typed memoryview*, that conceptually overlaps with the Python `memoryview` type and expands on it. As suggested by the name, a typed memoryview is used to *view* (i.e., share) data from a buffer-producing object. Because a typed memoryview operates at the C level, it has minimal Python overhead and is very efficient. A typed memoryview has a `memoryview`-like interface, so it is easier to use than working with C-level buffers directly. And because a typed memoryview is designed to work with the buffer protocol, it supports any buffer-producing object efficiently, allowing sharing of data buffers without copying.

Let's see an example.

Typed Memoryview Example

Suppose we want to work with a buffer of one-dimensional data efficiently in Cython. We do not care how the data is created at the Python level; we just want to access it in an efficient way.

Let's create a `def` function in Cython that has a typed memoryview argument:[2]

```
def summer(double[:] mv):
    """Sums its argument's contents."""
    # ...
```

The `double[:] mv` syntax declares `mv` to be a typed memoryview. The `double` specifies the memoryview's underlying data type, and the single colon in brackets indicates a one-dimensional memoryview object.

When we call `summer` from Python, we pass in a Python object that is implicitly assigned to `mv` as part of the usual function calling process. When an object is assigned to a typed memoryview, the memoryview attempts to access the object's underlying data buffer. If the passed object cannot provide a buffer—that is, it does not support the protocol—a `ValueError` is raised. If it does support the protocol, then it provides a C-level buffer for the memoryview to use.

Iterating through `mv` like a regular Python object is supported:

```
def summer(double[:] mv):
    """Sums its argument's contents."""
    cdef double d, ss = 0.0
    for d in mv:
        ss += d
    return ss
```

---

2. To follow along with the examples in this chapter, please see *https://github.com/cythonbook/examples*.

To play with this code (*memviews.pyx*) from IPython, we use `pyximport` to quickly compile this function at import time:

```
$ ipython --no-banner

In [1]: import pyximport; pyximport.install()
Out[1]: (None, <pyximport.pyximport.PyxImporter at 0x101c6c450>)

In [2]: import memviews
```

Let's create a million-element NumPy array to test:

```
In [3]: import numpy as np

In [4]: arr = np.ones((10**6,), dtype=np.double)
```

Now we can pass `arr` to `memviews.summer`:

```
In [5]: memviews.summer(arr)
Out[5]: 1000000.0
```

It also works with `array.array` objects. First, let's create a million-element array:

```
In [6]: from array import array

In [7]: a = array('d', [1]*10**6)

In [8]: len(a)
Out[8]: 1000000
```

We can pass `a` to `memviews.summer` and it works automatically in Python 3. In Python 2, we have to make sure we `cimport cpython.array` in our Cython source, which allows Cython to work with `array.array` objects:

```
In [9]: memviews.summer(a)
Out[9]: 1000000.0
```

This implementation of `summer` is not particularly efficient, however:

```
In [10]: %timeit memviews.summer(arr)
1 loops, best of 3: 262 ms per loop
```

When iterating through a typed memoryview, Cython essentially treats it as a general Python iterator, calling into the Python/C API for every access. We can do better.

C-Level Access to Typed Memoryview Data

Typed memoryviews are designed for C-style access with no Python overhead. A better way to add `mv`'s elements is:

```
def summer(double[:] mv):
    """Sums its argument's contents."""
    cdef:
        double ss = 0.0
```

```
    int i, N

N = mv.shape[0]
for i in range(N):
    ss += mv[i]
return ss
```

This version has much better performance: about 1 millisecond for our million-element array. When indexing into a typed memoryview with a typed integer, Cython generates code that bypasses Python/C API calls and indexes into the underlying buffer directly. This is the source of our large speedup. But we can do better still.

Trading Safety for Performance

Every time we access our memoryview, Cython checks that the index is in bounds. If it is out of bounds, Cython raises an IndexError. Also, Cython allows us to index into memoryviews with negative indices (i.e., index wraparound) just like Python lists.

In our summer function, we iterate through the memoryview once, and do not do anything fancy. We know ahead of time that we never index with an out-of-bounds or negative index, so we can instruct Cython to turn off these checks for better performance. To do so, we use the cython special module with the boundscheck and wraparound compiler directives (see "Compiler Directives" on page 28):

```
from cython cimport boundscheck, wraparound

def summer(double[:] mv):
    # ...
    with boundscheck(False), wraparound(False):
        for i in range(N):
            ss += mv[i]
    # ...
```

We modified our original summer definition by placing our loop inside a context manager (i.e., a with block) that turns off bounds and wraparound checking when accessing our memoryview. These modifications are in effect for the duration of the context manager. The result is a small performance improvement and more efficient code generation. It is up to us to ensure that we do not index out of bounds or with a negative index; doing so could lead to a segmentation fault.

To turn off bounds and wraparound checking for the entire function, we use the decorator form of the directives and remove the context manager form:

```
from cython cimport boundscheck, wraparound

@boundscheck(False)
@wraparound(False)
def summer(double[:] mv):
    # ...
```

```
    for i in range(N):
        ss += mv[i]
    # etc.
```

To turn off bounds and wraparound checking everywhere for an entire extension module, we use a compiler directive in a special Cython comment at the top of our file:

```
# cython: boundscheck=False
# cython: wraparound=False

def summer(double[:] mv):
    # ...
    for i in range(N):
        ss += mv[i]
    # etc.
```

We can also globally enable these directives when compiling by means of the --directive flag; see Chapter 2.

 The different scope levels for these directives—context manager, decorator, and module global—provide precise control over where the directives are in effect. They can be easily disabled for development and debugging, and easily enabled for production runs.

With these performance optimizations in place, the performance of our summer function is the same as that of the equivalent NumPy sum method:

```
In [1]: import numpy as np

In [2]: arr = np.ones((10**6,), dtype=np.double)

In [3]: %timeit arr.sum()
1000 loops, best of 3: 1.01 ms per loop
```

A C version of summer has the same performance as our typed memoryview version, when accounting for Python call overhead.

So, what have we learned? We saw how to declare a simple typed memoryview, we saw how indexing a typed memoryview with an integral argument efficiently accesses the memoryview's underlying buffer, and we saw how to use the boundscheck and wraparound directives to generate even more efficient code, understanding when it is safe to do so.

There are many more details to cover, starting with the syntax and semantics of typed memoryview declaration.

Declaring Typed Memoryviews

When declaring typed memoryviews, we can control many attributes:

Element type

The element type of a typed memoryview may be a numeric scalar type like int, float, or double complex; it may be a ctypedef alias; or it may be a structured type declared with cdef struct, for example. There is initial (and still developing) support for generic *fused types* as well—see the sidebar "Typed Memoryviews and Fused Types" on page 182.

Dimensionality

Typed memoryviews (currently) may have up to seven dimensions. To declare a three-dimensional typed memoryview, we use three comma-separated colons in the bracketed dimension spec after the element type—for example, double[:, :, :].

Contiguous or strided data packing

A strided dimension—declared with a single colon—in a typed memoryview is compatible with a strided (i.e., noncontiguous and regularly spaced) buffer dimension. This can result when the typed memoryview accesses the underlying data from a NumPy array that is a strided view of another array, for example. A contiguous dimension is more restrictive: the dimension must be contiguous in memory, and this is enforced when the typed memoryview accesses the underlying data at runtime. Because strided access is more general, it is the default.

C or Fortran contiguity

C- or Fortran-contiguous typed memoryviews are important cases with specific data packing constraints. *C-contiguous*—or *column-major*—layout means that the buffer as a whole is contiguous in memory, and, if multidimensional, that the memoryview's *last* dimension is also contiguous. *Fortran-contiguous*—or *row-major*—layout means that the entire buffer is contiguous in memory, and, if multidimensional, that the *first* dimension is also contiguous. When possible, it is advantageous from a performance standpoint to declare arrays as C or Fortran contiguous, as this enables Cython to generate faster code that does not have to take strided access into account.

Direct or indirect access

Direct access is the default and covers nearly all use cases—it specifies that this dimension can use straightforward indexing arithmetic to directly access the underlying data. If indirect access is specified for a dimension, the underlying buffer stores a *pointer* to the rest of the array that must be dereferenced on access (hence *indirect*). In part because NumPy does not currently support indirect access, this access specification is rarely used, and for that reason direct access is the default.

If we declare a typed memoryview with a single colon in each dimension's slot, the typed memoryview can acquire a buffer from an object of the same dimensionality and with either strided or contiguous packing.

For example, consider the default typed memoryview declaration for a three-dimensional object:

```
cdef int[:, :, :] mv
```

This is the most general and most flexible typed memoryview declaration. We can assign to mv, and thereby acquire a buffer from, any three-dimensional NumPy array with the int data type:

```
mv = np.empty((10, 20, 30), dtype=np.int32)
```

The mv typed memoryview can also acquire a buffer from a Fortran-ordered array, since each dimension has strided packing:

```
mv = np.ones((10, 20, 30), dtype=np.int32, order='F')
```

Lastly, it can acquire a buffer from a fully strided ndarray:

```
arr = np.ones((13, 17, 19), dtype=np.int32)
mv = arr[4:10:2, ::3, 5::-2]
```

When indexing into mv, Cython generates indexing code that takes the array's strides into account. If we are willing to trade some flexibility for speed, C- or Fortran-contiguous typed memoryviews can be indexed more efficiently.

Declaring a C-contiguous typed memoryview requires a simple modification to the strided version: all dimensions except the last are specified with a single colon, and the last dimension is specified with two colons followed by a literal 1. The mnemonic is that the last dimension has a unitary stride (i.e., is contiguous in memory), hence C contiguous.

For example, to declare a two-dimensional C-contiguous typed memoryview, we would say:

```
cdef float[:, ::1] c_contig_mv
```

We can assign a C-contiguous NumPy array to it. C contiguous is the default layout for all NumPy array-creation functions:

```
c_contig_mv = np.ones((3, 4), dtype=np.float32)
```

But assigning a Fortran-ordered or a strided array to c_contig_mv raises a runtime ValueError:

```
c_contig_mv = np.ones((3, 4), dtype=np.float32, order='F')
#=> ValueError: ndarray is not C-contiguous

arr = np.ones((3, 4), dtype=np.float32)
c_contig_mv = arr[:, ::2]
#=> ValueError: ndarray is not C-contiguous
```

In contrast to the C-contiguous version, a Fortran-contiguous typed memoryview has the unitary stride in the *first* dimension:

```
cdef double[::1, :] f_contig_mv = np.ones((3, 4), dtype=np.float64, order='F')
```

The f_contig_mv cannot acquire a buffer from a C-contiguous or strided buffer-supporting object.

One-dimensional contiguous typed memoryviews are simultaneously C and Fortran contiguous:

```
cdef float complex[::1] both_ways = np.zeros((100,), dtype=np.complex64)
# ...
both_ways = np.empty((73,), dtype=np.complex64, order='F')
```

These three typed memoryview declarations—fully strided, C contiguous, and Fortran contiguous—cover the vast majority of use cases. For the common case where all arrays are C contiguous, it is recommended to use C-contiguous memoryviews: it is the most common memory layout, it is required when we are working with external C or C++ libraries, and the performance improvements it allows are worth the extra syntax and small loss in flexibility. In many situations the ValueError that results when assigning a non-C-contiguous buffer to a C-contiguous typed memoryview is a feature: it noisily tells us when an incompatible (strided or Fortran-contiguous) array has sneaked through.

If the application is Fortran-centric, then Fortran-contiguous memoryviews are preferable.

NumPy provides the ascontiguousarray and asfortranarray conversion functions, which take an array-like object as an argument and return a guaranteed C- or Fortran-contiguous NumPy array, respectively. Each returns the argument unmodified when it is already C or Fortran contiguous, so they are as efficient as can be expected.

Fully strided typed memoryviews are valuable when we are iterating through an array once and the input array's layout is ambiguous. In these situations, the overhead of manually creating a contiguous copy for use by contiguous memoryviews may outweigh the performance gain from contiguous access.

Typed Memoryviews and Fused Types

We can use Cython's nascent *fused types* for a typed memoryview's element type to provide more generalization and flexibility. This comes with the usual restrictions for fused types (see the sidebar "Fused Types and Generic Programming" in Chapter 3). The fused type used with the typed memoryview must be used to declare at least one argument type so that Cython can determine which fused type specialization to dispatch to at compile time or runtime.

For instance, suppose we want to declare a cdef, cpdef, or def function that generalizes the preceding summer function to accept either a float or double strided and one-dimensional typed memoryview. We can do so using the `cython.floating` built-in fused type:

```
cimport cython

cpdef cython.floating generic_summer(cython.floating[:] mv):
    cdef cython.floating f, ss = 0.0
    for f in mv:
        ss += f
    return ss
```

Because the `cython.floating` fused type is used for the `mv` argument, it can also be used for the internal `f` and `ss` variable types.

With this definition, `generic_summer` can accept either a `float` or a `double` array, unlike the original `summer` function, which is restricted to buffers of `double` elements only:

```
import numpy as np
double_array = np.arange(10., dtype=np.double)
float_array = np.asarray(double_array, dtype=np.float)
print generic_summer(double_array)
#=> 1000000.0
print generic_summer(float_array)
#=> 1000000.0
```

Because `generic_summer` is a `cpdef` function, it can also be called from Cython with a typed memoryview argument:

```
import numpy as np
cdef double[:] double_array = np.arange(10., dtype=np.double)
cdef float[:] float_array = np.asarray(double_array, dtype=np.float)
print generic_summer(double_array)
#=> 1000000.0
print generic_summer(float_array)
#=> 1000000.0
```

The combination of fused types and typed memoryviews allows typed memoryviews to generalize not only the manner in which data is accessed, but also the underlying data type.

Using Typed Memoryviews

Once we have declared a typed memoryview, we must assign a buffer-supporting object to it. Doing so causes the typed memoryview to acquire (or *view*) a buffer from the righthand-side object. The assigned-to typed memoryview shares access with the object's underlying buffer.

If we forget to acquire a buffer with a typed memoryview, we cannot perform any operations with it that require a buffer. Doing so will result in runtime exceptions.

What operations do typed memoryviews support?

We can access and modify individual elements by indexing into the typed memoryview in a NumPy-like fashion:

```
cdef int[:, :] mv = obj
print(mv[10, -20]) # access
mv[0, -1] = 3 # modify
```

As we saw previously, typed memoryviews can be indexed efficiently, especially when we turn off bounds checking and wraparound checking:

```
from cython cimport boundscheck, wraparound

def mv_sum(int[:, ::1] mv):
    cdef int N, M, i, j
    cdef long s=0
    N = mv.shape[0]; M = mv.shape[1]
    with boundscheck(False), wraparound(False):
        for i in range(N):
            for j in range(M):
                s += mv[i,j]
    return s
```

To modify a memoryview in its entirety, thereby modifying the contents of the buffer it views, we can use slice assignment with an ellipsis (...); to modify a sliceable section, we can use regular slice assignment. Doing either copies data from the righthand side. The righthand side can be a scalar:

```
cdef double[:, :] mv = np.empty((10, 20))

mv[...] = math.pi
```

or it can be another memoryview with the same element type and of the right shape:

```
cdef double[:, :] mv1 = np.zeros((10, 20))
cdef double[:, ::1] mv2 = np.ones((20, 40))

mv1[::2, ::2] = mv2[1:11:2, 10:40:3]
```

If the shapes of the lefthand and righthand sides do not match, a runtime `ValueError` will be raised.

When we intend to copy data into a typed memoryview, slice assignment is necessary. If instead of slice assignment we had used regular assignment, then no copy would be made. Regular assignment with typed memoryviews results in another typed memoryview sharing the righthand side's underlying buffer. This behavior is conceptually —if not precisely—analogous to that of Python lists, where slice assignment copies data, and regular assignment simply creates another variable by which to access the same data.

We can also use the `copy` or `copy_fortran` method to generate a C- or Fortran-contiguous copy of a memoryview's buffer, respectively.

Once a buffer has been acquired, we can slice it like a NumPy `ndarray` to get another typed memoryview that shares the buffer:

```
cdef float[:, :, ::1] mv = obj

cdef float[:, :] two_dee_mv = mv[:, 0, :]
```

The usual start, stop, and step arguments are allowed with slicing:

```
two_dee_mv[...] = mv[4:10:2, ::3, -1]
```

Like NumPy arrays, typed memoryviews support partial indexing, which results in a typed memoryview slice:

```
cdef int[:, :, :] mv = obj

assert mv[10].shape == mv[10, ...].shape == mv[10, :, :].shape
```

Also as with NumPy arrays, we can insert new dimensions into typed memoryviews with `None`:

```
cdef double[:] mv = np.ones((50,))

assert mv[None, :].shape == (1, 50)
assert mv[:, None].shape == (50, 1)
```

Unlike NumPy arrays, however, typed memoryviews do not support universal functions, so no broadcasting operations are possible other than simple scalar assignment. But we can efficiently (i.e., without copying) make a NumPy array from a typed memoryview, since typed memoryviews themselves support the buffer protocol:

```
cdef float[:] rows = np.arange((100,), dtype=np.float32)
cdef float[:] cols = rows

# broadcasting sum
plane = np.asarray(rows[:,None]) + np.asarray(cols[None,:])
```

And lastly, to transpose a typed memoryview we use the `T` attribute, as with a NumPy `ndarray`. Transposing a C-contiguous typed memoryview results in a Fortran-contiguous one:

```
cdef int[:, ::1] c_contig = obj
cdef int[::1, :] f_contig = c_contig.T
```

 It is helpful to think of typed memoryviews as very flexible Cython-space objects that allow efficient sharing, indexing, and modification of homogeneous data. They have many of the core features of NumPy arrays, and what features they do not have are easily addressed by their efficient interoperability with NumPy.

But typed memoryviews go beyond the buffer protocol—they can be used to view C-level arrays as well.

Original Buffer Syntax

Before typed memoryviews, Cython had different syntax for working efficiently with NumPy arrays and other buffer-supporting objects. This original buffer syntax is still in use, but it has been superseded by typed memoryviews, which provide more features and cleaner syntax.

An example of the original buffer syntax, adapted from Cython's online documentation (*http://docs.cython.org/src/userguide/memoryviews.html#*), is:

```
cimport numpy as np

def convolve(np.ndarray[double, ndim=2] f,
             np.ndarray[double, ndim=2] g):
    cdef:
        np.ndarray[double, ndim=2] h
        # ...other static declarations elided...
    h = np.zeros((xmax, ymax), dtype=np.double_t)
```

The convolve function uses three NumPy buffers—f, g, and h—each of which is declared with Cython's original NumPy buffer syntax. This syntax uses np.ndarray to declare the type of the object exposing the buffer interface, and places the C data type for the array's elements inside square brackets after np.ndarray. Because these buffers are all two-dimensional, the ndim=2 attribute is included inside the square brackets.

The body of convolve loops over f and g to compute the two-dimensional convolution and store the result in h. The original buffer syntax also allows Cython to generate efficient indexing code.

We can translate convolve to use typed memoryviews instead. The body of convolve remains unchanged; only the array declarations need be modified:

```
def convolve(double[:, ::1] f, double[:, ::1] g):
    cdef:
        double[:, ::1] h
        # ...
    # ...
```

Here we use the syntax for C-contiguous typed memoryviews, which is appropriate for when we know the input arrays are standard unstrided arrays.

Besides a cleaner syntax, what benefits do typed memoryviews bring over the original syntax?

- Typed memoryviews can work with a wider range of buffer-supporting objects: NumPy arrays, Python `memoryview` objects, `array.array` objects, and any other type that supports the new buffer protocol. They can also work with C arrays. They are therefore more general than the NumPy array buffer syntax, which is restricted to work with NumPy arrays only.

- Typed memoryviews can be used in any scope. This includes module scope; arguments for `def`, `cpdef`, or `cdef` functions or methods; function or method local scope; and `cdef class` attribute scope. The NumPy buffer syntax can be used only in function-local scope and for `def` function arguments.

- Typed memoryviews have many more options that provide precise control: contiguous or strided data packing, C or Fortran contiguity, and direct or indirect data access. Some of these options can be controlled on a dimension-by-dimension basis. The NumPy array buffer syntax does not provide this level of control.

- In all circumstances, typed memoryviews match or exceed the original buffer syntax's performance.

Updating the original buffer syntax to use typed memoryviews is straightforward, as we saw in the previous example. Besides the small time and testing investment required to update, there are very few (if any) reasons to prefer the original buffer syntax to typed memoryviews.

Beyond Buffers

So far, we have assigned various types of Python objects to typed memoryviews: NumPy `ndarray` objects, `array.array` objects, `bytes` objects, and `bytearray` objects. NumPy arrays are the most common in practice, given NumPy's ubiquity, flexibility, and expressiveness. Beyond Python-space objects, however, typed memoryviews can also work with C-level arrays: either dynamic heap-allocated arrays or fixed-size stack-allocated arrays.

To view a C array with a memoryview, we simply assign the array to the memoryview. If the array is fixed size (or *complete*), the righthand side of the assignment can be the array's name only. Cython has enough information to keep track of the array's size:

```
cdef int a[3][5][7]
cdef int[:, :, ::1] mv = a

mv[...] = 0
```

In this example we declare `mv` as a C-contiguous memoryview, as fixed-size arrays are always C contiguous. The last line initializes the array `a` to all zeros, using slice assignment and broadcasting.

If we have a dynamically allocated C array rather than a fixed-size array, Cython does not know its extent, but we can still use it with typed memoryviews.

First, the dynamic array allocation:

```
from libc.stdlib cimport malloc

def dynamic(size_t N, size_t M):
    cdef long *arr = <long*>malloc(N * M * sizeof(long))
```

We can certainly use `arr` inside our function directly, but it would require that we manually do index calculations. For higher-dimensional arrays, this is inconvenient. Let's interact with our dynamic array via the typed-memoryview interface.

Suppose we try to assign our dynamic array to a typed memoryview, as in the fixed-size array example:

```
def dynamic(size_t N, size_t M):
    cdef long *arr = <long*>malloc(N * M * sizeof(long))
    cdef long[:, ::1] mv = arr
```

This does not compile, resulting in the error: "Cannot convert *long* * to memoryviewslice". Part of the reason is that Cython knows only that `arr` is a `long` pointer. We have to give Cython more information to indicate that `arr` is convertible to a typed memoryview. That hint comes in the form of a *typed memoryview cast*:

```
def dynamic(size_t N, size_t M):
    cdef long *arr = <long*>malloc(N * M * sizeof(long))
    cdef long[:, ::1] mv = <long[:N, :M]>arr
```

We use the memoryview casting syntax, `<long[:N, :M]>`, to provide Cython with the information it needs to assign `arr` to our memoryview. Notice that the type in the cast uses slice notation with stop values for each dimension. The stop values are necessary to communicate to Cython the shape we intend the typed memoryview to have.

 At the C level, there is no way to programmatically determine the length of a dynamically allocated C array via its head pointer. It is the responsibility of the programmer to know the right extent of the C array when casting a C array to a typed memoryview. If this is incorrect, buffer overruns, segmentation faults, or data corruption may result.

This rounds out the features of typed memoryviews and shows how they can be used with either buffer-supporting Python objects or C-level arrays, whether fixed size or dynamic. If a Cython function has a typed memoryview argument, it can be called with either Python objects *or* C arrays as arguments.

When returning a typed memoryview in a def function, Cython converts it to a regular Python memoryview without copying the buffer. In the preceding dynamic function, returning mv will work: the underlying arr C array is heap allocated, so it is not tied to the function's scope. If arr were fixed size (and therefore *stack* allocated), then it would be tied to the call stack, and returning a memoryview that viewed the array would be erroneous.

But there is still an issue with memoryviews that view heap-allocated C arrays: who is responsible for freeing the array when the memoryview is no longer needed? A related question: when a C or C++ library returns a dynamically allocated array, how can we return it as a NumPy array, and how can we properly manage its finalization?

Wrapping C and C++ Arrays

Suppose a C function make_matrix_c returns a dynamically allocated C array. Its declaration in Cython would be something like:

```
cdef extern from "matrix.h":
    float *make_matrix_c(int nrows, int ncols)
```

Suppose also that we want to return a NumPy array that views this array, allowing interaction with the underlying data from Python. Using what we know of typed memoryviews—and setting aside proper cleanup for the moment—we can use memoryviews to easily do what we want:

```
import numpy as np

def make_matrix(int nrows, int ncols):
    cdef float[:, ::1] mv = <float[:nrows, :ncols]>make_matrix_c(nrows, ncols)
    return np.asarray(mv)
```

This compiles and allows NumPy access to the C array, but it leaks memory. How do we properly clean up after ourselves?

Correct (and Automatic) Memory Management with Cython and C Arrays

First, we know (by construction) that we are responsible for this memory. If there is a possibility that we are sharing this array with other C code, then properly handling the shared array can become tricky. The difficult part is communicating to all interested parties who is responsible for cleanup. Because C has no automatic memory management features (like C++ shared pointers, for example), ensuring proper cleanup can be challenging. Often the cleanest solution in these situations is to make a copy of the data to clarify ownership semantics.

Knowing that we own this C array and are responsible for freeing it, how do we do so properly from Python? The C array is owned by a NumPy array. What we need is a way to automatically call the right destructor when the last viewing NumPy array is finalized by the Python runtime.

The NumPy/C API defines a `base` attribute on the `PyArrayObject`, which is designed for just this purpose. According to NumPy's documentation (*http://docs.scipy.org/doc/ numpy/reference/c-api.array.html#PyArray_BASE*), "If you are constructing an array using the C API, and specifying your own memory, you should use the function `PyArray_SetBaseObject` to set the base to an object which owns the memory." We will use a Cython-provided function rather than `PyArray_SetBaseObject` to accomplish the same end.

First, we need access to NumPy's C API. We can `cimport numpy` (mind the c) to access NumPy's C interface. Let's give it an alias to keep it distinct from the Python-level `numpy` package we already imported:

```
import numpy as np
cimport numpy as cnp
```

We know from Chapter 6 that the `cimport numpy as cnp` statement is a *compile-time* operation that gives us access to C-level constructs. Cython includes a `numpy` package alongside the `libc` and `libcpp` packages that are used by `cimport`.

We need to set the `base` to "an object which owns the memory." We can create a minimal extension type that does just that. It needs just one attribute to hold a reference to the array, and just one method, `__dealloc__`. This is the object that owns the memory, and its sole purpose is to call `free` on the array at finalization. Let's call it `_finalizer`:

```
cdef class _finalizer:
    cdef void *_data
    def __dealloc__(self):
        print "_finalizer.__dealloc__"
        if self._data is not NULL:
            free(self._data)
```

With our `_finalizer` class, we have everything we need to properly manage memory. The `print` statement is there just to ensure the array is deallocated appropriately. We can now create a convenience `cdef` function that creates a `_finalizer` and uses the `set_array_base` function from Cython's `numpy` C interface:

```
cdef void set_base(cnp.ndarray arr, void *carr):
    cdef _finalizer f = _finalizer()
    f._data = <void*>carr
    cnp.set_array_base(arr, f)
```

This function first creates an empty `_finalizer` object, then initializes its `_data` attribute, and lastly calls `set_array_base`.

Returning to our `make_matrix` function, we can use `set_base` to tie everything together:

```
def make_matrix(int nrows, int ncols):
    cdef float *mat = make_matrix_c(nrows, ncols)
    cdef float[:, ::1] mv = <float[:nrows, :ncols]>mat
    cdef cnp.ndarray arr = np.asarray(mv)
    set_base(arr, mat)
    return arr
```

The first line of our function calls make_matrix_c and stores the result in a float pointer. The next line creates a C-contiguous typed memoryview from the mat array.

The next line creates a NumPy array from our typed memoryview; this uses the buffer protocol behind the scenes to share the underlying C array. Then we use our set_base helper function to set the base attribute of our NumPy array to a _finalizer object. This ties everything together properly, and we can return our NumPy array as a result.

If we name our extension module *numpy_cleanup.pyx*, we can compile it using a distutils script:

```
from distutils.core import setup, Extension
from Cython.Build import cythonize
from numpy import get_include

ext = Extension("numpy_cleanup", ["numpy_cleanup.pyx"],
                include_dirs=['.', get_include()])

setup(name="numpy_cleanup",
      ext_modules = cythonize(ext))
```

Because we use the NumPy/C API (via the cimport numpy as cnp statement), we need to include some NumPy headers when compiling. That is the reason for the include_dirs option to the Extension call. NumPy provides a get_include function that returns the full path to its include directory.

After compiling:

```
$ python setup.py build_ext -i
running build_ext
building 'numpy_cleanup' extension
gcc -fno-strict-aliasing -fno-common -dynamic -g -O2
    -DNDEBUG -g -fwrapv -O3 -Wall -Wstrict-prototypes -I.
    -I/Users/ksmith/PY/lib/python2.7/site-packages/numpy/core/include
    -I/Users/ksmith/Devel/PY64/Python.framework/Versions/2.7/include/python2.7
    -c numpy_cleanup.c -o build/temp.macosx-10.4-x86_64-2.7/numpy_cleanup.o
gcc -bundle -undefined dynamic_lookup
    build/temp.macosx-10.4-x86_64-2.7/numpy_cleanup.o
    -o /Users/ksmith/examples/memviews/numpy_cleanup.so
```

We can try out our make_matrix from IPython:

```
$ ipython --no-banner

In [1]: import numpy_cleanup
```

```
In [2]: arr = numpy_cleanup.make_matrix(100, 100)
```

Let's check the `base` attribute:

```
In [3]: arr.base
Out[3]: <numpy_cleanup._finalizer at 0x100284eb8>
```

What we're interested in is that the finalizer's `__dealloc__` method is called at cleanup time. We can force IPython to wipe out any references to the `arr` NumPy array with `%reset`:

```
In [4]: %reset
Once deleted, variables cannot be recovered. Proceed (y/[n])? y
_finalizer.__dealloc__
```

We have the satisfaction of seeing the `"_finalizer.__dealloc__"` string output, indicating the array was, indeed, freed. It is left as an exercise for the reader to confirm that the finalizer's `__dealloc__` is called even when there are multiple views of the array.

There is a lot going on here. Interlanguage programming can require more effort to properly manage memory and resources, but Cython has the features and functionality to make it straightforward. The fact that we can do these low-level operations at the Cython level and do not have to resort to pure-C code saves us a tremendous amount of work. This is another instance of Cython making difficult things possible.

It is worth emphasizing that the most common use case is to use NumPy arrays to manage data, and to use the basic features of typed memoryviews to efficiently access and modify these NumPy arrays from Cython.

Summary

In this chapter we learned all about Cython's features for working with NumPy arrays, `array.array` objects, and objects that support the new buffer protocol. The central figure was Cython's typed memoryview, which provides a consistent abstraction that works with all of these Python types and gives us efficient C-level access to buffer elements. Typed memoryviews both use and support the buffer protocol, so they do not copy memory unnecessarily. They are highly efficient: we saw a simple example where using typed memoryviews provided a speedup of multiple orders of magnitude over pure Python.

We also learned how typed memoryviews can easily work with C and C++ arrays, either fixed size or dynamic. To pull everything together, we saw an example that uses a typed memoryview and a NumPy array to view a dynamically allocated C array. This required that we dip into the NumPy/C API to ensure that the dynamic memory is properly finalized at the appropriate time.

## CHAPTER 11

Cython in Practice: Spectral Norm

*The competent programmer is fully aware of the strictly limited
size of his own skull; therefore he approaches the programming task in
full humility, and among other things he avoids clever tricks like the plague.*

— E. Dijkstra

Like Chapter 4, this chapter's intent is to reiterate concepts and techniques to show Cython's use in context. Here we focus on using typed memoryviews to compute the *spectral norm* of a particular matrix. This is another example from the computer language benchmarks game (*http://benchmarksgame.alioth.debian.org/*), allowing us to compare the Cython solution's performance to other highly optimized implementations in different languages. The focus here is how to use typed memoryviews to achieve much better performance with array-heavy operations. That said, we will first cover what the spectral norm is and explore a pure-Python version before using Cython to speed it up.

Overview of the Spectral Norm Python Code

The *spectral norm* of a matrix A is defined to be the largest *singular value* of A; that is, the square root of the largest eigenvalue of the matrix $B = A^T A$, where A^T is the conjugate transpose of A. The spectral norm of a matrix is an important quantity that frequently arises, and it is often computed in computational linear algebra contexts.

To compute the spectral norm, we make use of one observation about B: if the vector u is parallel to the principal eigenvector of B, then the quantity $\sqrt{u^T B u / u^T u}$ is identical to the spectral norm of A. Therefore, if we compute $B^n u$ for positive integer n and random (nonzero) vector u, each application of B will align u more closely with the principal eigenvector. This provides an iterative solution to compute the spectral norm, and at its core it uses a matrix-vector multiply.

The particular matrix for which we will compute the spectral norm is defined as:

$$
\begin{vmatrix}
1/1 & 1/2 & 1/4 & 1/7 & \cdots \\
1/3 & 1/5 & 1/8 & & \\
1/6 & 1/9 & & & \\
1/10 & & & \ddots & \\
\vdots & & & &
\end{vmatrix}
$$

Given row i and column j—both zero-based—we can compute $A_{i,j}$ in a single expression:[1]

```
def A(i, j):
    return 1.0 / (((i + j) * (i + j + 1) >> 1) + i + 1)
```

Alternatively, we could compute $A_{i,j}$ up to a given maximum number of rows and columns and store the result in a two-dimensional array. Because the matrix is dense, the memory required to store it grows very quickly. For more direct comparison with the other language implementations, we will use the computed version defined in the preceding code block.

The core of the program computes $v = Au$ or $v = A^T u$:

```
def A_times_u(u, v):
    u_len = len(u)

    for i in range(u_len):
        partial_sum = 0.0
        for j in range(u_len):
            partial_sum += A(i, j) * u[j]

        v[i] = partial_sum
```

The definition of At_times_u is identical except for the partial_sum update:

```
def At_times_u(u, v):
    # ...
    for ...:
        for ...:
            partial_sum += A(j, i) * u[j]
    # ...
```

To compute $A^T Au = Bu$, we can first compute $v = Au$ using A_times_u and then compute $A^T v$ using At_times_u. That is what B_times_u does:

---

1. To follow along with the examples in this chapter, please see *https://github.com/cythonbook/examples*.

```
def B_times_u(u, out, tmp):
    A_times_u(u, tmp)
    At_times_u(tmp, out)
```

Because *A* is an infinite matrix, some approximation must be used. The spectral norm program takes an integer n from the command line that determines the number of rows and columns in *A*. It then creates an input vector u of length n initialized to 1, using the standard library `array` type:

```
def spectral_norm(n):
    u = array("d", [1.0] * n)
    v = array("d", [0.0] * n)
    tmp = array("d", [0.0] * n)
```

Here, u is the input vector; v and tmp are intermediates.

The core of the program calls B_times_u a net 20 times, all while managing the temporaries to handle swapping values:

```
def spectral_norm(n):
    # ...
    for _ in range(10):
        B_times_u(u, v, tmp)
        B_times_u(v, u, tmp)
```

After this loop is finished, the vectors u and v are both closely aligned with the principal eigenvector of B. The vector u has had one more application of B than v, so to compute the spectral norm of A, we compute $v^T u / v^T v$, which is equivalent to $v^T B v / v^T v$:

```
def spectral_norm(n):
    # ...
    vBv = vv = 0

    for ue, ve in zip(u, v):
        vBv += ue * ve
        vv  += ve * ve
```

The spectral norm is then a simple expression, which we return:

```
def spectral_norm(n):
    # ...
    return sqrt(vBv / vv)
```

Altogether, the entire script is about 70 lines of code. The pure-Python version is (subjectively) one of the easier implementations to understand among all submitted versions, but it is also consistently orders of magnitude slower than many other implementations. Cython is ideally suited to allow the Python version to keep its expressiveness and improve its performance to be competitive.

Performance Profiling

Our pure-Python version is in a source file named *spectral_norm.py*. If run as a script from the command line, it will pass the input argument to spectral_norm and print the result:

```
if __name__ == "__main__":
    n = int(sys.argv[1])
    spec_norm = spectral_norm(n)
    print("%0.9f" % spec_norm)
```

Let's try it out for small inputs:

```
$ python ./spectral_norm.py 10
1.271844019

$ python ./spectral_norm.py 50
1.274193837

$ python ./spectral_norm.py 100
1.274219991

$ python ./spectral_norm.py 200
1.274223601
```

The true solution to 10 significant digits is 1.274224152 (*http://bit.ly/challenge_prob lems*), so as n increases, we see that the accuracy of the computed spectral norm improves as well.

Let's run *spectral_norm.py* under a profiler (see Chapter 9) to see what occupies the runtime:

```
$ ipython --no-banner

In [1]: %run -p ./spectral_norm.py 300

    3600154 function calls in 3.836 seconds

Ordered by: internal time

  ncalls  tottime  percall  cumtime  percall filename:lineno(function)
 3600000    1.826    0.000    1.826    0.000 spectral_norm.py:15(A)
      20    1.013    0.051    1.934    0.097 spectral_norm.py:18(A_times_u)
      20    0.995    0.050    1.900    0.095 spectral_norm.py:32(At_times_u)
       1    0.000    0.000    3.835    3.835 spectral_norm.py:50(spectral_norm)
 ...
```

The column to focus on is tottime, which indicates the time spent in this function excluding time spent in called functions. Looking at the first three rows in the tottime column, we can conclude that the three functions A, A_times_u, and At_times_u together consume greater than 95 percent of the total runtime.

Cythonizing Our Code

With profiling data in hand, we can sketch out how we will use Cython to improve performance.

Before starting, first we rename *spectral_norm.py* to *spectral_norm.pyx*; this is the source of our Cython-generated extension module. We also create a minimal *run_spec_norm.py* driver script:

```
import sys
from spectral_norm import spectral_norm

print("%0.9f" % spectral_norm(int(sys.argv[1])))
```

We modify *spectral_norm.pyx* to work with this driver script, removing the if __name__ ... block.

We also need a *setup.py* script to compile *spectral_norm.pyx*:

```
from distutils.core import setup
from Cython.Build import cythonize

setup(name='spectral_norm',
      ext_modules = cythonize('spectral_norm.pyx'))
```

Let's compile and run our Cythonized version before doing anything else, to see what Cython can do unaided:

```
$ python setup.py build_ext -i
Compiling spectral_norm.pyx because it changed.
Cythonizing spectral_norm.pyx
running build_ext
building 'spectral_norm' extension
creating build
creating build/temp.macosx-10.4-x86_64-2.7
gcc -fno-strict-aliasing -fno-common -dynamic -g -O2
    -DNDEBUG -g -fwrapv -O3 -Wall -Wstrict-prototypes
    -I[...] -c spectral_norm.c -o [...]/spectral_norm.o
gcc -bundle -undefined dynamic_lookup
    [...]/spectral_norm.o -o [...]/spectral_norm.so
```

Again, this output is specific for OS X. Consult Chapter 2 for platform-specific options to pass when compiling using distutils.

Now that all the infrastructure is in place, running our program is straightforward.

First, let's see the runtime of our pure-Python version for comparison:

```
$ time python spectral_norm.py 300
1.274223986
python spectral_norm.py 300  3.14s user 0.01s system 99% cpu 3.152 total
```

The Cythonized version's performance may be surprising:

```
$ time python run_spec_norm.py 300
1.274223986
python run_spec_norm.py 300  1.10s user 0.01s system 99% cpu 1.111 total
```

Remarkably, for this spectral norm calculation Cython is able to improve performance by nearly a factor of three, with no modifications to the core algorithm. This is a great start, and using more Cython features will only improve performance.

Adding Static Type Information

The A(i, j) function is called millions of times, so improving its performance will yield a significant payoff. It takes integer arguments and computes a floating-point value in a single expression, so converting it to use static typing is straightforward. By converting it to a cdef inline function, we remove all Python overhead:

```
cdef inline double A(int i, int j):
    return 1.0 / (((i + j) * (i + j + 1) >> 1) + i + 1)
```

Using Cython's annotation support (see Chapter 9; output not shown here), we see that the body of A is still yellow. This is due to the division operation, which by default will raise a ZeroDivisionError if the denominator is zero. We already know that it is impossible for the denominator to be zero, so this check is unnecessary. Cython allows us to trade safety for performance by using the cdivision decorator to turn off the test for a zero denominator:

```
from cython cimport cdivison

@cdivison(True)
cdef inline double A(...):
    # ...
```

After compiling again, we see that our optimized A function leads to another factor-of-two performance improvement:

```
$ time python run_spec_norm.py 300
1.274223986
python run_spec_norm.py 300  0.51s user 0.01s system 99% cpu 0.520 total
```

But we can do even better—let's look at the matrix-vector multiplication functions.

Using Typed Memoryviews

The A_times_u and At_times_u functions work extensively with arrays inside nested for loops. This pattern is ideally suited to the use of typed memoryviews, covered in Chapter 10.

First we convert the untyped arguments of A_times_u to use one-dimensional contiguous typed memoryviews of dtype double:

```
def A_times_u(double[::1] u, double[::1] v):
    # ...
```

We then provide static typing information for all internal variables:

```
def A_times_u(double[::1] u, double[::1] v):
    cdef int i, j, u_len = len(u)
    cdef double partial_sum
    # ...
```

The body of A_times_u remains unmodified:

```
def A_times_u(double[::1] u, double[::1] v):
    # ...
    for i in range(u_len):
        partial_sum = 0.0
        for j in range(u_len):
            partial_sum += A(i, j) * u[j]
        v[i] = partial_sum
```

We make sure to provide static typing for all variables in the code body. Ensuring that u and v are contiguous typed memoryviews allows Cython to generate efficient indexing code for the innermost loop.

The At_times_u transformation is identical.

We leave both the B_times_u and spectral_norm functions unmodified. If you recall from our profiling run, the A, A_times_u, and At_times_u functions occupy more than 95 percent of the runtime. Modifying these functions to use Cython data structures and static types makes sense, but using Cython-specific features everywhere is not necessary and is an exercise in diminishing returns.

Because we use typed memoryviews for the u and v arguments, we can call the A_times_u and At_times_u functions with any Python object that supports the buffer protocol. So, whenever B_times_u calls A_times_u and At_times_u, the u and v typed memoryviews will acquire the underlying buffer from the provided array.array objects. They do so without copying data.

In Python 2, there is one more step to ensure array.array objects work with typed memoryviews. Near the top of the file, we add another compile-time import:

```
from cpython.array cimport array
```

After compiling with our Cythonized matrix-vector multiplication routines in place, we see that the runtime is now significantly faster than before:

```
$ time python run_spec_norm.py 300
1.274223986
python run_spec_norm.py 300  0.05s user 0.01s system 97% cpu 0.058 total
```

Using typed memoryviews and statically typing all inner variables in A_times_u and At_times_u has led to an additional factor-of-10 performance improvement.

As we saw in Chapter 10, we can generate slightly more efficient code inside A_times_u and At_times_u by turning off bounds checking and wraparound index checking:

```
from cython cimport boundscheck, wraparound

@boundscheck(False)
@wraparound(False)
cdef void A_times_u(...):
    # ...
```

Perhaps unexpectedly, these optimizations do not affect performance by any measurable margin.

Comparing to the C Implementation

We are using the same algorithm here as is used in all the other solutions to the computer benchmark game, which allows us to compare Cython's performance to C directly.

All C versions of the benchmark—including the serial version we compare to here—are freely available. We can compile and run the C version with an n of 5500, making sure to use the same optimization flags that we used for Python to ensure a fair comparison:

```
$ time ./spectralnorm.x 5500
1.274224153
./spectralnorm.x 5500  9.60s user 0.00s system 99% cpu 9.601 total
```

Our Cython version with n of 5500 run has identical output and identical performance (within measurement error):

```
$ time python run_spec_norm.py 5500
1.274224153
python run_spec_norm.py 5500  9.61s user 0.01s system 99% cpu 9.621 total
```

The fastest C implementation makes use of SIMD intrinsics to parallelize the core computation. There is nothing preventing us from accessing the same operations from our Cython code as well. Doing so requires that we declare the platform-specific SIMD-enabled functions to Cython and integrate them into the *spectral_norm.pyx* code.

Summary

This second *Cython in Practice* chapter reiterates concepts and techniques covered in Chapter 3 (static scalar types), Chapter 9 (profiling), and Chapter 10 (typed memoryviews). With it, we see how to speed up a nontrivial linear algebra computation to achieve C-level performance. Remarkably, Cython provides a factor-of-three performance improvement with no core modifications for this example. Using static typing and typed memoryviews, we are able to improve performance by an overall factor of 60, matching the runtime of a highly optimized serial-C implementation.

Parallel Programming with Cython

*On two occasions I have been asked, "Pray, Mr. Babbage, if you put into the
machine wrong figures, will the right answers come out?" I am not able rightly
to apprehend the kind of confusion of ideas that could provoke such a question.*

— C. Babbage

In previous chapters, we have seen several instances of Cython improving Python's
performance by factors of 10, 100, or even 1,000. These performance improvements
often accrue after minor—sometimes trivial—modifications to the initial Python version. For array-oriented algorithms, in Chapter 10 we learned about Cython's typed
memoryviews and how they allow us to work efficiently with arrays. In particular, we
can loop over typed memoryviews and obtain code that is competitive with C for loops
over C arrays.

All of these impressive performance improvements were achieved on a *single thread of
execution*. In this chapter we will learn about Cython's multithreading features to access
thread-based parallelism. Our focus will be on the prange Cython function, which allows us to easily transform serial for loops to use multiple threads and tap into all
available CPU cores. Often we can turn on this thread-based loop parallelism with fairly
trivial modifications. We will see that for embarrassingly parallel CPU-bound operations, prange can work well.

Before we can cover prange, we must first understand certain interactions between the
Python runtime and native threads, which involves CPython's global interpreter lock.

Thread-Based Parallelism and the Global Interpreter Lock

A term that frequently comes up in discussions of CPython's thread-based parallelism
is the *global interpreter lock*, or GIL. According to Python's documentation (*https://*

wiki.python.org/moin/GlobalInterpreterLock), the GIL is "a mutex that prevents multiple native threads from executing Python bytecodes at once." In other words, the GIL ensures that only one native (or OS-level) thread executes Python bytecodes at any given time during the execution of a CPython program. The GIL affects not just Python-level code, but the Python/C API as a whole.

Why is it in place? "This lock is necessary mainly because CPython's memory management is not thread-safe. (However, since the GIL exists, other features have grown to depend on the guarantees that it enforces.)"

Some points to emphasize:

- The GIL is necessary to help with the memory management of Python objects.
- C code that does not work with Python objects can be run without the GIL in effect, allowing fully threaded execution.
- The GIL is specific to CPython. Other Python implementations, like Jython, Iron-Python, and PyPy, have no need for a GIL.

Because Cython code is compiled, not interpreted, it is not running Python bytecode. Because we can create C-only entities in Cython that are not tied to any Python object, we can release the global interpreter lock when working with the C-only parts of Cython. Put another way, *we can use Cython to bypass the GIL and achieve thread-based* `parallelism`.

Before running parallel code with Cython, we first need to manage the GIL. Cython provides two mechanisms for doing so: the `nogil` function attribute and the `with nogil` context manager.

The nogil Function Attribute

We can indicate to Cython that a C-level function should be called with the GIL released. By necessity, such functions are from an external library or are declared `cdef` or `cpdef`. A `def` function cannot be called with the GIL released, as these functions always interact with Python objects.

To call a function in a GIL-less context, the function must have the `nogil` attribute, which we declare in the function's signature:[1]

```
cdef int kernel(double complex z, double z_max, int n_max) nogil:
    # ...
```

The `nogil` attribute is placed after the closing parenthesis of the argument list and before the colon. Inside the body of `kernel` we must not create or otherwise interact with

---

1. To follow along with the examples in this chapter, please see *https://github.com/cythonbook/examples*.

Python objects, including statically typed Python objects like `lists` or `dicts`. At compile time Cython does what it can to ensure that a `nogil` function does not accept, return, or otherwise interact with Python objects in the function body. It does a reasonably good job of this in practice, but the `cython` compiler does not guarantee that it can catch every case, so vigilance is necessary. For instance, we can smuggle a Python object into a `nogil` function by casting the object to a `void` pointer type.

We can declare external C and C++ functions to be `nogil` as well:

```
cdef extern from "math.h":
    double sin(double x) nogil
    double cos(double x) nogil
    double tan(double x) nogil
    # ...
```

Frequently, an external library does not interact with Python objects at all. In such cases, we can declare every function in an `extern` block as `nogil` by placing the `nogil` declaration in the `cdef extern from` line:

```
cdef extern from "math.h" nogil:
    double sin(double x)
    double cos(double x)
    double tan(double x)
    # ...
```

The `nogil` attribute simply *allows* the so-attributed function(s) to be called without the GIL in effect. It is still up to us to release the GIL before calling it, and for that, we use the `with nogil` context manager.

The with nogil Context Manager

To release and acquire the GIL, Cython must generate the appropriate Python/C API calls. Once the GIL has been released, it must be reacquired before interacting with Python objects, which naturally suggests a context manager (i.e., a `with` statement):

```
# ...declare and initialize C arguments...

with nogil: # run without the GIL in place
    result = kernel(z, z_max, n_max)

# GIL reacquired
print result
```

In this code snippet, we use the `with nogil` context manager to release the GIL before calling `kernel` and reacquire it after the context manager block is exited. The argument types and return type for `kernel` are C data types, by necessity. If we try to use Python objects in the `with nogil` block, Cython issues a compile-time error. For example, if we placed the `print` statement in the preceding example inside the context manager the cython compiler would complain, as the `print` statement coerces its argument to a `PyObject`.

One use of the `with nogil` context manager is to release the GIL during blocking operations (either CPU or IO bound), thereby allowing other Python threads to execute while a possibly expensive operation runs concurrently.

Suppose the `kernel` function had an `except 0` clause in addition to the `nogil` clause. In this case, Cython would generate the proper error handling code in the `nogil` context manager, and any errors would be propagated after the GIL was reacquired.

It is possible to acquire the GIL temporarily within a `with nogil` context by using a `with gil` subcontext. This allows, for example, a `nogil` function to acquire the GIL to raise an exception or to do some other operation involving Python objects.

Understanding what the GIL is and how to manage it is necessary, but not sufficient, to allow threaded parallelism with Cython. It is still up to us to actually run code that uses threads with the GIL released.

The easiest way to access thread-based parallelism is to use an external library that already implements it for us. When calling such thread-parallel functions, we simply do so inside a `with nogil` context to benefit from their performance.

But the jewel of this chapter is `prange`, and all this GIL work is necessary before we can use it.

Cython and OpenMP

Cython implements `prange` using the OpenMP API for multiplatform shared memory multiprocessing. OpenMP requires C or C++ compiler support, and is enabled by specific compiler flags. For instance, when using GCC, we must pass the `-fopenmp` flag when compiling and linking our binary to ensure OpenMP is enabled. OpenMP is supported widely by many compilers, both free and commercial. The most notable exception is Clang/LLVM, which has preliminary support in a separate fork. Work is ongoing to fully implement OpenMP for Clang and include it in the main release.

Using prange to Parallelize Loops

The `prange` special function is a Cython-only construct. Its name is meant to evoke a *parallel range*, although unlike the built-in `range`, `prange` can be used only in conjunction with a `for` loop. It cannot be used in isolation.

To access `prange`, we simply `cimport` it from `cython.parallel`:

```
from cython.parallel cimport prange
```

Let's see an example.

The *Drosophila melanogaster* of parallel programming examples is computing either the Mandelbrot set or its cousins, Julia sets. It is an embarrassingly parallel CPU-bound computation, ideal for speeding up with threads. Almost all compute time is spent executing a kernel function we call escape:

```
cdef int escape(double complex z,
                double complex c,
                double z_max,
                int n_max) nogil:
    cdef:
        int i = 0
        double z_max2 = z_max * z_max
    while norm2(z) < z_max2 and i < n_max:
        z = z * z + c
        i += 1
    return i
```

The details of escape are not central to this example; it is sufficient to know that this function determines the number of iterations required before a complex value's norm grows larger than a specified bound.

This function calls norm2, which is the square of the absolute value of its complex argument z:

```
cdef inline double norm2(double complex z) nogil:
    return z.real * z.real + z.imag * z.imag
```

Both escape and norm2 are declared nogil in anticipation of being run in parallel.

The escape function has an extra parameter, n_max, which limits the maximum number of iterations in our while loop. Without it, a point in a Julia set would cause the while loop to iterate forever, as these points *never* escape.

We call escape with fixed c, z_max, and n_max values on every point in the complex plane bounded by the four points $\pm 1.5 \pm 1.5i$. We can specify the resolution to control the number of complex points in this domain.

The complex value c parameterizes a Julia set and completely determines its characteristics. Varying c yields dramatically different Julia sets. A fun fact: if c is a point inside the Mandelbrot set, then its corresponding Julia set is connected and dense. If c is outside the Mandelbrot set, the corresponding Julia set is disconnected and nowhere dense. If c is at the boundary of the Mandelbrot set, the corresponding Julia set is fractal-like.

Let's define a function named calc_julia that takes a resolution, a c parameter, and some optional arguments that we pass through to the escape function:

```
def calc_julia(int resolution, double complex c,
               double bound=1.5, double z_max=4.0, int n_max=1000):
    # ...
```

First, we need to declare internal variables and the output array, named `counts`:

```
def calc_julia(...):
    cdef:
        double step = 2.0 * bound / resolution
        int i, j
        double complex z
        double real, imag
        int[:, ::1] counts
    counts = np.zeros((resolution+1, resolution+1), dtype=np.int32)
    # ...
```

Because we touch every point in the two-dimensional domain, nested `for` loops work well:

```
def calc_julia(...):
    # ...
    for i in range(resolution + 1):
        real = -bound + i * step
        for j in range(resolution + 1):
            imag = -bound + j * step
            z = real + imag * 1j
            counts[i,j] = escape(z, c, z_max, n_max)

    return np.asarray(counts)
```

Each loop iterates through the values 0 through `resolution`. We use the loop indexing variables `i` and `j` to compute the real and imaginary parts of the `z` argument to `escape`. The real work of the loop takes place inside our `escape` function, and we assign its result to `counts[i,j]`.

As we learned in Chapter 10, when looping through an array in this fashion, we can tell Cython to disable both bounds checking and wraparound checking when assigning to `counts[i,j]`:

```
from cython cimport boundscheck, wraparound

@boundscheck(False)
@wraparound(False)
def calc_julia(...):
    # ...
```

To compile our extension module (named *julia.pyx*), we use a `distutils` script named *setup_julia.py*:

```
from distutils.core import setup
from Cython.Build import cythonize
```

```
setup(name="julia",
        ext_modules=cythonize("julia.pyx"))
```

Let's create a test script to call `calc_julia` for an interesting value of `c`:

```
import julia

jl = julia.calc_julia(1000, (0.322 + 0.05j))
```

We can use `matplotlib` to plot our Julia set:

```
import numpy as np
import matplotlib.pyplot as plt

plt.imshow(np.log(jl))
plt.show()
```

Here we compute the logarithm of our Julia set to make the levels more easily distinguishable. We then pass the result to `imshow`, as shown in Figure 12-1.

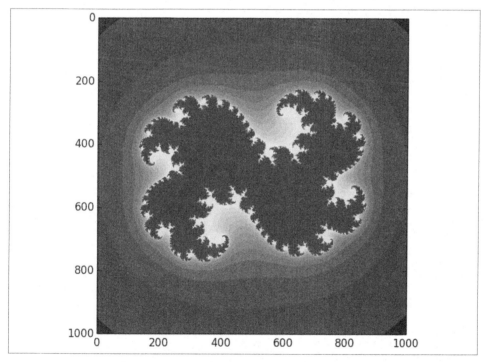

Figure 12-1. Julia set used for parallel computation

Performance-wise, it takes about 1.4 seconds to compute this Julia set on a domain with a resolution of 1,000 × 1,000 points.

Using prange

Upon inspection, it is clear that the escape computation does not depend on any previous loop iteration. This makes our loop an ideal candidate for parallelization, because each loop iteration is independent of all others.

As mentioned earlier, we first need to cimport prange from cython.parallel:

```
from cython.parallel cimport prange
```

Using prange is simple, provided we have already taken the necessary steps to ensure no Python objects are used inside the loop body. First we place the loop inside a with nogil block, and convert our outer loop's range call to prange:

```
def calc_julia(...):
    # ...
    with nogil:
        for i in prange(resolution + 1):
            real = -bound + i * step
            for j in range(resolution + 1):
                # ...
    # ...
```

This pattern is so common that prange has a nogil keyword argument that is equivalent to the preceding example:

```
def calc_julia(...):
    # ...
    for i in prange(resolution + 1, nogil=True):
        real = -bound + i * step
        for j in range(resolution + 1):
            # ...
```

Once we use prange, we must ensure that we compile with OpenMP enabled. The standard compilation and linking flag to give compilers like gcc is -fopenmp. We can add a compiler directive comment at the top of *julia.pyx*:

```
# distutils: extra_compile_args = -fopenmp
# distutils: extra_link_args = -fopenmp
```

When rerunning the distutils script from the command line, ensure that the -fopenmp flag is included in the compilation and linking commands:

```
$ python setup_julia.py build_ext -i
Compiling julia.pyx because it changed.
Cythonizing julia.pyx
running build_ext
building 'julia' extension
gcc -fno-strict-aliasing -fno-common -dynamic -g -O2
    -DNDEBUG -g -fwrapv -O3 -Wall -Wstrict-prototypes
    -I[...] -c julia.c -o [...]/julia.o -fopenmp
gcc -bundle -undefined dynamic_lookup
    [...]/julia.o -o [...]/julia.so -fopenmp
```

After taking these steps, we can run our test script as before, but this time the compiler enables threads when running the nested for loops, using all CPUs on our system to speed up execution. When we use this version of *calc_julia* and enable OpenMP, the runtime on an eight-core system improves to about 0.47 seconds, or a factor of three faster than the serial version. Not bad for a small amount of setup and an entirely trivial change to the source code. But we can do better: there are reasons why we are not utilizing more of the parallelism at our disposal.

prange Options

When prange is used with default parameters, it divides the loop range into equal-sized contiguous chunks, giving one chunk to each available thread. This strategy is bad for computing a Julia set: all points in red in Figure 12-1 (the fractal-like shape at the center for anyone reading in black and white) are in the set and maximize the number of loop iterations inside escape. The blue points (the outer area surrounding the fractal shape) are not in the set and require many fewer iterations. The unlucky threads assigned to the middle region get a chunk of the complex plane that contains many Julia set points, so these threads do the bulk of the work. What we want is to partition the work more evenly, or, in prange (and OpenMP) parlance, use a different chunksize, and possibly a different schedule.

Let's try using a static schedule with prange and give it a chunksize of 1. This assigns rows of the counts array to threads in a round-robin, or *cyclic*, fashion:

```
def calc_julia(...):
    # ...
    for i in prange(resolution + 1, nogil=True,
                    schedule='static', chunksize=1):
        # ...
```

With this modification, our runtime decreases to 0.26 seconds, about 5.5 times faster than the range-only version. Again, a nice payoff for a trivial change.

As indicated in the following list, there are other schedules besides static. Their behaviors allow control over different aspects of the threaded computation. The options are:

static

Iterations are assigned to threads in a fixed way at compile time. If chunksize is not given, the iterations are distributed in num_threads contiguous blocks, one block per thread. If chunksize is given, each chunk is assigned to threads in a round-robin fashion. This is best when the work is evenly distributed and generally known ahead of time.

dynamic

> Threads ask the scheduler for the next chunk dynamically at runtime. The `chunksize` defaults to 1. A `dynamic` schedule is best when the workload is unevenly distributed and unknown ahead of time.

guided

> Chunks are distributed dynamically, like with `dynamic`. Unlike with `dynamic`, the `chunksize` is not fixed but rather is proportional to the remaining iterations divided by the number of threads.

runtime

> The schedule and chunksize are determined by either the `openmp.openmp_set_schedule` function or the `OMP_SCHEDULE` environment variable at runtime. This allows exploration of different `schedules` and `chunksizes` without recompiling, but may have poorer performance overall as no compile-time optimizations are possible.

> Controlling the `schedule` and `chunksize` allows easy exploration of different parallel execution strategies and workload assignments. Typically `static` with a tuned `chunksize` is a good first approach; `dynamic` and `guided` incur runtime overhead and are appropriate in dynamically changing execution contexts. The `runtime` schedule provides maximum flexibility among all other `schedule` types.

We can use `prange` with `start`, `stop`, and `step` arguments, like `range`. In addition to the `nogil`, `schedule`, and `chunksize` optional arguments, `prange` also accepts a `num_threads` argument to control the number of threads to use during execution. If `num_threads` is not provided, `prange` uses as many threads as there are CPU cores available.

A performance boost of 5.5 for minor modifications to our Cython code is a nice result. This performance boost is multiplicative with the performance enhancements Cython already provides over pure Python.

Using prange for Reductions

Often we want to loop over an array and compute a scalar sum or product of values. For instance, suppose we want to compute the area fraction of our complex domain that is inside a Julia set. We can approximate this fraction by summing the number of points in the `counts` array that equal `n_max` and dividing by the total number of points. This gives us an opportunity to see how `prange` can speed up reduction operations, too.

Let's call our function `julia_fraction`. It takes a typed memoryview for the `counts` array and a `maxval` argument, by default equal to `n_max`:

```
@boundscheck(False)
@wraparound(False)
def julia_fraction(int[:,::1] counts, int maxval=1000):
    # ...
```

Our `julia_fraction` function needs to count up the number of `n_max` elements of our set, which we store in the `total` variable. We need the usual loop indexing variables as well:

```
def julia_fraction(...):
    cdef:
        int total = 0
        int i, j, N, M
    N = counts.shape[0]; M = counts.shape[1]
    # ...
```

The core of our computation is, again, nested `for` loops. Once we compute the cardinality, we return it divided by the `size` of the `counts` array:

```
def julia_fraction(...):
    # ...
    for i in range(N):
        for j in range(M):
            if counts[i,j] == maxval:
                total += 1
    return total / float(counts.size)
```

When running this serial version of `julia_fraction` for a Julia set with `c = 0.322 + 0.05j`, we get an area fraction of about 0.24. Because we normalize by the total number of points in the complex domain, this fraction is independent of resolution. For a complex plane with a resolution of 4,000 × 4,000 points, it requires about 14 milliseconds to run.

Let's substitute `prange` for `range` in the outer loop:

```
def julia_fraction(...):
    # ...
    for i in prange(N, nogil=True):
        # ...
    return total / float(counts.size)
```

With this trivial modification, runtime decreases to about 4 ms, an improvement of about a factor of 3.5. We can play with the `schedule` and `chunksize` as before, but they do not measurably affect performance. This may be related to the fact that this computation is likely memory bound and not CPU bound, so we cannot expect perfect speedup.

The generated code for this example uses OpenMP's reduction features to parallelize the in-place addition. Because addition is commutative (i.e., the result is the same regardless of the order of the arguments), additive reductions can be automatically parallelized. Cython (via OpenMP) generates threaded code such that each thread computes the sum for a subset of the loop indices, and then all threads combine their individual sums into the resulting total. The nice part is that we just have to change range to prange to see the performance boost.

For the record, the equivalent NumPy operation is:

```
frac = np.sum(counts == maxval) / float(counts.size)
```

It yields an identical result but takes approximately nine times longer to compute than the prange version.

Interestingly, if we nudge the c value to 0.326 + 0.05j, the area fraction drops to 0.0. This is consistent with the Julia set for this value of c, which is disconnected and nowhere dense.

Parallel Programming Pointers and Pitfalls

Cython's prange is easy to use, but as we see when computing the area fraction, prange provides a speedup of only 3.5, which is noticeably less than the speedup of 5.5 when we use prange to compute the corresponding Julia set. This boost is still far from perfect scaling on an eight-core system. We are glad for the extra performance boost, but in general it is very difficult to achieve perfect scaling, even when we have an embarrassingly parallel CPU-bound computation. This is true independent of using Cython: achieving ideal parallel scaling is just plain hard.

To better illustrate why perfect utilization is often elusive, consider a typical stencil operation like a five-point nearest-neighbor averaging filter on a two-dimensional C-contiguous array. The core computation is conceptually straightforward—for a given row and column index, add up the array elements nearby and assign the average to an output array:

```
def filter(...):
    # ...
    for i in range(nrows):
        for j in range(ncols):
            b[i,j] = (a[i,j] + a[i-1,j] + a[i+1,j] +
                          a[i,j-1] + a[i,j+1]) / 5.0
```

We can replace the outer range with prange, as we did with the Julia set computations. But for this straightforward implementation, performance is *worse*, not better, with prange. Part of the reason is that the loop body primarily accesses noncontiguous array elements. Because of the lack of locality, the CPU's cache cannot be as effective.

Besides nonlocality, there are other factors at play that conspire to slow down `prange` or any other naive thread-based implementation of the preceding loop.

There are some rules of thumb for using `prange`:

- `prange` works well with embarrassingly parallel CPU-bound operations.
- Memory-bound operations with many nonlocal reads and writes can be challenging to speed up.
- It is easier to achieve linear speedup with fewer threads.
- Using an optimized thread-parallel library is often the best way to use all cores for common operations.

With these warnings in mind, it is nevertheless useful to have `prange` at our disposal, especially given its ease of use. So long as our loop body does not interact with Python objects, using `prange` is nearly trivial.

Summary

Cython allows us to circumvent CPython's global interpreter lock, so long as we cleanly separate our Python-interacting code from our Python-independent code. After doing so, we can easily access thread-based parallelism via Cython's built-in `prange`.

We saw in this chapter how `prange` can provide extra performance boosts for loop-centric operations, and how `prange` provides control over how work is assigned to threads. Thread-based parallelism in other languages is error prone and can be very challenging to get right. Cython's `prange` makes it straightforward and comparatively easy to enable threads for many performance bottlenecks.

## CHAPTER 13

Cython in Context

> *The most important thing in the programming language is the name.*
> *A language will not succeed without a good name. I have recently invented*
> *a very good name and now I am looking for a suitable language.*
>
> — D. Knuth

In this last chapter, now that we have invested blood, sweat, and carpal tunnel syndrome in learning the depth and breadth of the Cython language, it is worthwhile to consider Cython in relation to other projects. As we have seen, Cython does many things well: it brings optional static typing to the Python language, it compiles Python to C, and it enables easy interoperability between Python, C, and C++. The greater Python world is diverse, and it is no surprise that many projects—new and old— overlap with Cython in some way. How does Cython match up, and what makes it relevant in the midst of these other options? When embarking on a new Python project, why should we use Cython?

Cython Versus Project X

Several Python projects fall under the category of "Python compiler." Each translates Python to another language (typically a lower-level natively compiled language) for some benefit. Some, like Cython, target C or C++; others target JavaScript; still others LLVM IR. Some are traditional in that they work ahead of time, while others are just-in-time compilers.

Cython's predecessor, Pyrex, is firmly in the traditional ahead-of-time compiler camp, and Cython inherits much of its design. But Cython has extended to acquire just-in-time compilation features, as we saw in Chapter 2.

The Cython core developers have discussed generalizing Cython to target other backend languages, but C and C++ are and will be Cython's primary targets.

Cython's close ties to C and C++ come with many advantages:

- C and C++ are extremely well established languages with many high-quality free and commercial compilers, and these compilers have benefited from several *decades* of optimization effort to generate very efficient binaries.

- C and C++ (and, in HPC contexts, Fortran) are the go-to languages as soon as performance is an important consideration, meaning many existing high-performance libraries are written in these languages.

- C and C++ are still actively growing and evolving; both languages have had recently updated standards to incorporate new features and expanded standard libraries.

C and C++, as a rule, choose control and performance over safety and ease of use. For instance, neither language provides automatic garbage collection (although there are ways to approach that via C++ smart pointers). By providing a Python-like language that is compiled to C and C++, Cython simplifies the task of programming in and with these languages.

Other Ahead-of-Time Compilers for Python

Three other ahead-of-time Python compiler projects are worth noting:

Nuitka
Nuitka (*http://nuitka.net/*) is a more recent Python-to-C++ compiler that supports all Python constructs from 2.7 through 3.3. One of its main focuses is on automatically compiling an entire Python application into a binary executable or extension module. It has future plans for automatic type inference, `ctypes` integration, and some way to inform Nuitka of type information it cannot determine unaided.

Shedskin
Shedskin (*https://code.google.com/p/shedskin/*) is an experimental Python-to-C++ compiler that compiles to a standalone binary without any CPython dependencies. It places some restrictions on the Python it can compile—reassigning a variable to an object with a different type is not allowed. This restriction allows Shedskin to use sophisticated type inference to determine the C++ type of a variable. Like Nuitka, it works with pure Python and therefore does not support static typing, but its type inference mitigates this to some extent. It does not support calling out to external C++ code, however.

Pythran
Like Shedskin, Pythran (*http://pythonhosted.org/pythran/*) is a Python-to-C++ compiler for a subset of the Python language. Like Cython, Pythran provides a way

to add type information to Python code via inline comments to help it generate more efficient C++. It also has features to make use of SIMD instructions and automatic parallelization over multiple cores. It is firmly in the scientific computing camp, and focuses its optimizations there. It has some support for NumPy arrays, but not quite as much as Cython. It does not support interfacing with external libraries.

Each of these projects provides a way to automatically generate C or C++ source from Python code and automatically compile an extension module. None goes as far as Cython does by extending the Python language, preferring instead to maintain pure-Python compatibility. None has the longevity, widespread user base, or breadth of Cython. In particular, all ignore interfacing existing C and C++ code with Python, which is one of Cython's major strengths.

Python Wrapper Projects

As discussed in Chapters 7 and 8, Cython has first-class support for interfacing Python with external C and C++ libraries. When combined with the rest of the Cython language—particularly its static typing features—this support makes Cython a powerful tool to provide highly optimized wrappers.

Several standalone projects automate the process of generating Python bindings for C and C++. The best-known projects in this space are SWIG and Boost.Python:

SWIG

SWIG (*http://swig.org/*) is the king of the hill with regard to automatically wrapping C and C++. It has been around since the 1990s, can generate wrapper code for *20* different target languages—both mainstream and obscure—and offers sophisticated customization features to the end user via typemaps. For all its strengths, it can be difficult to use for advanced needs. Cython cannot hold a candle to SWIG's full breadth of wrapping prowess. But Cython does have strengths when compared to SWIG: because Cython focuses specifically on Python, its wrappers are better optimized and have less runtime overhead when compared to SWIG's. Also, because Cython provides a full Python-like language to help wrap external code, it can be easier to use in advanced cases. SWIG automates the wrapping process almost entirely, and is therefore easier to use than Cython to wrap large libraries. If users require extensive customization when wrapping a library, however, the advantage of SWIG over Cython is less clear.

Boost.Python

The Boost project has the Boost.Python (*http://bit.ly/boost_lib*) library to enable easy interoperability between C++ and Python. It uses sophisticated C++ template metaprogramming to generate Python wrappers for C++ libraries. As with Cython (and unlike with SWIG), each C++ class, function, and method must be specified separately to be wrapped. To help with this, it provides high-level C++ constructs to help in the wrapping effort. Boost.Python also provides features to allow the direct manipulation of Python objects in C++ in a high-level way.

There are several other wrapping tools for Python, but SWIG and Boost.Python are the main contenders. Neither can compile existing Python code to C or C++, so they lack what Cython provides there. Each can be thought of as providing an interfacing *domain-specific language* to control how the wrappers are generated. Cython, in comparison, has features to describe the external interface, but uses the full Python and Cython languages to accomplish the interfacing.

To further narrow the gap, an up-and-coming project named XDress (*http://xdress.org/index.html*) automatically generates Cython wrappers for C and C++ libraries, making Cython easier to use for large C- and C++- wrapping projects.

Just-in-Time Compilers for Python

At the other end of the spectrum are the just-in-time (JIT) Python compilers. These stress ease of use and automatic compilation at runtime, with very little user input required. Python JITs are a very active area of development, especially since the advent of the LLVM project (*http://llvm.org/*).

Some of the more widely known Python JITs are:

PyPy
PyPy (*http://pypy.org/*) is the oldest Python JIT compilation project in widespread use. It offers ease of use and improved performance for unmodified Python code. It can yield nice speedups for certain classes of operations, particularly operations on built-in Python containers. PyPy does not offer the same level of control that Cython provides—PyPy does what it does, and if the speedup is not satisfactory, there is little that can be done. Cython, in contrast, often requires more effort to provide static type information, but it also allows the end user to try many different approaches, moving more code into C or C++ to improve performance. PyPy's extension module support—including NumPy, SciPy, and the like—has traditionally been its greatest weakness, although efforts are under way to address this. Because Cython merges Python and C, and because generating extensions is its *modus operandi*, it is in a much better position when it comes to interfacing.

Numba
Numba (*http://numba.pydata.org/*) is an LLVM-based JIT compiler that is focused on speeding up array-oriented and math-heavy Python code. Like all JIT compilers, it provides this speedup automatically from within a single code base, so it is easier to use than Cython in this respect. Cython can achieve nice speedups for this same subset of operations, but it requires some static type information to help the cython compiler generate efficient code. On the other hand, Cython's ability to speed up non-numeric Python code (using the built-in containers and non-numeric data

types) allows Cython to speed up general Python code that is not Numba's primary focus.

Pyston

Pyston (*https://github.com/dropbox/pyston*) is another Python JIT compiler project, currently in its infancy, that aims to speed up general Python code, like PyPy. It takes a different approach than PyPy, however, and like Numba, it is based on the LLVM project. From the outset it aims to support interoperability with CPython extension modules.

In general, Cython is not as easy to use as JIT compilers, given that it typically relies on inline static type declarations to generate efficient code. (The pyximport package and the %%cython magic support in IPython do provide some degree of automatic compilation for Cython code, making Cython easier to explore.)

On the other hand, because JIT compilers stress ease of use and work with pure-Python code, they do not provide the same level of control that a hybrid language like Cython does. Cython allows the user to determine where on the Python-to-C spectrum to implement an algorithm; because of this, it is often possible to achieve better performance by pushing more code into C or C++. Cython also provides code annotations to help indicate where code is likely to be inefficient. When we are using a JIT compiler, it is up to the compiler implementation to provide all optimizations. If the performance is not satisfactory, then end users have little at their disposal to remedy the situation.

Cython also does not place any runtime dependencies on end users (other than the Python runtime itself). This is in contrast to JIT compilers, which require the JIT compiler infrastructure at runtime. Because Cython generates a standalone C or C++ source file, a package developer can distribute just these generated files (or precompiled binaries) to end users. The extension module requires only the Python runtime and any wrapped library components; Cython itself is not required when we are running a Cython-generated extension module.

Summary

Cython is difficult to categorize succinctly: it is an ahead-of-time compiler, but the pyximport package and %%cython IPython magic (Chapter 2) introduce aspects of just-in-time compilers. Cython has powerful features to call into external C and C++ libraries, making it competitive with specialized binding generator projects like SWIG and Boost.Python. Perhaps the best way to think of Cython is in the name itself: it fluidly blends C and C++ with Python. It combines capabilities from all the major topics covered in this chapter, and it does so in such a way that all components work well with one another.

The open source Python world has widely adopted Cython, for good reason: it has demonstrated its breadth and depth of features time and again in this competitive environment, where life and death are based on technical merit and overall value. Large and widely used projects such as Sage, Pandas, scikits-learn, scikits-image, and lxml use Cython to provide highly optimized algorithms for all of their performance-critical components. Projects such as MPI4Py, PETSc4Py, and (again) Sage use Cython for its powerful wrapping features. Cython is also used pervasively in research and closed source projects where performance improvements and interfacing Python with C or C++ are necessary.

With this one multifaceted tool in hand, we can confidently bring Python's dynamism to C and C++, and bring the performance of C and C++ to Python.

Index

Symbols

% (percent sign), % or %%, preceding magic commands, 19

& (ampersand), address-of operator, 38

* (asterisk)
  ** operator, 76
  in pointers, 38

+ (plus sign), addition operator, 94

-> (arrow operator), accessing struct member in a pointer to a struct, 39

. (dot)
  accessing nonpointer struct variable or pointer to a struct, 39
  using dot operator on C or C++ pointer, 143

< >, Cython casting operator, 90

A

*a syntax to dereference pointers, Cython and, 38

__add__ method, 94

annotations, 164
  def and cpdef functions, 169
  examples, 165, 168, 169, 198

api keyword, 127

arguments (function)
  cpdef functions, 51
  mixing dynamically and statically typed in Cython, 48

arithmetic operations, Python versus C semantics, 6, 42

arithmetic special methods, 94

array.array type, 140, 173
  creating million-element array to test typed memoryview, 177
  working with typed memoryviews, 199

arrays, 171
  assignment to typed memoryviews, 181, 187
  creating NumPy array to test typed memoryview, 177
  in ctypes package, 173
  NumPy, 172
    memoryview from empty array, 175
    memoryview of multidimensional array, 174
  typed memoryviews acquiring buffers from, 181
  types implementing new buffer protocol, 172
  using NumPy arrays to manage data, 192
  viewing a C array with a memoryview, 187
  wrapping C and C++ arrays in Cython, 189
    correct memory management with, 189

arrow operator (->), accessing struct member in pointer to a struct, 39

assignment
  assigning struct fields, 57
  dynamically typed variables in Cython, 34
  statically typed variables and, 35

We'd like to hear your suggestions for improving our indexes. Send email to index@oreilly.com.

automatic memory management, 45

B

basestring type, 66
Behnel, Stefan, 9
bint type, 40
bool type, 40
Boost C++ library, 155
Boost.Python, 217
bounds checking, turning off, 28, 178, 200
boundscheck compiler directive, 178
Bradshaw, Robert, 9
buffers
    acquisition by typed memoryviews, 180, 183
    original buffer syntax in Cython, 186
        benefits of typed memoryviews over, 186
    power of new buffer protocol, 172
        memoryview type, 173
    Python buffers and new buffer protocol, 172
build systems, 26
    CMake and Cython, 26
    make-based, using with Cython, 26
    SCons and Cython, 26
builtin_function_or_method type, 48
bytearray type, 173
    memoryview of, 174
bytecodes, 31
bytes type, 41
    memoryview of a bytes object, 174
    no differences in Python versions, 66
    support for new buffer protocol, 173

C

C-contiguous typed memoryviews, 180, 186
    declaring, 181
C/C++
    arithmetic operations, 42
    arrays, wrapping in Cython, 189
        correct memory management with, 189
    C standard library (libc), Cython declaration
        for, 107
    C++ standard library (libcpp), Cython dec-
        laration for, 107
    C-level initialization and finalization for ex-
        tension types, 85
    cdef declarations for common types, 36
    code generated by cython compiler, 54
    code, wrapping with Cython, 8

common C++ STL containers, definition
    file, 107
comparing C with Python and Cython per-
    formance, 2
compilation, 11
compiled code, 32
compilers, 13
converting Python data structures to structs,
    73
Cython and, 1
Cython's close ties to, advantages of, 216
dynamically allocated arrays, 189
efficiency of code, Cython versus pure C
    equivalent, 5
efficiency of compiled programs at runtime,
    33
exposing Cython code to C, 126
external functions wrapped in Cython, de-
    claring as nogil, 203
functions, 46
header files, similarities of definition files to,
    109
inline keyword, 51
prerequisite knowledge for Cython, xii
Python wrapper projects, 217
spectral norm implementation, comparing
    to Cython, 200
static typing, 32
type coercion and casting, 55
type correspondence with Python types, 40
wrapping C libraries with Cython, 115–134
    constants, other modifiers, and control-
        ling what Cython generates, 125
    declaring and wrapping structs, unions,
        and enums, 119
    declaring external C code in Cython, 115
    declaring external C functions and type-
        defs, 118
    error checking and raising exceptions,
        128
    wrapping functions, 121
    wrapping structs with extension types,
        122
wrapping C++ libraries with Cython, 135–
    157
    exceptions, 144
    memory management, RAII, and smart
        pointers, 154

simple example, MT_RNG class, 135–144

stack and heap allocation of C++ instances, 145

templates, 147–154

working with C++ class hierarchies, 146

__call__ method, 143

callbacks

and exception propagation, 133

using except clause with cdef callbacks, 128

casting

and subclasses, 90

in Cython, 55

using checked casting operator, 56

memoryview casting syntax, assigning array to a memoryview, 188

cdef keyword

api keyword with, 127

C functions in Cython defined with, 49

exception handling and, 51

cdef class statement, 81

cdef cppclass block, 143

cdef extern blocks in definition file, 106

cdef extern from declarations, 118

cdef extern statement

C++ namespaces and, 137

namespace clause, 136

declaring instance attributes in extension type, 82

defining enums with, 58

defining extension type methods, 86

defining function pair to convert between Python and C data types, 73

defining function with nogil attribute, 202

functions defined with, no Python function call overhead, 169

public keyword used with, 126

readonly declaration of instance attributes in extension type, 83

static type declaration with, 34

C pointers in Cython, 37

declarations for common C types, 36

declaring struct variables in Cython, 120

mixing static and dynamic variables, 39

Python types, 41

struct and union declarations, 57

@cdivision decorator, 198

chained comparisons, 98

char * type, 40, 41

conversion to unicode object, 66

checked casting operator, 56, 91

cimport statement, 101, 105

cimporting from cython namespace, 38

for Cython definition file in Python package, 111

importing definition file, 106

multiple named cimports, 108

providing alias to definition file and declarations, 106

Python-level objects and, 106

using cimport and import for namespace-like object having same name, 108

using cimport and import with different functions with same name, 108

using instead of include, 110

using with a module in a package, 108

using with an alias, 108

using with an object from a dotted module name, 108

using with C++ STL template classes, 108

__cinit__ method, 85, 123, 137

classes (Python)

attribute access, 83

comparing with extension types, 79

converting to extension types in Cython, 80

classmethod constructor, 85

CMake build system, 26

code annotation, 165

code examples from this book, xv

repository, 2

code, organizing (see Cython, organizing code)

command line

Cython standalone executables, running from, 27

setting compiler directives with --directive or -X option, 28

comments, directive, 28

comparison special methods, 96

compiled versus interpreted languages, 11

compiler directives, 28

boundscheck and wraparound, 178

cdivision, 42, 169

cdivision_warnings, 43

comprehensive list of, 29

c_string_type, 66

c_string_type and c_string_encoding, 41

embedsignature, 53

in directive comments, 28
infer_types, 37
nonecheck, 92
overflowcheck and overflowcheck.fold, 40
profile, enabling globally in Cython module, 163
setting from command line, 28
using for distutils script to compile C++, 139
compilers
C or C++ compiler support, for OpenMP, 204
compiling with OpenMP enabled, 208
cython and C/C++, 13
just-in-time (JIT) Python compilers, 218
Windows, 17
compiling Cython, 11–29
C functions wrapped in Cython, 121
C++ project, 138
C/C++ compiler, 13
compilation pipeline, 12
C/C++ code, compiling into shared library, 12
transforming Cython source into C or C++, 12
distributable compiled package, 113
extension type into extension module, 123
interactive Cython with IPython, 19
manually, 24
on-the-fly with pyximport, 21–24
options, 11
using Cython with other build systems, 26
CMake, 26
make-based systems, 26
SCons, 26
using distutils and cythonize, 14
distutils on Mac OS X and Linux, 15
distutils on Windows, 16
setup.py distutils script, 15
complex types, 41
computer language benchmarks game, 69, 193
conditional compilation, 64
conjugate method, 41
const keyword (in C), 36
constants, 125
DEF constants in Cython, 63
constructors (Python), 85
containers
C++, conversions to and from Python analogues, 152

Cython support for built-in containers, 171
looping over, 62
context manager
compiler directives, setting, 29
nogil, 203
turning off bounds and wraparound checking, 178
contiguous data packing, typed memoryviews, 180
cpdef keyword
cpdef function example, 111
Cython-compiled functions, injecting Python signature, 53
defining extension type methods, 86
defining functions with, 50
exception handling and, 51
limitations of, 51
cppclass keyword, 136
cProfile module, 159
run call, using to profile integrate function, 160
CPython
and relation to Cython, 2
automatic memory management, 45
python-config utility, 26
cpython declaration package, 107
cpython.array, 177
ctypedef keyword, 118
combining struct and union declarations with, 57
declaring C struct, 123
declaring C structs, unions, and enums, 120
declaring typedefs in Cython, 118
fused statement, 60
type aliasing with, 59
ctypes package, arrays in, 173
Cython
adoption of, 67
use in data analysis and scientific computing, 68
array features, 171
power of new buffer protocol, 172
support for Python buffer protocol and NumPy arrays, 172
bridging Python 2 and Python 3 divide, 64–67
strings and string types, 66
bringing static typing to a dynamic language, 34

C pointers in, 37
cdef keyword, static type declaration with, 34
comparing with Python and C performance, 2
    pure-C code, 5
    reasons for Cython performance improvements, 5
compilation, 11
concerns over C type limitations, 7
Cython-only features, 9
declarations and definitions, 104
declaring and using structs, unions, and enums, 56
example, converting Python N-body simulator code to, 71–77
exposing Cython code to C, 126
extension types (see extension types)
for loops and while loops, 61
    example, 62
    guidelines for efficient loops, 61
functions
    C functions defined with cdef, 49
    defining with cpdef, 50
    embedsignature compiler directive, 53
    exception handling, 51
    kinds of, 46
    Python functions defined with def keyword, 46
fused types and generic programming, 59
in context, 215–220
    Cython versus Project X, 215
    just-in-time (JIT) Python compilers, 218
    other ahead-of-time compilers for Python, 216
    Python wrapper projects, 217
installing, 14
interfacing with external code, 7
memoryviews and buffers, 175
OpenMP and, 204
organizing code, 101–113
    cimport statement, 105–109
    compiling Cython modules in Python packages, 110–113
    implementation (.pyx) and declaration (.pxd) files, 102
    include files and include statement, 109
origins of, 9
preprocessor, 63
stack and heap allocated C++ objects in, 146

standalone executables, 27
static typing for speed, 43
statically declarable Python types, built-in, 44
support for full range of C declarations, 36
type inference, automatic, 36
versus CPython, 2
why it speeds up Python code so well, 31
wrapping C code with, 8
wrapping C libraries with, 115–134
cython compiler, 1
    --annotate flag, 165
    --directives flag, 179
    --embed flag, 27
    -2 and -3 flags, 65
    called by distutils setup.py script on Mac OS X, 16
    generated C code, 54
    generating and compiling C/C++ code, 24
    options, 24
%%cython magic command, 20
Cython.Build package, 113
cython.floating fused type, 183
cython.operator.dereference operator, 38
cython.operators magic module, 142
@cython.profile(True) decorator, 163
cythonize command, 15, 15
    compiling Cython modules in Python package, 113

D

data structures (Python), 72
    converting to structs, 73
__dealloc__ method, 86, 123, 138
declarations, 104
    Cython support for full range of C declarations, 119
    extern block, 115
def keyword
    Cython-compiled functions, injecting Python signature, 53
    for C functions wrapped in Cython, 121
    Python functions in Cython defined with, 46
        exception handling and, 51
    returning a typed memoryview from a def function, 189
    wrapping a cdef function in a def function, 50
DEF keyword, 63

definition (.pxd) files, 101
    cdef extern blocks in, 106
    cimporting, 106
    contents of, 104
    created from Python modules converted to Cython, 111
    excluded content, 105
    for C++ container classes, 151
    only C-level declarations in, 103
    predefined, for Cython, 107
    simulator.pxd (example), 103
definitions, 104
__del__ method, 94
delete operator (C++), 138
dependencies
    build systems and, 27
    managing with pyximport, 22
    pyximport example with external dependencies, 23
dereference Cython operator, 143
dereferencing pointers, 38
dimensions (typed memoryviews), 180
direct or indirect access, typed memoryviews, 180
directive comments, 28
distutils, 14
    compiling N-body code using setup.py script (example), 71
    compiling spectral_norm.pyx (example), 197
    compiling with, on Mac OS X and Linux, 15
    compiling with, on Windows, 16
    compling C++ class wrapped in Cython, 138
    setup.py script for, 15
    using cythonize function with, 113
distutils.sysconfig module, 26
division and modulus operations, C versus Python, 42
-DMS_WIN64 compiler flag, 17
domain-specific language, 218
double complex C-level type (Cython), 41
double type, 44
    conversion between Python float type and, 8
dynamic dispatch, 33
dynamic library (.pyd) files, 12
dynamic typing, 32
    Cython's use of general Python method lookups on dynamically typed objects, 90
    dynamic variables initialized from statically declared Python types, 42
    untyped dynamic variables in Cython, 34
dynamic_particles object (example), 43

E

element type (typed memoryviews), 180
embedsignature compiler directive, 53
enums
    aliases for names in Cython, 125
    declaring and wrapping in Cython, 119
    defining in Cython, 58
__eq__ method, 96
error checking, external C functions wrapped in Cython, 128
Ewing, Greg, 9
except clause, 52, 128
    except *, 53
    except?, 52
    using when declaring cdef callbacks, 133
exception handling
    custom exception handler translating C++ exceptions to Python, 145
    functions and, 51
exceptions
    C++, 144
        bad_alloc exception, converting to Python MemoryError (example), 144
        mapping to Python exceptions, 144
    propagation, callbacks and, 133
    raising Python exception from C function error code, 128
executable binary, compiling with Cython, 27
extension modules, 12, 32
    building and compiling for N-body simulator (example), 72
    compiling extension type wrapping C++ class, 138
    compiling fib.c file into, with cython (example), 25
    distutils Extension objects returned by cythonize, 15
    using, 17
extension types, 79–99
    accessing instance attributes, 83
    C++ smart pointers as attributes in, 156
    C-level initialization and finalization, 85
    cdef and cpdef methods, 86
    comparing with Python classes, 79
    defined, 80
    in Cython, 80

inheritance and subclassing, 89
    casting and subclasses, 90
    extension type objects and None, 91
properties in Cython, 92
special methods, 94
    iterator support, 98
    rich comparisons, 96
    __radd__ method and, 94
wrapping C structs with, 122
wrapping C++ class, 137
    creating and initializing C++ object, 137
    pointer to heap-allocated C++ object, 137
extern block statement, 115
    declaring C struct, 122
    declaring every function as nogil, 203
    declaring external C functions and typedefs,
        118
    misconceptions about, 117
    removing unnecessary C modifiers, 125
extern keyword, bare extern declarations, 116

F

fib function (example)
    C implementation, wrapping in Cython, 8
    converting from Python version to Cython,
        2
    performance, comparing for different imple-
        mentations, 3
finalization, C-level, Cython support through
    __dealloc__ method, 86
finalizer class, 190
    calling __dealloc__ method at cleanup, 192
float complex C-level type (Cython), 41
float type (Python), 44
    conversion between C double and, 8
    converting to C float, 41
floating fused type, 59
floating-point numbers, 6
for loops
    expanded, in annotated integrate (example),
        166
    in annotated integrate with static typing (ex-
        ample), 168
        func argument and, 168
    in Cython, 61–63
        converting to use static types, 74
        ensuring efficiency of, 61
        example, 62
    Python versus compiled languages, 6

    using prange with, 204
format attribute (memoryview), 175
Fortran-contiguous typed memoryviews, 180,
    181
function call overhead, 5
function pointers, 36
function type (Python), 48
functions
    alias for C function name in Cython, 125
    and embedsignaure compiler directive, 53
    C functions in Cython with cdef keyword, 49
        problems with Python objects and C
            types mapping, 50
        restriction on, 49
    C++ templated functions, 148
        rotate, 150
    calling in GIL-less context, nogil attribute,
        202
    declared in definition file, 106
    declaring external C functions in Cython,
        118
    declaring local variables in, with cdef, 35
    def and cdef, combining with cpdef, 50
    def function in Cython with typed memory-
        view argument, 176
    defined in Cython, mixing dynamically and
        statically typed arguments, 48
    enabling type inference for, 37
    exception handler to translate C++ excep-
        tions to Python, 145
    exception handling and, 51
        Cython except clause for cdef or cpdef
            functions, 52
    external C functions wrapped in Cython, er-
        ror checking and raising exceptions, 128
    external C/C++ functions, declaring as no-
        gil, 203
    for defining DEF constants, 64
    overloaded C++ functions, wrapping, 141
    Python, performance gains when compiled
        with Cython, 7
    raising C++ exceptions, 144
    wrapping external C functions in Cython,
        121
        C functions taking function pointer call-
            backs, 128
fused types, 59
    typed memoryviews and, 182
    wrapping C++ templated functions, 148

G

gcc, 13
    calls to, in Mac OS X compilation with distu-
        tils, 16
    instructing to create shared library, 25
__get__ method, 93
get_config_var function, 27
global interpreter lock (GIL), 201
    nogil context manager, 203
    nogil function attribute, 202

H

header files
    often-used, predefined definition files for,
        107
    similarities of definition files to, 109
heap allocation
    C arrays, memoryviews viewing, 189
    of C++ instances, 146
    stack allocation versus, 6

I

identity (objects), 79
IF compile-time statement, 109
IF-ELIF-ELSE statement, 64
imag attribute, 41
implementation files, 101
    converting Python modules into, 111
    definition of all objects in, 104
    importing with cimport statement, 105
    simulator.pyx (example), 102
        breaking up into subcomponents, 103
import statement, 101, 106
    using import and cimport for namespace-
        like objects having same name, 108
    using import and cimport with different
        functions with same name, 108
    using instead of cimport for extension type
        or cpdef function, 106
include files, 101
    C++ STL container classes, 152
    using in platform-independent design, 109
#include preprocessor directive, 109, 117
@include preprocessor directive, 116
include statement, 109
    using cimport instead of, 110
    using twice with same source file, 110

Includes directory, Cython, 107
indexes (typed memoryview), 178
    C- or Fortran-contiguous typed memory-
        views, 181
indexing into a pointer at location 0, 38
infer_types compiler directive, 37
inheritance
    extension classes, 89
    working wih C++ class hierarchies, 146
__init__ method, 85
inline keyword, 51
installing Cython
    source code download and installation, 14
    via packaged software distribution, 14
instance attributes (extension types), 81
    accessing, 83
    making both readable and writeable from
        Python, 84
    not accessible from Python, 82
instance dictionary, 79
int type
    correspondence between Python and C int,
        39
    grouping C ints into dynamic Python tuple,
        39
    Python, 40, 44
        conversion to C int, 8
integers
    integral type conversions and overflow, 40
    Python versus C integral types, 48
integral fused type, 59
    integral_max implementation (example), 59
integrate module
    adding static type information to, 162
    adding static typing to integrate, 167
    annotating integrate without static typing,
        165
    compiling sin2 function, 162
    converting to extension module, 161
    profiling Cythonized version, 161
    profiling pure-Python version, 160
    profiling statically typed version, 162
    writing cdef version of integrate and turning
        on cdivision, 169
integrators, 69
interpreted versus compiled execution, 31
interpreted versus compiled languages, 11
interpreter (Python)
    dynamic dispatch, 33

embedding in Cython-generated source file, 27

initialization by external C code calling into Cython code, 126

IPython
    installation, 14
    interactive Cython with magic commands, 19
    introspection features, providing details about extension module, 17

__iter__ method, 98

iterators
    C++ templates, 150
    extension type special methods for, 98
    iterating through a typed memoryview, 177
    using standard C++ container objects in Cython, 154

J

just-in-time (JIT) Python compilers, 218

L

__le__ method, 96

Linux
    C/C++ compiler, 13
    compiling executable binary with python-config, 27
    compiling with distutils, 15

%load_ext magic command, 19

local variables, declaring in a function with cdef, 35

long type (in C), 44

looping, in Python versus compiled languages, 6

loops
    Cython for loops and while loops, 61
        example, 62
        guidelines for efficient loops, 61
    parallelizing with prange, 204
    Python for loops and while loops, 6

__lt__ method, 96

M

Mac OS X
    C/C++ compiler, 13
    compiling executable binary with python-config, 27
    compiling with distutils, 15

macros, 63
    declaring C macro in Cython, 118

magic commands, 19

magic numbers, 63

main function
    embedding Python interpreter in, 27
    running in nbody extension module (example), 71

make-based build systems, using Cython with, 26

make_ext function, 23

make_setup function, 23

math operations, Python versus C and Cython, 6

memory management
    automatic, in Python and Cython, 45
    C++ shared pointers working wih Python reference counting, 155
    correct, with Cython and C arrays, 189
    smart pointers in C++, 154
    stack versus heap allocation, 6

memory-bound operations, performance and, 7

memoryview type, 173
    attributes querying underlying buffer's metadata, 174
    format strings, 175
    memoryview of immutable bytes object, 174
    memoryview of mutable buffer like bytearray, 174
    modifying mutable memoryview, 174
    slicing with arbitrary start, stop, and step values, 174
    support for structured data types, 175

memoryviews, typed, 176
    C-level access to data, 177
    declaring and controlling attributes, 179
    example of, 176
    fused types and, 182
    returning NumPy array to view C arrays, 189
    trading safety for performance, 178
    using, 183
        original buffer syntax and, 186
        to access and modify NumPy arrays from Cython, 192
        with C-level arrays, 187
        with functions in spectral norm, 198

methods, 79
    calling in extension types, 85
    cdef extension type methods, 86

cpdef extension type methods, 86
defined in cdef class extension types, 83
overloaded C++ methods, wrapping, 140
special, 94
    arithmetic methods, 94
    iterator support, 98
    rich comparisons, 96
mingw compiler, 17
modifiers, C-level, removing in Cython, 125
modules, 101
Cython, organizing and compiling in Python
    packages, 110–113
using cimport with a module in a package,
    108
modulus, computing, C versus Python, 42
more_inference(), 37
msvc compiler flag, 17
mult function, 54
    C code generated by cython compiler, 54

N

N-body simulator (example), 69–77
converting pure Python code to Cython, 71
    converting data structures to structs, 73
    Python data structures and organization,
        72
    running Cythonized version, 75
Python code, 69
namespaces
declaring C++ namespace with Cython
    namespace clause, 136
nested, declaring to Cython, 137
ndim attribute (memoryview), 174
new operator, 137
__next__ method, 98
nogil function attribute, 202
None object, 91
    not None clause in Cython, 92
nonecheck compiler directive, 92
    setting for extension module, 28
Nuitka, 216
NULL pointer (in C), 91
Numba, 218
numeric fused type, 59
NumPy
arrays, 172
    memoryview of multidimensional array,
        174

ascontiguousarray and asfortranarray func-
    tions, 182
ndarray object, 172
structured dtype, 175
numpy declaration package, 107
NumPy/C API, 190
including NumPy headers when compiling,
    191

O

objects (Python), 37, 79
working with in Cython, 44
OpenMP, 204
compiling with OpenMP enabled, 208
operator overloading
in C++, Cython support for, 142
Python syntax for, 143
operators
C++ operators implemented as external
    functions, 144
overloading, support with Cython extension
    types, 94
overflow, integral type conversions and, 40
OverflowError, 40

P

packages, 101
Python, organizing and compiling Cython
    modules in, 110–113
parallel programming with Cython, 201–213
parallel programming pointers and pitfalls,
    212
thread-based parallelism and the global in-
    terpreter lock, 201
    nogil context manager, 203
    nogil function attribute, 202
using prange for reductions, 210
using prange to parallelize loops, 204
    prange options, 209
Pareto principle, 7, 68
particles, 42
appending Particle object to dynamic_parti-
    cles object, 43
performance
Cython N-body simulator versus Python
    version (example), 75
Cython-generated C code versus hand-
    written C, 13

fib function (example), comparing for different implementations, 3
  function call overhead, 5
gains, Python code compiled with Cython, 7
Python versus statically typed compiled languages, 1
pointers
  C pointers in Cython, 37
    dereferencing, 38
    pointers to structs, 39
  dereferencing, 143
  NULL pointer in C, 91
  smart pointers in C++, 154
    declaring smart_ptr template class interface to Cython, 155
  to heap-allocated C++ object in extension type, 137
polymorphism
  in extension types, 89
  using in C++, 147
prange function, 204
  using, 204–213
    guidelines for, 212
preprocessor, 63
print function (C language), wrapping in Cython, 125
profile compiler directive, 163
profile module, 159
profiling examples
  Cythonized version of spectral norm, 197
  pure-Python N-body simulator code, 71
profiling tools, 159–170
  performance profiling and annotations, 164–170
  runtime profiling, 159–164
    Cythonized version of integrate, 161
    enabling profile compiler directive globally in extension module, 163
    imported functions and, 163
    selectively profiling functions, 163
  using annotations and runtime profiling together, 170
projects using Cython, 67
properties
  extension type, in Cython, 92
  in Python, 92
property function, 92
public keyword, adding to C-level type variable, or function declared with cdef, 126

pure-Python mode (Cython), 12
.pxd files, 101
.pxi files, 101
.py files, 102
PyArrayObject, base attribute, 190
PyArray_SetBaseObject function, 190
.pyd files, 12
PyIntObject, 44
PyList_Append function, 43, 56
PyList_SET_ITEM function, 43, 56
PyLongObject, 44
PyNumber_Multiply function, 54
PyObject_Call function, 43
PyObject_GetAttr function, 43
PyPy, 218
Pyrex, 9, 215
Pyston, 219
Python
  arithmetic operations, 42
  calling cdef function defined in Cython, 50
  classes, comparing with extension types, 79
  comparing with C and Cython performance, 2
  correspondences of types with C/C++ types, 40
  Cython code in pure-Python mode, 12
  differences from C-like languages, 1
  distutils package, 14
  dynamic typing, 32
  foundational projects, Cython use in, 67
  functions, 46
  implementations in other languages, Cython versus, 2
  integral types, conversions to C and overflow, 40
  N-body simulator code (example), 69
    data structures and organization, 72
  performance gains when compiled with Cython, limitations of, 7
  prerequisite knowledge for Cython, xii
  properties in, 92
  types, statically declaring variables with, 41
  using Cython wrapper for C++ class, 139
  versions, Python 2 and Python 3, 64–67
    strings and string types, 66
  wrapper for C implementation of fib function (example), 8
  wrapping in C, 126
Python Imaging Library (PIL), 173

python-config utility, 25, 26
    compiling executable binary on Mac OS X
        or Linux, 27
Python/C API, 2
    calling into, versus equivalent operation in
        straight-C code, 164
    implementation of built-in types, 79
Pythran, 216
.pyx files, 101
.pyxbld file extension, 22, 139
.pyxdeps file extension, 22
pyximport, 21
    compiling and importing Cython code, 22
    compiling Cython source into extension
        modules in Python package, 112
    compiling extension module from wrapped
        C++ class, 139
    controlling and managing dependencies, 22
    example with external dependencies, 23
py_fact function (example), 46
    accessing and using fact.py_fact, 47
    defining pure-Python version, 47
    putting in fact.pyx file and compiling, 47
    two versions, comparing, 47

Q

qsort C function (example), wrapping in Cy-
    thon, 128

R

__radd__ method, 94
real and imag attributes, 41
reductions, using prange for, 210
reference counting, 45
    support by shared_ptr smart pointer, 154
%reset magic command, 192
return types
    cdef functions, 49
    cpdef functions, 51
__richcmp__ method, 96
rotate templated function (C++), 150
%run magic command, 160
runtime language version, 65

S

Sage project, 9
SCons build system, 26

SDK C/ C++ compiler, Windows, 17
__set__ method, 93
setup.py script, 15
    build_ext subcommand, 16
    invoking from command line on Mac OS X
        or Linux, 15
shape attribute (memoryview), 174
shared-object (.so) files, 12
shared_ptr smart pointer, 154
Shedskin, 216
signature (function), 53
    injecting compiled function's Python signa-
        ture with embedsignature, 53
sin2 function (example), 160
    compiling in Cython, 162
    using C library sin instead of Python
        math.sin, 163
source files, Cython file types, 101
source language version, 65
special methods (see methods, special)
spectral norm (example), 193–200
    comparing Cython's performance to C im-
        plementation, 200
    Cythonizing the code, 197
        adding static type information, 198
        compiling and running Cythonized ver-
            sion, 197
        creating main.py driver script, 197
        setup.py script to compile .pyx file, 197
        using typed memoryviews, 198
    overview of Python code, 193–195
    performance profiling of pure-Python ver-
        sion, 196
sqrt function, 76
stack allocation
    of C++ instances, 145
    versus heap allocation, 6
standalone executables, 27
static keyword (in C), 36
static typing, 32
    for speed, 43
static variables with C types and C semantics, 35
std::string type, 41
    conversion to unicode object, 66
Stein, William, 9
str type (in Cython), 41
    built-in string type in Python 2.6 and 2.7,
        172
    equivalent Python types, 66

strided data packing (typed memoryviews), 180
strides attribute (memoryview), 175
strides of an array, 175
strings
    differences in Python 2 and Python 3, 66
    static string types, reference counting and,
        45
structs
    aliases for names in Cython, 125
    converting Python data structures to, 73
    declaring and using in Cython, 56
        initializing a struct, 57
        nested and anonymous declarations, 58
    declaring and wrapping in Cython, 119
    for instance attributes in extension types, 82
    pointers to, 39
    wrapping with extension types, 122
subclassing
    C++ classes, 147
    casting and subclasses, 90
    extension types, 89
super function, 89
SWIG, 217
symplectic integrators (example), 70
SystemError exception, 56

T

templates (C++), 147–154
    included STL container class declarations,
        151
    iterators and nested classes, 150
    templated classes, 149
    templated functions and Cython's fused
        types, 148
temporary variables, 45
thread-based parallelism and the global inter-
    preter lock, 201
    nogil context manager, 203
    nogil function attribute, 202
%timeit magic command, 47, 160
try/except block (Python), 144
tuples (Python)
    grouping static C ints into, 39
    N-body simulator (example), 72
    unpacking, 73
type aliasing with ctypedef, 59
type inference, automatic, in Cython, 36
typed memoryviews (see memoryviews, typed)

typedefs
    aliases for names in Cython, 125
    declaring in Cython, 118
types
    coercion and casting, 55
    complex types, 41
    conversion, C code wrappted in Cython, 8
    correspondences between built-in Python
        types and C/C++ types, 40
    cpdef function arguments and return types,
        51
    dynamic versus static typing, 32
    dynamically typed Python function, convert-
        ing to Cython, 2
    floating-point type conversions, 41
    for defining DEF constants, 64
    fused types in Cython, 59
    implementing new buffer protocol, 172
    integral type conversions and overflow, 40
    object type, 79
    Python built-in types, 79
        having same name as C types, 42
    Python types having direct C counterparts,
        44
    statically declaring variables with a Python
        type, 41

U

Unicode encodings, conversion of C strings to,
    66
unicode type, 41
    equivalent Python types, 66
unions
    aliases for names in Cython, 125
    declaring and using in Cython, 56
        nested and anonymous declarations, 58
    declaring and wrapping in Cython, 119

V

value (objects), 79
variables
    C++ reference variables, 148
    declaring with struct type in Cython, 57
    dynamic and static, important difference be-
        tween, 35
    statically and dynamically typed, mixing, 39
    statically typing in Cython, 34
    untyped dynamic variables in Cython, 34

using temporary Python variables, 45
vector templated class, 149
    using vector's iterator from Cython, 150
virtual machine (VM), 31
Visual Studio, 17

W

while loops
    in Cython, 61
        efficiency of, 62
    in Python, 6
Windows systems
    C/C++ compiler, 13
    compiling with distutils, 16
wraparound checking, turning off, 29, 200
wraparound compiler directive, 178
wrapping C libraries with Cython, 115–134
    constants, other modifiers, and controlling
        what Cython generates, 125
    declaring and wrapping C structs, unions,
        and enums, 119
    declaring external C code in Cython, 115
        no automation of wrapping, 117
    declaring external C functions and typedefs,
        118
    error checking and raising exceptions, 128
    wrapping C functions, 121

wrapping C structs with extension types, 122
wrapping C++ libraries with Cython, 135–157
    C++ templates, 147–154
        included STL container class declara-
            tions, 151
        iterators and nested classes, 150
        templated classes, 149
        templated functions and Cython's fused
            types, 148
    exceptions, 144
    memory management, RAII, and smart
        pointers, 154
    simple example, MT_RNG class, 135
        compiling with C++, 138
        declaring class interface for use in Cy-
            thon, 136
        operator overloading, 142
        overloaded methods and functions, 140
        using the wrapper from Python, 139
        wrapper extension type, 137
    stack and heap allocation of C++ instances,
        145
    working with C++ class hierarchies, 146

X

XDress, 218
XML parser (lxml), use of Cython, 68

About the Author

Kurt W. Smith has been using Python in scientific computing ever since his college days, looking for any opportunity to incorporate it into his computational physics classes. He has contributed to the Cython project as part of the 2009 Google Summer of Code, implementing the initial version of typed memoryviews and native Cython arrays. He uses Cython extensively in his consulting work at Enthought, training hundreds of scientists, engineers, and researchers in Python, NumPy, Cython, and parallel and high-performance computing.

Colophon

The animal on the cover of *Cython* is a South African python (*Python sebae natalensis*). Also known as the South African rock python or the natal rock python, it was first identified by Sir Andrew Smith in 1833 and is variously labeled a subspecies of or a distinct but closely related species to the African rock pythons native to parts of the African continent farther north. The South African python is found in areas near permanent bodies of water from Kenya to South Africa, and, though generally smaller than its more northern relative, can grow to a length of 20 feet. The subocular mark that appears as a rule on the northern variation is smaller or entirely absent on the South African python.

The nonvenomous South African python regularly consumes animals as large as goats, which it kills by coiling itself around prey and constricting the coil with every inward breath of its victim. As with the heat-sensitive organs between the eyes and nostrils of pit vipers, pits in and around scales on the lips of the African rock python permit these snakes to hunt warm-blooded prey in the dark. Attacks on humans are rare but not unprecedented.

A female South African python lays a clutch of up to 100 hard-shelled eggs in the spring. Like other python mothers, she will then coil herself around the clutch until the eggs hatch 2 to 3 months later. Recent evidence suggests African rock python mothers will even continue to defend the brood for weeks or months after the eggs have hatched.

Like the Burmese python, the African rock python has arrived in recent years as an uninvited guest to the Florida Everglades, where it poses a significant threat to native wildlife. Along with several other decidedly unwelcome nonnative reptile species, it has been targeted by local officials in eradication efforts.

Many of the animals on O'Reilly covers are endangered; all of them are important to the world. To learn more about how you can help, go to *animals.oreilly.com*.

The cover image is from Wood's *Natural History*. The cover fonts are URW Typewriter and Guardian Sans. The text font is Adobe Minion Pro; the heading font is Adobe Myriad Condensed; and the code font is Dalton Maag's Ubuntu Mono.

Have it your way.

O'Reilly eBooks

- Lifetime access to the book when you buy through oreilly.com
- Provided in up to four, DRM-free file formats, for use on the devices of your choice: PDF, .epub, Kindle-compatible .mobi, and Android .apk
- Fully searchable, with copy-and-paste, and print functionality
- We also alert you when we've updated the files with corrections and additions.

oreilly.com/ebooks/

Safari Books Online

- Access the contents and quickly search over 7000 books on technology, business, and certification guides
- Learn from expert video tutorials, and explore thousands of hours of video on technology and design topics
- Download whole books or chapters in PDF format, at no extra cost, to print or read on the go
- Early access to books as they're being written
- Interact directly with authors of upcoming books
- Save up to 35% on O'Reilly print books

See the complete Safari Library at safaribooksonline.com

©2014 O'Reilly Media, Inc. O'Reilly logo is a registered trademark of O'Reilly Media, Inc. 14373

Get even more for your money.

Join the O'Reilly Community, and register the O'Reilly books you own. It's free, and you'll get:

- $4.99 ebook upgrade offer
- 40% upgrade offer on O'Reilly print books
- Membership discounts on books and events
- Free lifetime updates to ebooks and videos
- Multiple ebook formats, DRM FREE
- Participation in the O'Reilly community
- Newsletters
- Account management
- 100% Satisfaction Guarantee

Signing up is easy:

1. Go to: oreilly.com/go/register
2. Create an O'Reilly login.
3. Provide your address.
4. Register your books.

Note: English-language books only

To order books online:
oreilly.com/store

For questions about products or an order:
orders@oreilly.com

To sign up to get topic-specific email announcements and/or news about upcoming books, conferences, special offers, and new technologies:
elists@oreilly.com

For technical questions about book content:
booktech@oreilly.com

To submit new book proposals to our editors:
proposals@oreilly.com

O'Reilly books are available in multiple DRM-free ebook formats. For more information:
oreilly.com/ebooks

O'REILLY®

©2014 O'Reilly Media, Inc. O'Reilly logo is a registered trademark of O'Reilly Media, Inc. 14373

CPSIA information can be obtained at www.ICGtesting.com
Printed in the USA
BVOW09s1530021215

429155BV00016B/112/P

9 781491 901557